# STANDARDS OF THE GUQIN

An English Language Introduction to the
Chinese Seven-Stringed Zither

英
語
琴
統
初
階

Juni L. Yeung          楊儶立 著

**Toronto Guqin Society**          多倫多古琴社

**Fifth Edition**

# Not a copyright statement page.

As long as you're not selling it, you can 'pirate' it. How awesome is that?

Print ISBN: 978-0-9866225-0-2
E-book ISBN: 978-0-9866225-3-3
Ringbound Print ISBN: 978-0-9866225-5-7

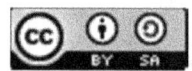Cover design by Juni Lefeuille Yeung.

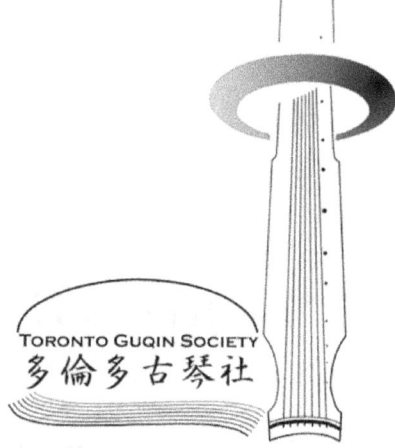

Published by Toronto Guqin Society,
visit us at http://torguqin.wordpress.com.

Printed by Lulu.com

Typeset in 20/18/13/12/8 Book Antiqua.
Chinese characters typeset in 36/12 PMingLiU.
Chinese characters in tables typeset in 36/12 DFKai-SB.
Chinese calligraphic titles bitmapped, originally typeset in 70/12 Arisawa-Kaisho.
Guqin tablature (Jianzipu) generated by Guangling Shenqi, http://guanglingsan.com.
Staff and cipher generated using Noteworthy Composer.

# Fifth Edition Acknowledgments

Over six years have passed since the last edition, a whole new generation of students have gone and come. Faces new and old fade into the song of yesteryear as new challenges and prospects rise anew. Mr. Hs'in-Ts'ai (Maya) Sun 孫新財 of Taichung, may you rest in peace.

Thank you to Prof. Victor Chun-yan TSE 謝俊仁教授 of Chinese University of Hong Kong Department of Ethnomusicology for your book review of the Fourth Edition, where you pointed out the deficiencies and inaccuracies in it, and thus inspired this rewrite. A further thanks for then reading over this revision's draft, and saved it from a fatal misunderstanding of the basic concepts. Thanks to your diligence, I am able to maintain the rigor and finesse from an academic institution even after having left it for so long.

A distant thank you to Ke Qihan 柯棋翰 of Beijing, whom we've never actually met - or even conversed yet. Both of us have perused through mountains of works by Chinese ethnomusicologists, but it was your study notes, posted openly on your website (kqh.me) that helped summarize and finish the rewritten sections, so thank you.

Thank you, fellow qinster and stringmaker extraordinaire Lawrence P. Kaster, for grammar-checking this edition of the book and ensuring readability of its passages. English isn't an agglutinated language, and it takes a certain tact to mark and divide ideas to their rightful breaks and stops. That often gets forgotten when the manuscript gets mulled over in the matter of days to weeks on end.

# Third & Fourth Edition Acknowledgments

*To my dear students past and present*, who have patiently stood by me in times of joy and distress, meticulously going through every pore of this work and suggesting edits. Thank you for putting up with my days of incomprehensible rambling, and for making sense out of chaos into method – this method. That means especially you all for combing over this mistake-ridden work, Junhai (Shuyi) Yang, Jingying (Ellin) Li, Zhaoheng Huang, Yanjun Qi, Jamie Liu, and Brian Blugerman.

The Third edition marked a new milestone in Chinese instrument tutorial books by actually explaining the relationship between theory and performance, and it would not have been possible without your guidance and study together. My respects to you, dear friends and comrades: Jim Binkley, Peiyou (Judy) Chang, John Thompson.

For the Fourth edition, I particularly thank David Badagnani of the Cleveland Chinese Music Ensemble for pushing me into the proverbial deep end of Chinese musicological studies, leading my way to the warm guidance Mr. Chiang-Shan Lin of Taipei Municipal Chinese Orchestra and masterful critques of Mr. Hs'in-Ts'ai (Maya) Sun of Taichung. The completely revised chapter on modes, modality, and tuning would not have been possible without the searing enlightenment from your decades of research and dissemination, leading us away from the misdirection of Eurocentric Orientalism that has plagued scholarly analysis for the past century. I have but only bit off a small corner of your colossal intellect to chew, and any misinterpretation or mistakes I may have presented in this edition remain the result of my own ignorance.

# First & Second Edition Acknowledgements

To my father, who bought my first instrument and supported my self-study of the music; and to my mother for her lifetime's worth of sage advice;

To Yanna Zhu, John Thompson, and everyone at the NAGA mailing list and Facebook International Guqin Society for your untiring support of this project;

To Jim Binkley and Charles Tsua, who tirelessly peer-revised every bit of content in this book;

and

To Gavin and Kenric, and to April – the initial sparks of my flame. My friends, my inspiration; my rivalry, and my first passion.

Thank you administrators and community members at guanglingsan.com, for your work on the *Guangling Shenqi* software and *jianzipu* database. You have made the second edition and onward possible.

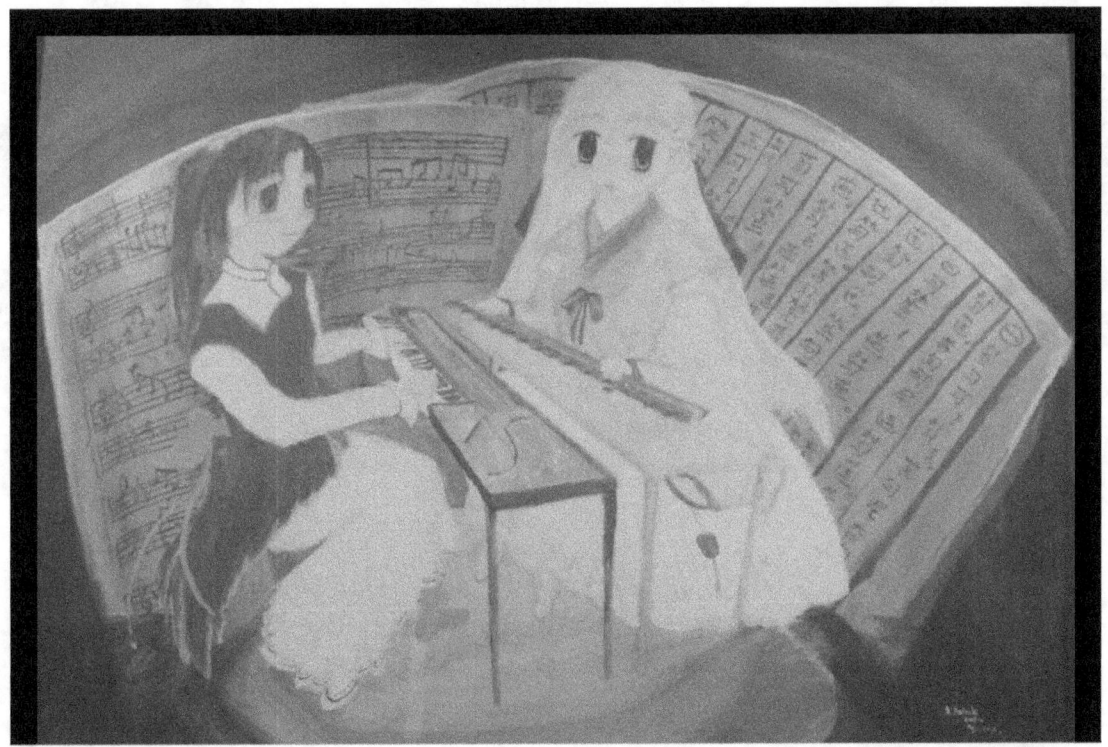

"Les Jeunes-Filles en *Heptachordia Sinesis* et *Clavichordia*" (琴の少女達)
Acrylic on Canvas, 42" x 30", painted by the author, completed Dec 25, 2007.

# Fifth Edition Foreword

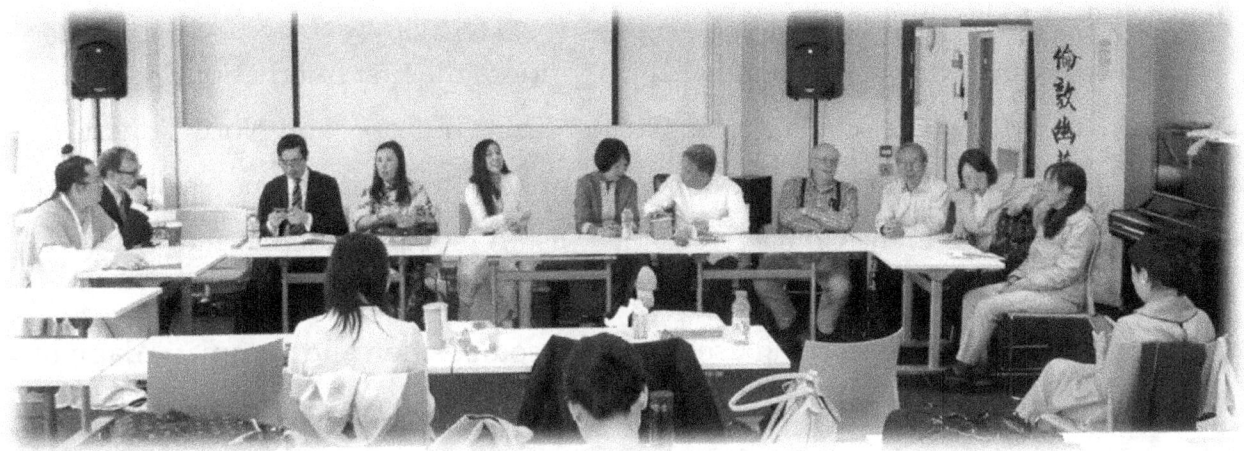

*"Come on guys, it's not rocket science!" – Music Teachers*
*"Come on guys, it's not music theory!" – Rocket Scientists*

Over the past decade and a half, I have built upon this collection of notes and summaries pertaining to the arts, theories, technologies, and progress on this seven-stringed zither. Further down the rabbit hole this book goes as each revision reveals new insights to tones, modality, tuning, and musical analysis. Now, in this latest edition, the content can truly be called 'no bars withheld' as I rearrange the music theory curriculum into a micro-to-macroscopic narrative that accounts for how and why systems and designs came to be in ancient China. This content traditionally is the stuff of university monographs and often to the point of focusing towards a particular period of research, not a 'beginner' technical manual of a Chinese instrument. Since for the majority of performance-based or conservatory-stream instrumentalists who are not pursuing a university degree would probably never come into contact with such works, I feel the compellation and responsibility to at least provide the materials here. Like a late-imperial Confucian canon excerpted reader, this book serves all levels as a learning tool as well as reference material for the experienced. It is my hope that with this edition, the content is detailed and correct enough to stand the tests of time.

There are still major theory topics yet to be covered by this book, such as the the specific topic of "Qin temperament" or *qin lü*, specifically referring to the history and challenges of using *zhunfa* (measurement method), *huifa* (harmonic marker method), and comparison with actual *sanfen sunyi-fa*. Perhaps a future publication in English will continue the existing scholarship from Guanzi to Zhu Xi to Chen Yingshi, but to date the most authoritative work on the subject is still Chen Yingshi's *Qinlü Xue* 《琴律學》 published in 2015 in Chinese.

The previous edition was published just prior to the first International Guqin Conference in 2018, where scholars from Greater China, Europe, and North America attended and presented various topics on qin aesthetics and performance, as well as qin culture and pedagogy in the China versus the West. A global pandemic and five years later, a Second International Guqin Conference presented advances in artificial intelligence (AI) technologies being used in guqin composition and automatic dapu of any given jianzipu score. It has been since the second edition (2012) I have updated the progress in the field, so along with the history overview it has been overhauled in this version. Despite the innovations, the fundamental visions for an accessible, widely accepted digitized jianzipu have still yet to materialize. This may lead to questions about how stable exactly our foundations for qin digital humanities is based on as it reaches for the clouds.

This edition sees another two pieces added to the repertoire, including a modern composition by my student Brian Blugerman (pictured 1st from right, in the Fourth Edition foreword). Now the book contains traditional, adapted, and new composition works, rounding off the need for a balanced and total representation of the performance environment of the 21st century. As a testament to 20 years of teaching and almost 15 years into this book project, I stop my pen here as my sights settle for new and experimental shores with heptatonism in the qin of the 9 or 10-stringed variety, and declare this work satisfactorily complete. Until, perhaps, new insight and corrections from colleagues and students amount to yet another revision.

Juni L. Yeung, M.A. (Toronto)

September 11, 2024

英語琴統初階

# Fourth Edition Foreword

*"There is a limit to our life, but to knowledge there is no limit. With what is limited to pursue after what is unlimited is a perilous thing; and when, knowing this, we still seek the increase of our knowledge, the peril cannot be averted."*

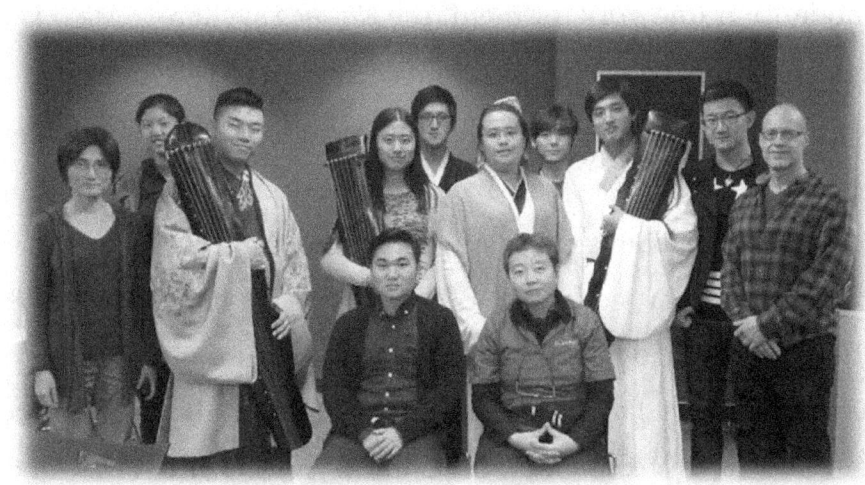

- Zhuangzi

In the second edition, I started to introduce Chinese music from the conceptual level using the language native to the tradition, and in the third edition presented the history of temperament from the Chinese history of science and discovery. The mood and the ingredients are here, and all that's left are the tools that shape the music.

The only problem was – is, none are absolutely certain how those tools look like, or precisely how they're used.

This revision originally intended correct small errata for all the previous edits, but instead ended up into the forays of the most hotly-contested at the forefront of Chinese musicological scholarship. It certainly did not help when even my mentors scoffed and advised me to steer clear of the most authoritative books in the field, because the *very system of knowledge itself* has been overturned numerous times in the past twenty years, rendering every existing primer in Chinese and English as outdated if not outright fallacious in their eyes. As people investigated the fringes of Han Chinese music in the margins of regional opera and rediscovery of Tang court music, trying to describe or provide a coherent narrative of "a Chinese music theory" seemed impossible. The learning environment for this topic was litigative and unwelcoming – but that only further proves the importance of the topic, and that dire need for student-friendly material to gradually wade into the depths of the various musicologies over the course of Chinese music history.

The content on modality in this revision does not cover the heptatonic banquet music 28 mode (燕樂二十八調) naming system, which is used today in Tang/Song

Standards of the Guqin                                                                 3 music and Japanese *gagaku* – but not in the guqin tradition, save for titular mentions in *Jieshidiao Youlan* and Jiang Kui's *Baishi Daoren Gequ*. This also means that the prevalent modality framework for them (the *zhi-diao* system 之調制) is intentionally omitted to prevent confusion from the *wei-diao* system 為調制 taught here. Because of this decision, I am conflicted to leave in descriptions of perfect-transition external tunings as pentatonic pitch-*diao*, which originated from grandmaster Gu Meigeng's *Qinxue Beiyao*, and uses a *zhi-diao* method of sorting the tunings – hence, I write this as an early *caveat*.

This year marks the 13th year since the conception of this book as a project, and the 8th year since publication. As my own studies and research head off towards the direction of *dapu* and analysis, any writings in that subject would be beyond the purview of this primer. Perhaps this is not the end, but a lead to the beginning of something new. If this book does inspire more questions than answers, and provokes students to be curious enough to discover on his or her own accord and volition, then my own decade of learning and sharing would not have been for naught.

Juni L. Yeung, M.A. (Toronto)

July 7, 2018

# Third Edition Foreword

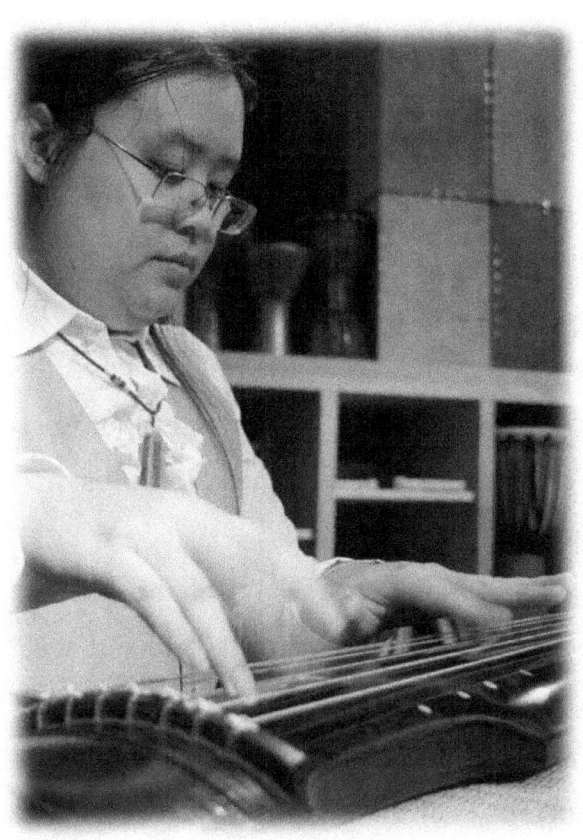

*"At fifteen my heart was set on learning; at thirty I stood firm; at forty I had no more doubts."*

- Confucius

What I had initially planned as a one-off project back in 2005 has now become a lifetime endeavour – teaching the guqin and revising this book is a humbling realization of my humanly mistakes, errors, and vices. I dare not say that what I teach may be absolute truth, but I at least strive to correct my wrongs.

This third edition was conceived under such a mentality: no new content was planned, and the objective was to simply correct problematic statements in the text and fix the myriad misprints and faults in the second edition music score. My students have been invaluable in this process – only the freshest pair of inquiring eyes and curious minds would scour through the lines of *jianzipu* and five-line staff and discover the elusive missing ledger line, or a mistype of the left hand position in a repetitive phrase. Errata of this nature are but the easiest to fix, but conceptual and pedagogical issues are much harder to detect and address.

Admittedly, the most difficult part for me was to restructure and rebuild the system from the middle, as rewriting or even resequencing the chapters would affect how information is presented. In the end, instead of writing a lesson in Repertoire A on how to tune Standard Tuning using harmonics and cross-checked with Xianweng Cao, it became an entire chapter on the subject I have avoided to detail in the past two editions, spilling all of my knowledge and energy to explaining the history and issues of temperament. Now, I can unabashedly claim that all of my knowledge on this matter has been poured onto those few pages in the most coherent presentation I can muster.

Since I intend this book to be popularly readable in high-school level language, it was a challenge to parse and paraphrase sources of this knowledge, often riddled in mathematic formulas and musical jargon – not to mention that both the language and knowledge in this field is uncertain and contentious, making the research and preparation of this material a humbling experience of confusion and nausea amongst visits and emails to scholars and trips to the Cheng Yu Tong East Asian Library and Music Library at the University of Toronto.

As this volume expands, I see myself following the footsteps to my distant grandmaster Gu Meigeng's magnum opus, the *Qinxue Beiyao*. Notwithstanding the expansive repertoire in over 900 pages of handwritten manuscript, the book is the only one in all contemporary Chinese manuals which explains the intricacies of temperament and modal transpositions, beyond even the material covered in this work. Perhaps, in the future, an official translation of that work shall be called for.

In retrospect, the second edition has stood its trial by fire, and all the things that contribute into this edition's maturity are marks of my personal shortfalls and setbacks. Personally, I confess that these past three years, being a graduate student at the Chinese University of Hong Kong and later again at my *alma mater* University of Toronto has made me fundamentally realize my limit and mortality – if the evolution of this book is a legacy of my youth and eagerness to learn, my only fear now is losing this momentum as I reach the point of life where I come to "stand firm" with my meager achievement and be satisfied with the delusion of the present as having achieved perfection.

Juni L. Yeung, M.A. (CUHK)

May 6, 2016

# Second Edition Foreword

*"A cultural Renaissance means that our ancestors'*
*achievements must be surpassed, with daily innovation*
*upon their principles."*

– Xishan Qinkuang (alias),
Hanfu movement thinker (1978-2008)

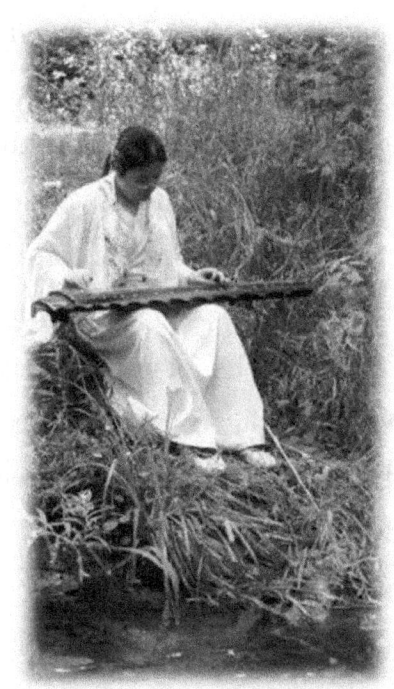

Two years have passed since the initial completion
of the *Standards* book, but it was known, if not already
assumed, that work was far from done. Ever since the
book was first uploaded to Lulu.com, there has been over
14 (!) minor revisions to the details pertaining to this book,
some related to font and printing issues, but more so on the finer details of the
instruction text, from grammar to changes in facts.

However, making revisions to the musical score then were next to impossible. As
all scores were handwritten and then scanned during the five years of the writing of
this book on-and-off, the running list of "bugs" meant that continual tweaks using
conventional white-out and ink was simply too daunting a task to fix.

That has changed, with the computerization of *jianzipu* input. Two decades ago,
qin master and computer scientist Chen Changlin attempted to formulate a guqin
tablature system for digital recording and MIDI-sequence playback, but nothing
substantial was produced for the generic user in the market. The original attempts tried
and failed to catalogue every possible left and right hand combination for *jianzipu*, as
with over hundreds of left and right hand movements on over hundreds of positions
(half and whole tones) over the seven strings, the potential was beyond the capabilities
of any computer codepage, with millions of combinations. Relating this to the sound is
also an issue: take any *jianzi* with both left and right hand information – and there are
two to three sounds or timbres possible for it: Harmonic, pressed (plucked or left hand
slapped), or even open (for releases).

While as of writing these words in 2012 we have still not yet tackled the latter
challenge of computer parsing of *jianzipu* into playable music, a new solution for typing
the tablature has arisen. Thanks to the community at guanglingsan.com forums, a
Cloud-based database and client software was developed to allow its users to assemble

custom tablature and output them as vector graphics. With this part of the puzzle complete, filling in the rest was easy with existing market software for staff music. Only by full integration of both these aspects, however, can we consider the mission of digitizing qin music as complete.

Aside from the complete revamping of all scores in this second edition, the other major update is the addition of two scores in Repertoire A and the creation of Repertoire D, focusing solely on the *dapu* process. Typically no qin manuscript includes a methodology for teaching this, and the pedagogy of this art can usually be found in doctoral dissertations deep within the ethnomusicology realm. *Standards of the Guqin* does not try to disprove the advanced nature of this study, nor dismiss the claim from others that the dapu process should be a subjective and intuitive experience that should not be taught by the written word (as many Chinese arts do). Instead, we present some basic considerations by professionals in a sequential tutorial, and encourage students to pursue investigative and critical study beyond the contents of this book.

It is my wish to see that the publication of this new edition will lead to further written and creative results for the qin in the English language, branching into categories covered by this book in specific detail. Most importantly, however, is that this "Prime of the Four Scholarly Arts" will blossom beyond its native cultural borders and resonate all under heaven.

I dare not say that with this new edition that my work is finished or error-free. I pledge my readers and users of this book to pick out any shortcomings or errata so that we can better this work for the sake of all to come.

Juni L. Yeung, B.A. (Toronto)

July 8, 2012

# Foreword

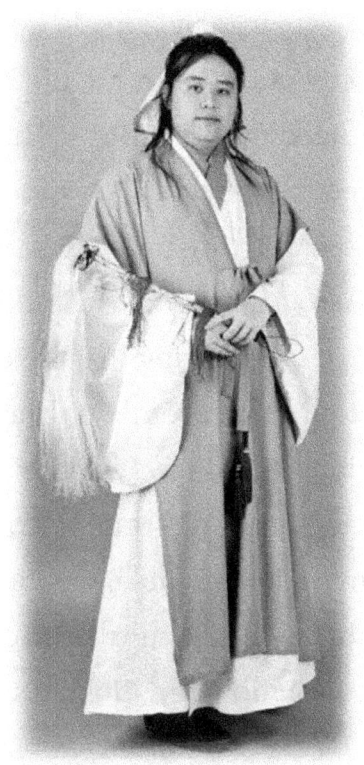

As a fourth-generation Hong Konger who started learning about my own heritage after immigrating to Canada, it was unusual to have an elementary grade-schooler prefer this exclusive musical tradition over more popular (and Western) forms of music. My first contact with the qin came from my father's tape copy of one of the "Old 8" – 8 tapes' worth of recordings by master players from the mid-20th Century, as well as a trio of *Yangguan Sandie* with erhu and xiao from a digital encyclopaedia. When I did my Grade 5 music project on the instrument, with the wealth of information from the Internet, I was aghast to learn there were less than 100 professional players surviving today. In addition to my interest, I also felt a sense of responsibility that there was a necessity to keep this tradition alive.

Like most children of this age and background, I began my music studies with the piano, and despite nearly completing the top examination level, I found no sense of enjoyment (let alone enlightenment) from the music. The force feeding of examination repertoire and studies left a confused state of mind and an itching distaste for the binary interface of the keyboard. Only after mastering the guqin have I come to appreciate clavier music, particularly of the Renaissance to early-Baroque period. Despite the negatives, the rudiments of Western music theory have undoubtedly contributed a foundation for writing this book.

In the summer of 2003, on a visit back to Hong Kong, I was given my first guqin from my father, who obtained it from a friend who bought it in Guangzhou. I read the small handbook that came along with Professor Li Xiangting's instructional VCD, but failed to grasp the technique from watching the video due to my then weak Mandarin skills. At the same time, UNESCO had officially declared the instrument and its tradition an "Intangible and Oral Heritage of Humanity", and its popularity in China began to soar. Thanks to this trend, resources were increasingly easier to find online, and Web 2.0 infrastructure allowed international players to connect directly for the first time.

In 2005, I made my public debut in the Toronto Kiwanis Music festival, as the only guqin player in the Non-Western plucked strings category, surrounded by guzheng competitors. The curious and puzzled expressions of my fellow competitors led me to realize that something must be done to debunk the mistake of confusing these two instruments, which led to the founding of the University of Toronto Guqin Association in the fall of that year.

Realizing that the qin community is a small and exclusive one, there was no doubt that promotion and teaching new players is the only way to expand it. When I first started teaching the instrument in the International Student Centre at the University of Toronto, I quickly encountered the problem of having little to no teaching materials suitable for students illiterate in the Chinese written language. At the time, the three major English sources were: John Thompson's website and *Shenqi Mipu* (Zhu, 1425) translation, Jim Binkley's website (and later book), and Fredric Lieberman's *Mei'an Qinpu* (Wang, 1931) translation. The general inaccessibility to a complete curriculum compelled the need to develop Standards of the Guqin, which started out as a compilation of materials and essays on various aspects of playing, open-sourced and placed online.

Asides from simply being "another qin manuscript" except written in English, I recognized the differences of attitude towards learning in Anglophone and traditional Chinese society. This book focuses on acquiring applicable techniques and understanding the music from musical and historical contexts, much like the traditional oral tradition in China. However, this book also encourages the student to "play critically"– being unbounded by Chinese schools or traditional sects, one is open to interpreting classical texts and scores with a different perspective.

The name of this book is taken from the Song Dynasty text Qin Tong 《琴統》 by Xu Li 徐理, as well as the personalized Ming version *Xilutang Qintong* 《西麓堂琴統》 by Wang Zhi 汪芝, who both emphasized discrete knowledge of music theory and technique over abstract art theories (the focus among players at the time). It is my hope that through this work, players will grasp an understanding of the tradition from its own context, without losing sight of how it can be bridged to other practices.

Juni L. Yeung, B.A. (Toronto), FXKQS
April 18, 2010.

英語琴統初階

# Table of Contents

# How to Read this Book and Learn the Art

*Standards of the Guqin* is a monograph that teaches content in key concepts and related ideas by showing the full breadth of what *qinxue* 琴學 or qin studies embodies, and is not hesitant at times from showing the full depth of forefront scholarship involves.

Like the classical qin manuscripts of imperial times, the textual part of this work is written in *themes and topics* rather than *by lessons* from basic to complicated. As digital natives of the 21ˢᵗ century, the student shouldn't try to memorize by rote every piece of information in here (except with the music – do practice plenty until the sounds and motions become second nature to you), or to expect that one will comprehend and appreciate every nuance from the first read, but rather grasp the basic concepts first, put them into practice, then come back for more as your experience and repertoire increases.

The contents of this book should provide for roughly 2 years of study and instruction, based on my experience with students who receive hourly instruction once a week with regular, diligent practice. Here is a timetable of what to learn over time, and what would be a logical progression of material to read and understand.

Month 1: Encountering the Qin
- Basic information (Encountering the qin, notation overview)
- Familiarizing Left hand thumb/ring press, right hand index/middle finger single stroke fingering names
- Xianweng Cao (2~3 weeks instruction + practice)
  - Revision / contingency time for slower learners (week 4)

Month 2: Harmonic Mastery
- Read *From Standard Tuning – The Default Setting of Strings* section
- Harmonic Tuning Technique (3~4 weeks)
  - Familiarizing with tuning pegs and mechanisms (week 1)
  - Attempt to tune the instrument based on a given pitch within one lesson (week 1)
  - Precisely and clearly play harmonic overtones, without muffling its timbre (week 1), and pairing tones with clear sense of purpose for tuning (week 2)

- Tune all 7 strings without teacher's assistance within 30/15/10 minutes, with progressive familiarity and dexterity (week 2~4)
- Ultimately aim for tuning all strings from loosened state to performance ready within 90~120 seconds. (month 2~3)
  - Liangxiao Yin (3~4 weeks, start 2 weeks into teaching harmonic tuning)
    - Contingency/Review of previous material (1 week)

## Month 3: Basic Repertoire, First Test

- Liangxiao Yin (Refer to list from previous month)
- Qiufeng Ce (Week 2, 2 weeks)
- Read Pre-20th century qin history
- Zhao Yin (Week 4, 3~4 weeks)


## Month 4-6: Towards Tuning Modulation

- Finish Repertoire A (Guanshan Yue, Liu Shang) within 2 months
- Ensure that all previous repertoire can be played by memory
  - Optional: Selected or total dictation of the piece on paper, or explain the technical highlights of each piece
- Preliminary read on the Temperaments, Modes and Tunings chapter
  - Learn half to all of Repertoire B within timeframe (synonymous assignment with Rep. A above)
  - Can explain fundamental principles and types of tuning modulation

## Month 6-12: Basic Level Mastery

- By now, the student has finished most or all of Repertoires A&B, and has familiarity with *jianzipu* literacy and sight reading, and expertise with performance in several tunings
- If not already encountered in first half-year, the student should acquire hands-on experience with instrument cleaning to component replacement and maintenance
- Learn and memorize half of Repertoire C (Gufeng Cao + 1 piece of choice)

- Technique learning should start shifting from quantity to quality: Enhancing smoothness of hand motions and body expression; note timbre, musicality and 'melodic tension' control
- If confident with theory content, read *Songxia Guantao dapu report* and begin attempting Repertoire D (month 11~12)
- The student should start acquiring a reading list of books on the guqin, as well as other repertoire collections to expand horizons

Month 12-24: Building a Holistic Qin Player

- Finish remaining content in this book
- By now most new pieces are selected from other compendia
- Familiarity with sight reading *and interpreting* historical manuscripts
- Engage & contribute to local/global community of qin players
- Based on the Central Conservatory Examination List, select pieces from levels 4-8 to study and play (as intermediate students), totalling to a performance time of 1 to 1.5 hours

# Encountering the Qin

## A Few Basics Before we Begin

Reading qin scores requires memorization of numerous symbols which may appear alien even to the native Chinese reader. However, knowledge of Chinese characters for the numbers one to ten (一 二 三 四 五 六 七 八 九 十) by heart is a must. Eleven, twelve and so on are expressed as 10-1 or 10-2 (十一, 十二…) in Chinese. Knowledge of the numbers is crucial to reading the tablature itself.

This curriculum expects the student to acquire primarily hand-eye coordination and sight-reading skills in the learning process, but also pays emphasis on ear training on proper pitch.

The Western music tradition recognizes the widespread usage of Italian terms in musical language. While this work will try to provide an explanation in native English as much as possible, it is assumed the student will understand (or will look up a music dictionary) when such terms are used.

## Romanized Chinese Conventions

While English and other European books in sinology and China (the guqin being one of its myriad subjects) prior to 1979 may use the British-developed Wade-Giles system (and publications from Harvard University in their own system), *Hanyu Pinyin* is the standard convention today for depicting the reading of Putonghua, or spoken Mandarin Chinese, in Latin characters. English readers without familiarity may tend to misinterpret and mispronounce its Slavic-based consonant system. For more information, please refer to external material on pronunciation.

Tones in this book are written as numbers after the Pinyin letters rather than as diacritic markers on top of the main vowel. "Māo" for example would be written as mao1. Here are some tips:

- All vowels are read short, not long.
- A diphthong (two vowels together, such as "*jia*") is still one syllable.
- C's (as in *ce*) are read ts- as in "ts-e." Ch are the same as in English.
- Q's (as in *qia*) are a sharper, tongue-based version of ch-, such as *Ciao* in Italian. The old Wade-Giles writing *Ch'* gives a clearer idea to English speakers – *Quan* in Pinyin would be *Ch'uen* in W-G.
- X's (as in *xi*) are read hs- as in "hs-ee."

- The ü vowel may be written as "v", as in "Lü → Lv." They are interchangeable, and should not be mistaken with u without the umlaut (Lu = "Loo").

## Romanized Japanese Conventions

As another major source of qin scholarship past and present, Japanese works may also be studied or referenced. Although the Japanese government promotes the use of Kunrei-shiki romanization, this work continues with popular convention of using modified Hepburn Romanization without the use of long vowel diacritics (e.g. Toukyou rather than Tōkyō) for visibility and ease of typing.

## Qin vs. Zheng

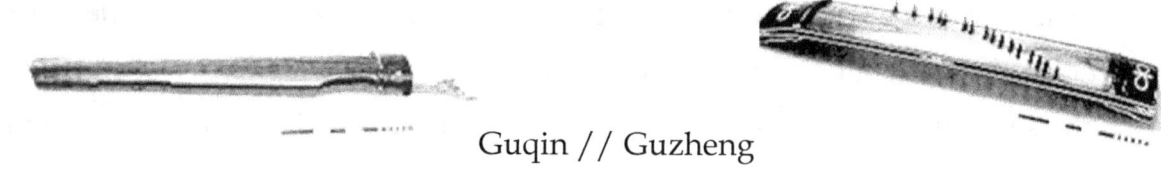

Guqin // Guzheng

(http://www.geidai.ac.jp/~odaka/gcat/japanese/tubezithers.html)

Know the difference between a guqin and a guzheng – this is a common mistake to many people. The guqin has only seven strings and is considerably smaller than the guzheng. The guzheng evolved from splitting the 25-string *se,* and has over the ages regained more strings (from 13 to 21), and has movable bridges that determine the tone of each string. A guzheng can be up to twice the size of a standard guqin.

It is usually difficult to describe the timbre differences between qin and zheng music, although some differences are notable: the qin capitalizes on colourful variations of *vibrato* and *portamento* slides, as well as its over 100 harmonic positions; while the zheng capitalizes on its string count and offers a larger tonal range when performing large continuous strokes on multiple strings and more readily-available higher pitches on an unmodified string.

Given our modern environment and resources, go and try to network with other guqin players in your area – ask around, and utilize the Internet. Numerous websites are linking players worldwide in forms of forums and newsgroups. Some links are provided at the back of this book, under "Further Reading".

英語琴統初階

## The Instrument

### The Body

The guqin (Ku Ch'in in Wade-Giles) is composed of two wooden boards glued together and lacquered to give its shiny and smooth surface. Since the sound emanates from the underside of the instrument, the top board is a rounded piece of a light, porous wood. The bottom is a flat piece of a heavier, dense wood. In China, Paulownia (*tong*) and Catalpa (*zi*) wood are often used for the top and bottom respectively. The wood must be completely dry in order to produce the crisp sound and be able to survive over the ages, hence the wooden pillars and beams of old buildings are often

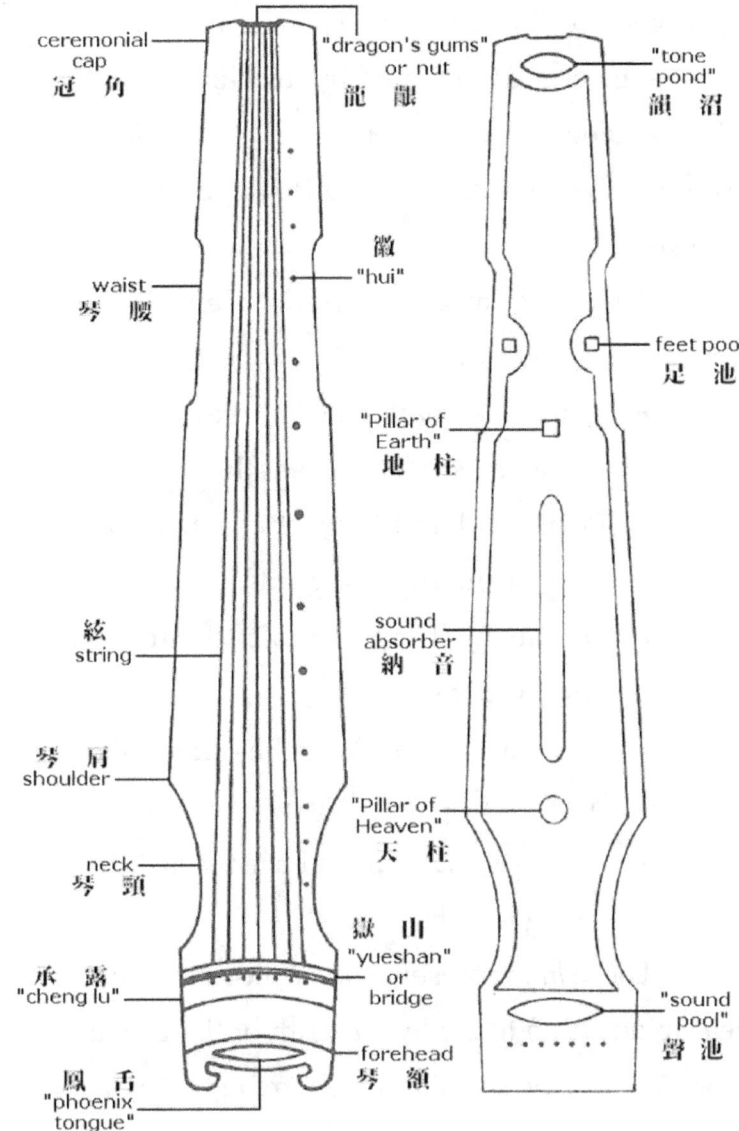

considered prime material for making instruments. In more recent times, pine and spruce woods have been used in making guqin as well. The *Yueshan* bridge and even the *Longyin* dragon gums is often made with sandalwood or some kind of extra-hard tonewood for maximum durability.

The Yin-Yang School of ideology considers the roundedness and flatness, lightness and heaviness, hardness and softness, and various other characteristics of the woods to represent the characteristics of "round heaven and square earth".

### Hui, the harmonic markers

The guqin has thirteen round markers (徽, "hui", insignia) above the first string, made of mother-of-pearl or small inlaid pieces of precious stone or metal. These markers are laid out to represent the positions of harmonic overtones, and present harmonics at different pitches, fifths, and octaves. The distances are calculated by dividing the effective length of the string (from the *Yueshan* or bridge to the *Longyin* end) in a Pythagorean pattern.

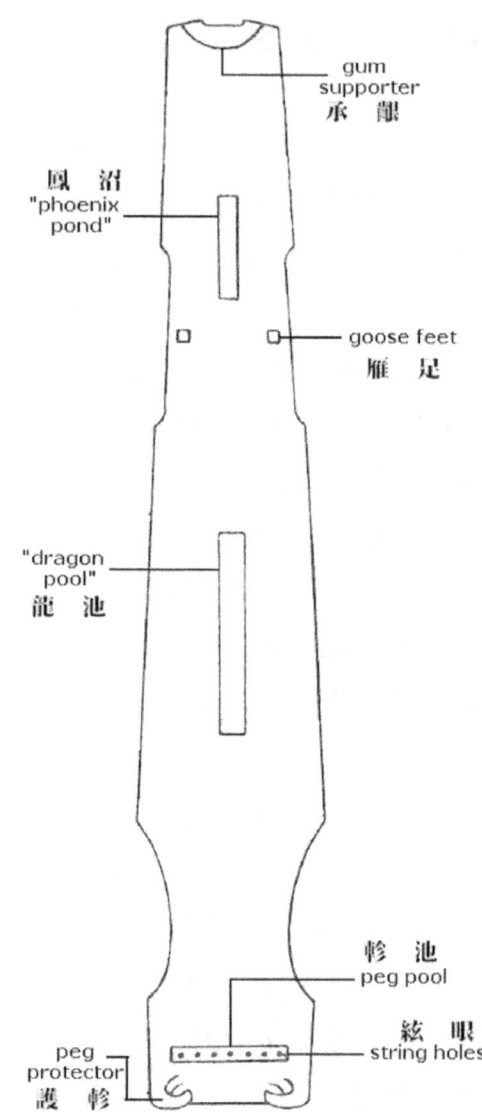

*Hui* are counted from right to left. They are calculated as follows:

- ➤ The 7th *hui* marks the halfway point of the string's effective length.
- ➤ Positions 4 and 10 mark the quarters,
- ➤ 1 and 13 mark the eighths.
- • Divide the string length into threes to get positions 5 and 9.
- • Positions 2 and 12 are the outer halves of these thirds. (Sixths)
- • Positions 3,5,8, and 11 are fifths of the string length.

These *hui* represent the 12 months of the year in addition to the leap month of the Lunar calendar. The often enlarged centre *hui* (7th) also symbolizes the universal sovereignty. The thirteen *hui* are counted from the right to left, starting from the *Yueshan*.

From *hui-wai* ("outside", a finger's width left of 13th hui) to 7th *hui* is known as lower register (*Xiazhun*, 下準), 7th hui to 4th hui is known as middle register (*Zhongzhun*, 中準), and 4th hui and up is considered upper register (*Shangzhun*, 上準). While it is possible to create every semitone by stopped notes, commonly 8 usable positions are recognized (the pentatonic sounds, two lowered tones, two raised tones, and the *gong* on the higher octave).

英語琴統初階

<u>The Strings</u>

Seven strings span across the top board, traditionally named "gong 宫, shang 商, jue 角, zi 徵, yu 羽, wen 文, wu 武" starting from the lowest string positioned furthest away from the player. The first five names represent the five 'proper' sounds of the Chinese (pentatonic) scale, while Wen and Wu originate from the first two kings of Zhou Dynasty. According to Yin-Yang school teachings, these strings also relate to other natural hierarchies and elements. In order, the five sounds reflect "sovereign/master, subject/servant, people, subject-matter, object". Today, the strings are simply referred as strings 1 to 7, with 1 (the 'gong' string) being the lowest in tone and 7 (the 'wu' string) as the highest. For the sake of clarity and to avoid confusing with left hand positions, string numbers are usually expressed using Roman numerals (I, II…VII).

Over the ages, musicians and kings attempted to add more strings onto the instrument while citing the Wen and Wu kings as a role model, but were all deemed as unnecessary and redundant, and the seven-stringed design persevered.

By the Tang Dynasty, the basic structure of the instrument had become established. As the guqin was perfected in its technical and musical design, the original nomenclature of the first

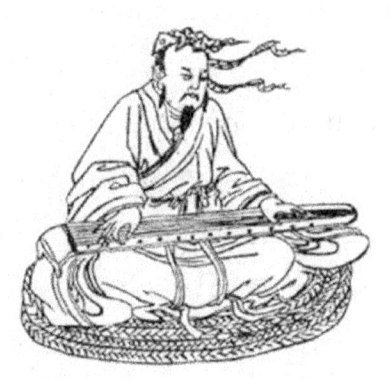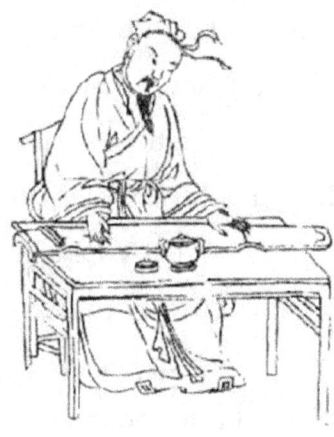

**On the floor or in a chair, guqin is meant to be played sitting down. Image from Taigu Yiyin (1280) and Xilutang Qintong (1525), compiled courtesy of silkqin.com.**

five strings sparked debate. This will be explained in further detail in the "Tunings" section.

## Body Posture

Prior to the advent of chairs, the player supported the instrument cross-legged, with the instrument on both shins and the end standing on its goose feet on the ground, or put onto a low table. When chairs became prevalent in the Chinese lifestyle sometime during the Tang Dynasty, guqin playing took the form of the regular table-and-chair posture as we know it today.

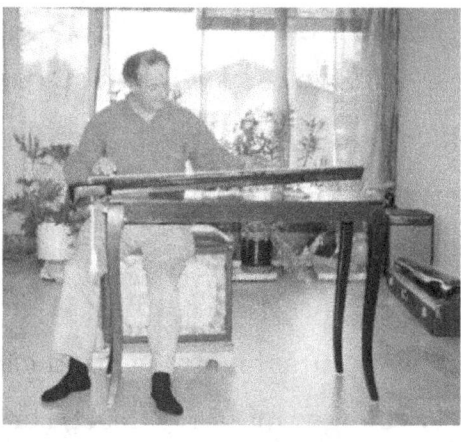

**When table height is too high, elevate the chair to compensate. Sit forward, and plant your feet to the floor. Photo from UTQA archives, student David Powell performing.**

When choosing a table for playing the guqin, a hard but somewhat permeating surface (such as an old hardwood desk) is ideal. Tablecloths may muffle sounds and glass tables may make tones sound too piercing, and should be avoided. When authentic guqin tables aren't available, a desk at "writing" or "keyboard" height is ideal. The right side of the table should always be left open to let the instrument hang over the edge. If one has to use a dining table, a phone book or two on the chair should be sufficient to counteract the height difference. Chairs with adjustable heights are also an option.

Place the instrument as pictured. The tuning pegs should hang out and not touch the side of the table. The saying is "Position your heart in line with the 5th hui on the qin", so adjust your seat accordingly. Sit straight with a slight forward tilt and plant your feet firmly to the ground. Imagine that *qi/ch'i* energy is derived from the ground, up the feet and spine, over the top of the head and falling onto the fingers, which is injected into the instrument and back into the ground through the table. This forms a cycle and is the most ergonomic way to play the instrument.

Avoid leaning on the back of the chair, looking back and forth towards the hands, or using too little/too much energy playing, as this will tire your joints, neck and spirit.


## Finger Posture

Right hand fingers act like little hammers with a slight whipping motion, moving straight back and forward when playing single notes. This is so that the notes are played with strength and confidence. The finger joint closest to the palm should be the only joint that bends significantly in a stroke. *Tiao* (index finger outward) should always be supported by the thumb on the index finger pad for a firm enunciation. The ancients

22                                            英語琴統初階

assigned notes to fingers according to the characteristics of the sound each finger produces, therefore the fingering (or the style) should be carefully observed.

- The index finger is agile and produces a balanced sound.
- The middle finger supports the index finger and produces a stronger note.
- The ring finger adds complexity and is soft-spoken in tone.
- The thumb adds a sense of affirmation to the musical phrase, especially working together with another finger.

Modern players tend to replace ring finger movements with the middle finger, but often forget the difference in tone quality and volume between these two fingers. Hence it is important that if one does replace the fingering, the effect of the ring finger (gentle, soft-spoken) must be emulated, or use the original fingering.

After every pluck, the fingers should stop just before the adjacent string on an outward movement, or perch on the adjacent string if an inward movement (stopping that string). If there is no string adjacent, control the hand so it does not wander too far off. The right hand should not fly high with exaggerated movements.

Left hand movements are the key to the qin's expression. One should press firmly for stopped tones, and touch gracefully for harmonics. When using the ring finger, the left edge between the fingernail and flesh should be used. Northern Chinese schools teach students to turn their wrist to the left so the finger can lean sideways, but Southern schools keep their hands flat.

# Notation Overview

## Jianzipu: The Simplified Character Notation System

Guqin scores are written since the late Tang Dynasty (9 c. C.E.) in a system known as "*Jianzi-pu* (減字譜, Chien Tzu P'u in Wade-Giles, means 'reduced-ideograph notation')". Although often purported as something unique to the guqin, numerous other Chinese instruments have or once had a single-character tablature or fingering notation system. Surviving ensemble scores for *yayue* (court or temple music) in the Tang, Song, and Ming have seen customized fingering tablature for the *se* (the 25-string bridged zither and predecessor of the *guzheng*), pipa, and xun (the clay ocarina).

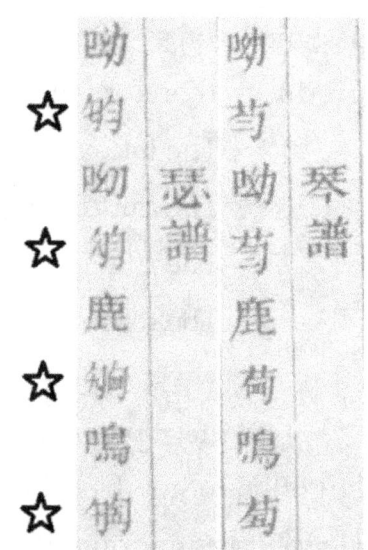

Qin (right) and Se (left) score, with the tablature highlighted in stars. Image: Xiaoya: Luming from *Shijing Yuepu* (1788).

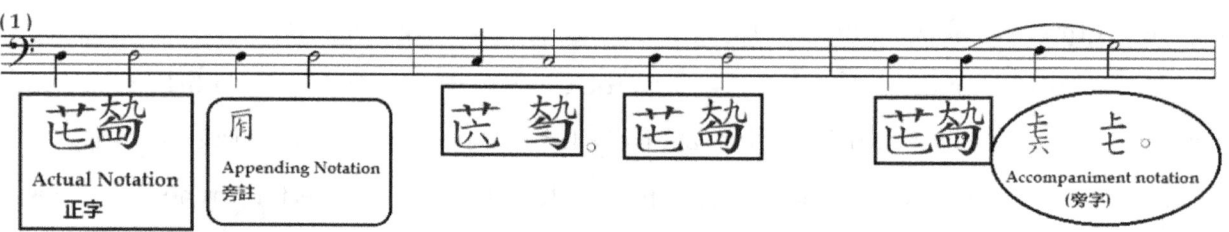

The *jianzipu* system consists of compounding a series of left and right hand movement in simplified Chinese ideographs into one Chinese-like character.

There are three main categories of notation in *Jianzipu*:

- Actual notation (正字) records the "proper tones," or distinct tones produced by explicit left and right hand motioning,

- Accompaniment notation (旁字) records the "resonance" or the sound(s) after the pronounced tone by the left hand, and

- Appending notation (旁註) annotates rhythm modifiers, or other special movements that refers or modifies upon previously mentioned Actual Notation.

英語琴統初階

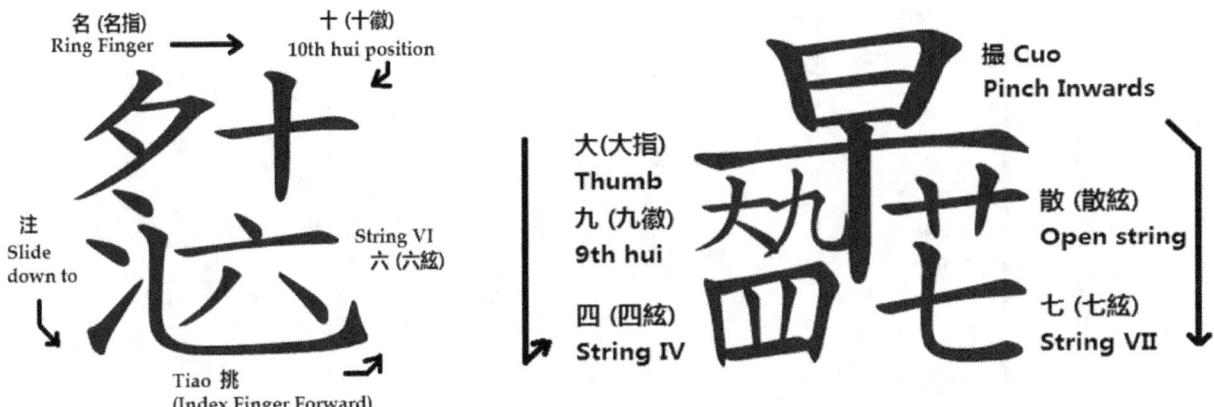

**Actual Notation involving a single string (left), and multiple-strings (right).**

Actual notation contains the most substantial information pertaining to performanceand hence is the most complex. It consists of three mandatory components and several optional modifiers. In most cases, the left hand portion is on the top and the right hand instructions are on the bottom. The example image here shows on the top half that the left ring finger is to slide down to the 10th *hui* as the right ring finger plucks outward on string VI, implying that the left hand should press on that string.With notes involving multiple strings plucked simultaneously by the right hand, such as a *cuo* pinching movement, the fingering movement encapsulates the information for the two strings, each with their own left hand information attached to the string number (if they're missing, assume previous).

With such massive amounts of information crammed into one character, it is possible to obtain crucial information within a single glance and optical parsing, despite its rather complicated verbal iteration. The following examples demonstrate how complex syntax is parsed and read:

| | Left hand position | Lower string modifier | Lower string number | Compound R.H. Mvt. | Left hand position | Upper string modifier | Upper string number |
|---|---|---|---|---|---|---|---|
| 芍 | open 散 *san* | | | gou 勾 *gou* 右指法 *right hand movement* | | | I 一絃 *yi (xian)* |
| 卓 | thumb 6.2 大六二 *da  liu-er* (六徽二分) short for: liu-hui er-fen | slide up to 綽 *chuo* | VII 七絃 *qi (xian)* | CUO 撮 *cuo* | open 散 *san* | | III 三絃 *san (xian)* |
| 發 | ring 7.6 名七六 *ming  qi-liu* | | VII 七絃 *qi (xian)* | PO-LA 潑剌 *po-la* | open 散 *san* | | VI 六絃 *liu (xian)* |
| 曇 | thumb 6.2 大六二 *da  liu-er* | | VII 七絃 *qi (xian)* | CUO 撮 *cuo* | ring 7 名七 *ming qi* | harmonic 泛 *fan* | III 三絃 *san (xian)* |
| | 左手 Left hand position | 下絃手法 Lower string modifier | 下絃數 Lower string number | 複合右指法 Compound R.H. Mvt. | 左手 Left hand position | 上絃手法 Upper string modifier | 上絃數 Upper string number |

**Parsing the syntax of jianzipu, from the simple to the very complicated.**

With the exception of string number, other components in the actual notation may be omitted on subsequent characters. It is assumed that the new fingering would follow from the most recently mentioned state. The example to the right shows the left thumb at the 9th *hui* with the right middle finger plucking inward (*gou*), but is not written on the subsequent two characters. In this case, whatever elements that are missing are assumed to retain the previous definition, until a new definition is stated. Left hand position and finger information is always written as a pair, except in accompaniment notation such as sliding moves.

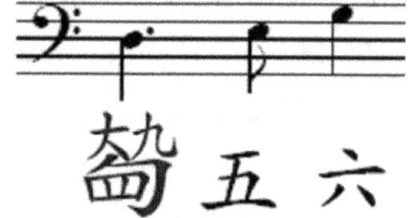

The "Assume Previous" rule in example.

### Accompaniment and Appending Notation

Both accompaniment and appending notation modify or work from given positions, usually one or two previous characters in actual notation. In some cases (especially where a passage referenced is more than a pair of notes), a 「 (*Kai Yinhao* – or the Chinese *open quotation* mark) will denote where the appending notation will refer to. For pieces with multiple long repeat passages, pairs of encircled Chinese characters act as the quotation marks and are referred to as "from ⊖ to ⊡ ."

英語琴統初階

# Fingering – Right Hand

| Script | Name | Details |
|--------|------|---------|
| | | *Basic Fingering (single string with single sound)* |
| 乇 | 托<br>Tuo1 | **Thumb** plucking in an **inward** movement, towards centre of the palm.<br><br>(NOTE: Since the thumb is the opposing finger, there is some debate as to what "inward" means. Most people today agree on "inward" defined as "toward the center of the palm" and vice versa, but many pre-20th century handbooks and some schools today teach "inward" as "towards the player's body". One must make sure which definition is taken when interpreting or playing a piece by examining the original document's fingering section.<br>*Standards of the Guqin* goes with the first and modern definition, with "centre" as "middle of the palm".) |
| 尸 | 擘<br>Bo4 | **Thumb** plucking in an **outward** movement. See above note. |
| 木 | 抹<br>Mo3 | **Index** finger plucking in an **inward** movement, towards the centre of the palm. |
| し | 挑<br>Tiao1 | **Index** finger plucking in an **outward** movement.<br>Posture: The finger should be supported by the thumb before pushing out. |
| 勺 | 勾<br>Gou1 | **Middle** finger plucking in an **inward** movement. |
| 切 | 剔<br>Ti1 | **Middle** finger plucking in an **outward movement.** |
| 丁 | 打<br>Da3 | **Ring** finger plucking in an **inward** movement. |
| 夲 | 摘<br>Zhai1 | **Ring** finger plucking in an **outward** movement. |

| Single-string movements (multiple sound movements) | | |
|---|---|---|
| 杚 | 抹挑 | **First *mo* 木 then *tiao* し**. Writing two movements together does not imply that the notes necessarily be played faster, but that they are musically related to the same phrase. |
| 冩 | 勾剔 | As above, but with the middle finger. |
| 㪯 | 打摘 | As above, with the ring finger. |
| 叕<br>or<br>兴<br>Or<br>厶 | 疊蠲<br>Die3<br>Juan1 | On a single string: 勹木 in **rapid succession on the same string**. Produces two quick but clear sounds.<br><br>**On multiple strings**: Perform a quick 木 on all involved strings, while using the middle finger to stop the previous string as the next is played.<br><br>The shorthand symbol for this movement is not to be confused with Quanfu and Banfu (全扶,半扶). |
| 夻 | 抹勾<br>Mo3<br>Gou1 | Similar to above, but has implication to play slower, making the two sounds distinct from each other. |
| 类 | 半輪<br>Ban1<br>Lun2 | 勹 勽 in rapid succession on the same string. Knuckles should be bent and lined against each other, firing off in an unrushed manner. Speed of playing this movement depends on context of the piece. |
| 合 | 輪<br>Lun2 | 勹 勽 し in rapid succession on the same string. Produces 3 sounds. Knuckles should be bent and lined against each other, pronouncing clearly and unmuddled. Speed of playing this movement depends on context of the piece. |

| | | |
|---|---|---|
| 北<br>《《《<br><br>Or<br><br>小 ·<br>《《《 | 背鎖 or<br><br>小鎖<br><br>Bei1<br><br>Suo3<br><br>or<br><br>Xiao3<br><br>Suo3 | 木𠃊勹 in rapid succession on the same string. Produces 3 sounds.<br><br>Different masters have different explanations on the *suo* patterns. While variations may seem endless and confusing when cross-referencing different schools of teaching, the basic pattern must be noticed: the rhythm for dividing the series of notes are fixed, and are played out from combinations of 𠂆 and in-out sequences (such as 杏 ). The formula for *suo* rhythms are:<br><br><br><br>Rhythm Patterns of Suo |
| 矢<br>《《《 | 短鎖<br><br>Duan2<br><br>Xuo3 | 木𠃊勹 男木 on the same string. Produces 5 sounds. **See above** regarding rhythm. |
| 長<br>《《《 | 長鎖<br><br>Chang2<br><br>Xuo3 | (木𠃊) 木𠃊勹 男木𠃊勹 on the same string. **Produces 7 sounds** (**sometimes** specified as **9 sounds** if followed by the term 九声). **See above** regarding rhythm. |
| *Multiple-String Movements (single/double-sound movements)* | | |
| 厂 | 歷<br><br>Li4 | A 𠃊 movement on two (or more) consecutive strings. The focus is on being light, brisk, and clear. |
| 𡚦 | 如一<br><br>Ru3 Yi1 | "As one (sound)", perform a 男 on two strings simultaneously to produce one whole sound. This character is usually written in subscript (and looks like accompaniment notation) which includes one pressed and one open string. e.g. (4th string at 7.6 *hui*, open 3rd string 𡚦) |

| 早 | 撮 Cuo1 | There are two variations of this movement: 勹乚 on two separate strings to produce 1 sound for smaller distances (2~4 strings apart), OR 勹乇 on two separate strings to produce 1 sound for larger distances (5 strings apart or more, usually used for perfect octaves). |
|---|---|---|
| 辱 | 反撮 Fan2 Cuo1 | Same as above, reverse motion: 木㫖 for smaller distances (this movement may require some practice), OR 尸㫖 for larger distances. **Appears only after a 早.** |
| 足貟 | 齷齪、 Wo4 Chuo4; Or 摟圓 Lou3 Yuan2 | Simultaneously on two strings, perform a 木 and 勹, producing 1 sound. This is like the 早, but gentler in sound (from using inward movements, hence avoiding hard nail sounds). e.g.: 足一三 = [勹一] + [木三]  The alternative symbol of 貟 is 團. |
| 㳀 | 潑 Bo1 | Index, middle, and ring fingers move **inward** simultaneously to **produce 1 sound**. The fingers are lined up close to each other and act as one moving body part to produce a powerful sound from the string(s). |
| 申 | 剌 La2 | Index, middle, and ring fingers move **outward** simultaneously to **produce 1 sound.** The fingers are lined up close to each other and act as one moving body part to produce a powerful sound from the string(s). |
| 㪇 | 潑剌 Bo1 La2 | A combination of the above, playing 㳀 followed by a 申, producing 2 sounds. |
| 団 | 打圓 Da3 Yuan2 | Play 乚勹 (at normal speed, then pause) 乚勹乚 (quickly, then pause) and 勹 (drift out) on the **two previously mentioned strings**. This character is always written in subscript, following the two indicated strings. |

英語琴統初階

| | | |
|---|---|---|
| 單 | 彈<br>Tan3 | Pluck outwards forcefully on the two strings indicated using middle and index finger, digging deeper than usual with the nails into the string and stop before the next string. An alternative name for this is 支 (鼓, *Gu3*)<br>Usually, this movement is played multiple times:<br>㧞 *Shuang Tan*: "Tan" twice, using both or middle then index fingers.<br>三<br>口口 *San Tan:* "Tan" thrice: ring, middle, then index fingers. |
| 声<br>玄 | 牽<br>Qian1 | Pluck inwards on the two strings indicated using the index and middle finger, essentially the opposite action of Tan above.<br>Quick reference: (木 1 2) |
| *Multiple-String Movements (Multiple-sound movements)* | | |
| 六<br>厷<br>高<br>弗<br>蒲 | 滾<br>Gun3 | "To roll", a series of 勹 played continuously. The accompanying string numbers indicate the starting point **to** the final string.<br>This symbol is not to be confused with the number six. |
| | 臨<br>Lin2 | Similar to above, but played with ㄴ (the index finger). Traditionally defined as only used for harmonics. |
| | 沸<br>Fu2 | "To Bubble/Flow", A series of 木 played continuously. The accompanying string numbers indicate the starting point to the final string. |
| | 滾沸<br>Gun3<br>Fu2 | A combination of 六 and 弗, producing a back-and-forth wave of sounds. |

| | | |
|---|---|---|
| 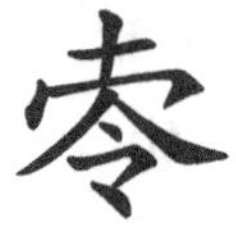 索 | 索鈴<br>Suo3<br>Ling2 | "A string of bells", Similar to 六, but played as a series of し (index) instead of 芍 (ring). Usually played with harmonic notes. |
| 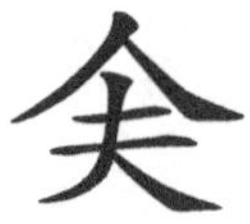 全 | 全扶<br>Quan2<br>Fu2 | On two consecutive strings, 木 on the top string. As the 木 continues to the bottom string, the middle finger **stops** the top string sound by touching it, then proceeding with 勹 on the two strings. When playing the bottom 勹, the ring finger **stops** the top string's sound by touching it. **Produces 4 sounds in one continuous chain.** |
| 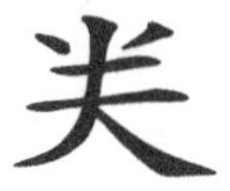 关 | 半扶<br>Ban4<br>Fu2 | On two consecutive strings, 木 on the top and bottom strings, with middle finger stopping top string by touching it during the 木 on the bottom string. **Used for harmonics only, produces 2 sounds in one continuous chain.** |
| 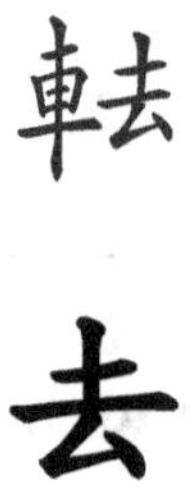 �<br>去 | 却轉<br>Que4<br>Zhuan3 | On two consecutive strings, play using ring and middle finger outwards (strings B-A-B-A) and finish with the thumb resting on the higher (B) string to silence it. Opposite movement equivalent of Quan-fu. **Produces 4 sounds in one continuous chain.**<br>Quick reference: ( 芍2 芍1 另2 芍1 伏) |
| 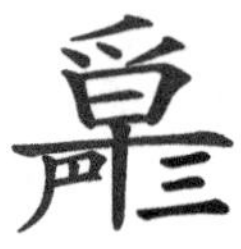 鼉 | 搯撮三聲<br>Tao1<br>Cuo4<br>San1<br>Sheng1 | On the aforementioned two strings (of which one is pressed), perform a 冈 and 已 with the left hand (refer: Left hand "*Yan* 罨, to cover "and "*Tao-qi* 搯起, to dig up"), 早 the two strings, 冈 and 已 **two more times**, and another 早. **Produces 8 sounds.**<br>(Quick reference: 冈 已 早, 冈 已 冈 已 早) |
| 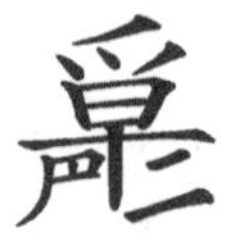 鼉 | 搯撮二聲<br>Tao1<br>Cuo4<br>Er4<br>Sheng1 | On the aforementioned two strings (of which one is pressed), perform a 冈 and 已 with the left hand two times, followed by 早 on the two strings.<br>(Quick reference: 冈 已 冈 已 早) |

| | | |
|---|---|---|
| 繇 | 搯潑剌<br>三聲<br>Tao1<br>Bo1 La2<br>San1<br>Sheng1 | On the aforementioned two strings (usually consecutive, of which one is pressed), perform a 冈 and 巳 with the left hand, followed by a 𣃥, 冈 and 巳 two more times, ending with a 中. **Produces 8 sounds.**<br>(Quick Reference: 冈 巳 𣃥, 冈 巳 冈 巳 中) |
| 韋 | 摘潑剌<br>Zhai1<br>Bo1 La2 | On the mentioned two (consecutive) strings, perform a 芍 on the lower string, then the upper string, and then a 鞸 on both strings. **Produces 4 sounds.** |
| 小<br>日勹<br>勹门 | 小間勾<br>Xiao3<br>Jian1<br>Gou1 | Involves 3 strings, of which the top 2 must be consecutive (e.g. strings 3, 4, 5 or 2, 3, 6). Begin with 勹 on the middle string, followed by 丁 on the top string, finally a 乚 on the lower string. **Produces 3 sounds.** (e.g. 勹 3, 丁 2, 乚 6)<br>**NOTE: Some textbooks may explain the _Jian Gou_ movements to be simply a 乚 and 勹 with 1 string in the middle for the smaller and 2 strings for the larger movement. This is a mistaken interpretation.** |
| 大<br>日勹<br>奀门 | 大間勾<br>Da4<br>Jian1<br>Gou1 | Involves 3 strings, of which the top 2 must be consecutive (e.g. strings 4, 5, 7 or 5, 6, 7). Begin with a 木 on the middle string, followed by 勹 on the top and middle strings. As the middle finger hits the lower string, ring finger **stops** the top string, followed by 丁 on the two strings. Finally, 乚 the remaining (lower) string. **Produces 5 sounds.**<br>(e.g. 木 5, 勹 4, 勹 5, 丁 4, 乚 7).<br>See above note for details. |

*Others*

| | | |
|---|---|---|
| 伏 | 伏<br>Fu2 | "To prostrate oneself". Use palm of right hand to cover the vibrating strings to abruptly stop the sound. This movement is usually used in conjunction with 中, therefore also has a variant known as 㐱 (_la fu_ 剌伏). The covering motion creates a slapping sound like the ripping of silk, and performing this movement at 4th/5th _hui_ would amplify this effect. |

# Fingering – Left Hand

| | | Written on top of primary tablature |
|---|---|---|
| 大 | 大指<br><br>Da4 Zhi3 | Left hand thumb.<br><br>**Tip: Using a "half-flesh, half-nail" area of the thumb to press on the string produces the best result. When playing multiple strings, the thumb joint can also be used.** |
| 亻 | 食指<br><br>Shi2 Zhi3 | Left hand index-finger. |
| 中 | 中指<br><br>Zhong1<br><br>Zhi3 | Left hand middle finger. |
| 夕 | 名指<br><br>Ming2<br><br>Zhi3 | Left hand ring finger.<br><br>**Tip: Rotate the finger so that it is on the left side, using near the "half-nail, half-flesh" area to press on the string. This would allow greater control to press or touch the string properly and accurately.** |
| 足 | 跪指<br><br>Gui4<br><br>Zhi3 | Literally "kneeling finger", left hand ring finger's second joint (the upper joint, closer to the fingernail).<br><br>**Tip: Instead of applying pressure from the palm down to the finger, practice using the finger to exert downward force on its own. To do this, pretend as if the finger joint is kicking out onto the board.** |
| 尤 | 就<br><br>Jiu4 | Assume the same left hand fingering as from the previous description (on the music score).<br><br>**Tip: Unless otherwise stated, *jianzi-pu* without left hand fingering automatically assumes whatever movement was stated before. Watch for any *budong* 不動 symbols beforehand – this symbol most likely refers to that context.** |
| 扔 | 不動<br><br>Bu2<br><br>Dong4 | (Left hand) immobile. Keep left hand on string and position in preparation for a note on the same position further down in the piece. |

英語琴統初階

## Left hand position numbers and marking

Left-hand positions are traditionally written in 徽位 *hui-wei* (*hui* position) shorthand for a longer phrase, such as 七八 (7-8) being "between 7 and 8" and 九上 being "[a bit] above 9", and are the standard in Ming dynasty textbooks. Despite the seemingly imprecise description, it implied that the player knows where the exact tone is in the vicinity. The basis of descriptions is always with the closer *hui*, unless it is roughly halfway in between two of them.

Since the *Dahuange Qinpu* (1673), manuscripts began to adopt a new system called 徽分 *hui-fen* (*hui* decimal), which describes a position by dividing the distance between two *hui* into ten equal parts. What used to be described as 七八 7-8 in the old system, for example, is now 七六 7.6.

For 0.5 positions, the character 圡 (Shorthand for 半) is used instead of 五, example such as 8.5: 圡 .

Position 13.2 is also known as 卜 ("outside", *wai*, 外).

| | | | |
|---|---|---|---|
| 卄 | 散<br>San3 | | Open String. Play with right hand only (Left hand not pressing or touching). |
| 宀,安 | 按<br>An4 | | Stopped/Pressed note. Press down string firmly onto board (in preparation for a series of notes ahead). Not to be confused with the adjective Ding (steady.) |
| ㇒ | 泛<br>Fan4 | | Harmonics. Place finger accurately on the marked position on the string (touching, but applying no force whatsoever) while plucking with the right hand.<br><br>**Tip: As tradition describes, "like a dragonfly skimming on a surface of water", the touch must be light in order to make the sound crisp and clear (which lasts about 6~8 seconds on a typical instrument). As skill improves, try removing the left finger quickly after obtaining the sound.** |
| 㢟正 | 泛起/止<br>Fan4 Qi3<br>/Zhi3 | | Begin / stop playing described notes as harmonics. These characters are written in subscript, and both must be used to bracket a selection of movements that is to be played as harmonics. A ㇒ note in the middle of the bracketed sentence cancels the effect for that note, however. |

*Table header:* *Tone Quality, written on top of primary tablature or in subscript*

| | | | Basic glissandos (slides), written in subscript |
|---|---|---|---|
| 上 | | 上<br>Shang2 | A firm upward glide from the previous position to the marked positions, e.g. *shang* 7.6 (from a position lower than 7.6).<br>At times, a number may be attached before the *shang* symbol, indicating how many stops the player makes in order to reach the position, e.g. *2 shang 7* (from 9th *hui*) would involve sliding firmly up from 9th → 7.6 (or 7.9 depending on string)→ 7th. These multi-step slides require familiarity of the pentatonic scale and its corresponding positions represented on each string. |
| 下 | | 下<br>Xia4 | A firm downward glide from the previous position to the marked positions, e.g. *xia* 9 (from a position higher than 9). At times, a number may be attached before the *xia* symbol, indicating how many stops the player makes in order to reach the position described below, *e.g. 2 xia 9* (from 7th *hui*) would involve sliding firmly down from 7th → 7.6 (or 7.9 depending on string) → 9th. |
| 乜 | | 拖<br>Tuo1 | "Drag." Slide left hand in a dragging manner to indicated location. |
| 弓 | | 引<br>Yin3 | "Lead to." Drag naturally (unhurried, up once or twice) to exact location. Not to be confused with *tan* 彈, the right hand movement. |
| 卜占 | | 綽<br>Chuo4 | Sliding up onto tone. Begin from a slightly lower position (away from the bridge) and slide up to position as the sound is produced.<br>For example, a *Chuo* on 9th *hui* would mean pressing the string at half to one tone lower than the tone on 9 (anywhere from 10 to 9.5 is acceptable), pluck as the left finger slides up to 9 and hold. |
| 氵 | | 注<br>Zhu4 | Sliding down onto note. Begin from a slightly higher position (closer to the bridge) and slide down to position as the sound is produced. |

英語琴統初階

| | | |
|---|---|---|
| | | For example, a *Zhu* 9 would mean pressing the string at certain distance higher than 9 (7.9 is acceptable), pluck as the left finger slides down to 9 and hold. |
| 隹 艮 | 進 Jin4 | Advance. After playing a pressed note, slide up one note (on the pentatonic scale) while ensuring an audible volume after the transition. |
| 艮 | 退 Tui4 | Retreat. After playing a pressed note, slide down one note (on the pentatonic scale) while ensuring an audible volume after the transition. |
| 乍 | 復 Fu4 | "Return". From a previous advance or retreat movement, return back to original pressed note position. Advance-return can be written together as 雋 and retreat-return as 暑. |
| 徠 | 往來 Wang3 Lai2 | "Back and forth". Repeat the last pair of positions (if applicable) by sliding back and forth without rounding off for two (or three) times. Otherwise, advance or retreat one tone away from last specified location. |
| *Left-Hand Notes* | | |
| 閃 电 虏 庵 | 罨/掩 Yan3 | "To cover". Assuming that a previous note was a pressed note, using the indicated left hand finger, strike down and hold onto the indicated string (likely the same one) and position, **producing one sound.** |
| 虜 庵 | 虛罨 Xu1 Yan3 | "Empty cover". Similar to the above, only that a pressed note was **not** previously played. The left finger would have to produce one sound from relying solely on striking the string, instead of altering a previous tone. |
| 虔 | 虛按 Xu1 An4 | After obtaining a certain sound (assuming open string), lightly press on the marked position as if playing a harmonic (which will restrain the sound), then remove finger. |
| 扎 | 推出 Tui1 Chu1 | "To push out". Using indicated left finger (usually middle), push out and release the string, **producing one open note.** |

| | | |
|---|---|---|
| 弁 | 分開<br><br>Fen1<br>Kai1 | "To divide apart". Usually played in context of a compound right hand movement such as *mo-tiao* 杢 , but separating the two sounds. Play the first sound, perform a 隹, then play the remaining note while coming back down. |
| | *Vibratos (Yin and Nao)* | |
| 亇<br><br>ゥ | 吟<br><br>Yin2 | A small-degree vibrato performed closely around the actual tone (¾ tones or less on the pentatonic scale). Begin by playing the actual tone, **then** move slightly back and forth for **two to three** revolutions, finishing on the original position. The movement is described as "in style of reciting a poem", and the movement should be rounded, natural (as to human speech), and gradually decreasing. A graphical representation is presented below:<br><br> |
| 犭 | 猱<br><br>Nao2/<br>Rou2 | A medium-degree vibrato performed **only either above or below** the actual tone (about 1 note on the pentatonic scale). Begin by playing the actual tone, **then** move slightly back and forth, finishing on the original position. The movement is described as "like a sloth climbing a tree", and the movement should be rounded and gradually decreasing in tone variation. An adjective may accompany the *Nao* to indicate its direction. A graphic representation is presented below:<br><br> |

| | | |
|---|---|---|
| 立 | 撞<br>Zhuang4 | "To collide (or bump)". After plucking the string, quickly slide up a halftone or so and back, with the return approach pressing on the string more firmly. The result is 1 actual tone, followed by 2 empty tones.<br> 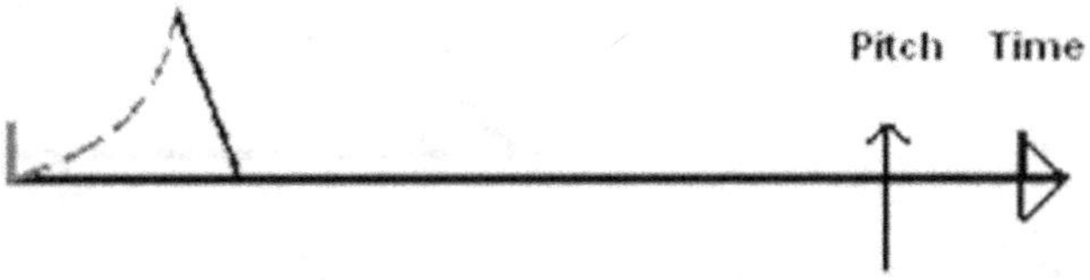<br> |
| 豆 | 逗<br>Dou4 | "To provoke", "To skilfully vie for (something)". Move 0.1 to 0.2 of a tone up before actually plucking with the right hand, then after obtaining the sound, continue **firmly** moving upwards, followed by a quick, empty fall back to the original intended tone position. The note should not be played too heavily in order to prevent a convoluted sound. The result is 1 tone slightly higher than intended (produced by the right hand) **merged** into an empty tone (the actual pitch).<br> 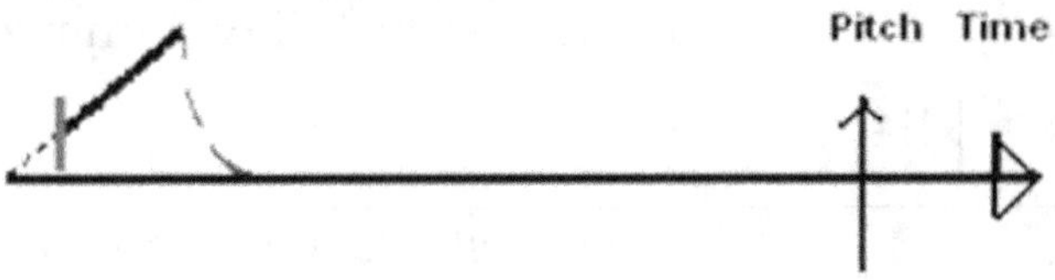<br> |
| 史 | 使<br>Shi3 | Assuming that a previous pressed note was played, perform a *chuo* **followed** by a *yin* (as below) or *nao*. Then perform a *zhuang* from the raised position back to the original sound. This move is different from *xu-zhuang* and *dou* because **the right hand does not play immediately before this movement.** Make sure that this movement is played continuously and very smoothly. The diagram below will attempt to explain the movement: 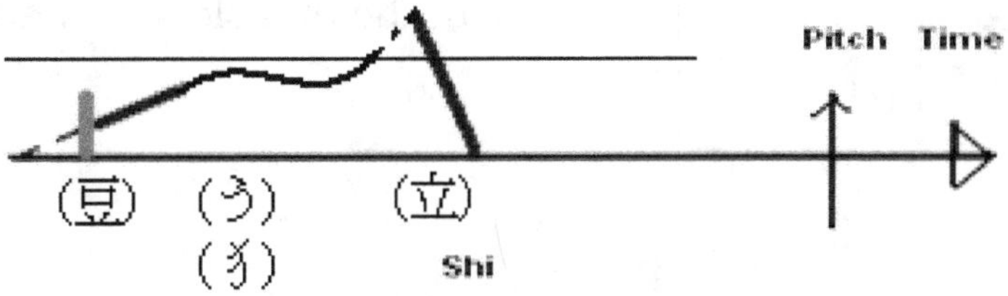<br><br> |

| | | |
|---|---|---|
| 奐 (symbol) | 喚<br>Huan4 | After obtaining the pressed note, move slightly upwards, then quickly down past the original pitch by about 1 or 2 positions in a **firm manner**, then return to original position in a **light** manner. The movement should be light-hearted, as it resembles "a swan calling for rain".<br><br>Pitch Time<br>Huan |

### Adjectives to vibratos & common examples

The following adjectives are added as prefixes to the previously mentioned vibrato and portamento movements. For example, a hurried *yin* is read "*ji-yin.*"

| | | |
|---|---|---|
| (symbol) | 绰<br>Chuo4 | Perform a *chuo* then the vibrato indicated on the pressed string. |
| (symbol) | 注<br>Zhu4 | Perform a *zhu* then the vibrato indicated on the pressed string. |
| (symbol) | 急<br>Ji4 | "Hurriedly." Play with urgency and rushed feeling. |
| (symbol) | 緩<br>Huan3 | "Unrushed, slow." Play at ease and in a relaxed pace. |
| (symbol) | 長<br>Chang2 | "Long." Extend the sound of the pressed note for a longer time. |
| (symbol) | 細<br>Xi4 | "Small." The pitch variation is more subtle than the standard variant. (For example, if the pitch originally goes up 1 pentatonic note, it is now ½ a tone.) |
| (symbol) | 緩急<br>Huan3<br>Ji4 | "Unrushed, then hurriedly." Play the note with the *vibrato* two times, with the first slowly, then the second time quickly. |

| | | |
|---|---|---|
| 双双<br>丁<br>双<br>立 | 雙<br>Shuang1 | "Double." On the same string, play the accompanying *vibrato* **twice** (in the same manner, unlike *huan-ji*). |
| 宁宂 | 定<br>Ding4 | "Fixed." Compared to the regular variant, the pitch amplitude is smaller as the wrist stays in a fixed position, instead making small jumps with the fingertip, and is almost unnoticeable by the eye. |
| 迂 | 遊吟<br>You2<br>Yin2 | "Wandering *yin*". This *yin* is larger in amplitude and slower in speed, as if a person is wandering leisurely. Used exclusively for *yin*. |
| 徕徕<br>丁 扌 | 往來<br>Wang3<br>Lai2 | "Back and forth." Advance one full tone and back for two or three cycles, emphasizing on the distance with a rounded treatment on direction change. |
| 飞飞<br>丁 扌 | 飛<br>Fei1 | "Flying." Perform the *vibrato* at twice the amplitude of a normal one. |
| 莎荡 | 蕩<br>Dang4 | "Wavy." Perform the vibrato longer and stronger than usual, similar to objects yielding to the wind or splash waves from a stone thrown into a pond. |
| 音音<br>扌 丁 | 撞吟/猱<br>Zhuang4<br>Yin2/<br>Nao2 | Perform a *zhuang* (See next section) followed by the *vibrato* (without striking a tone on the right-hand again after the *zhuang*). |
| 虜虜<br>虛虜 | 虛<br>Xu1 | "Empty." Perform the *vibrato* without the right hand plucking beforehand. |
| 車 | 連<br>Lian2 | "*Legato*, connected". |

| | | |
|---|---|---|
| 午 | 滸<br>hu3 | After playing a pressed note, pause briefly and glide up lightly several positions (usually 3 or 4 notes on the pentatonic scale, but not strictly controlled). |
| 坙 | 輕<br>Qing1 | "Lightly." |
| 禾 | 重<br>Zhong4 | "Heavily." |
| 更 | 硬<br>Ying4 | "Firmly." Similar to *Shang* (up), but quicker and should have a firmer remaining sound than after a *shang* movement. |
| 尚 | 淌<br>Tang3 | "Pouring." When playing a *shang*, push note back down (return to or beyond original position) just before the note drifts out. |
| *Replacement and Release Techniques* | | |
| 巳 | 起<br>Qi3 | "To rise up". General term that can be further defined, but otherwise lifting up or releasing the left finger pressing on string. Other definitions include: *Tao-qi, Dui-qi, Zhua-qi, Dai-qi, Pié-qi, Tong-qi.* |
| 㠯 | 搯起<br>Tao1 Qi3<br>or<br>搯起<br>Qia1 Qi3 | Pick-up, lit. "hold/gather up" While the thumb is pressing on a previously mentioned position, the ring finger presses onto the indicated position on the notation, then the thumb **lifts itself while slightly dragging the string** to produce a pressed sound (the pitch is whatever the location the ring finger is on). In recent years, it is also often read as 搯起 Qia1 Qi3, as a result of character misrecognition and/or printing discrepancies. |
| 芑<br>㲍 | 對起<br>Dui4 Qi3 | "Match and release." Essentially the same as a *tao-qi*, but implies the first note (the tone involving the left thumb pressed position) is plucked before this release is performed, while *tao-qi* does not. **Modern scores use this and tao-qi interchangeably.** |

英語琴統初階

| | | |
|---|---|---|
| 𢒩 | 拶對起<br>Za1 Dui4<br>Qi3 | A variant of the *duiqi*, referring to a position being pressed by the left thumb to be replaced by another finger (eg. ring finger), by way of pressing on a lower position and immediately sliding up to replace the position. |
| 爪 | 爪起<br>Zhua3<br>Qi3 | "To hook up". Remove thumb from pressed string by slightly arching it inwards (a clawing manoeuvre), pulling the string slightly backwards, then lift up, producing **one open note**. |
| 帒 | 帶起<br>Dai4 Qi3 | "To bring up". Remove ring finger from pressed string by slightly pulling string backwards and lift up, producing **one open note**. |
| 撇 | 撇起<br>Pie2 Qi3 | After obtaining the pressed note (with the left thumb), perform a *chuo*, and then claw up with the thumb in a diagonal direction, producing an open note in the process. This move is now **obsolete**, as modern pieces use *zhua-qi* in replacement. |
| 方 | 放<br>Fang4 | Release. Similar to 帶起, produces one open note. Difference is in the hand movement: instead of going upwards away from the instrument, the hand moves directly onto the next pressed position of a different string. |
| *Unison-matching movements* | | |
| 㪃 | 放合<br>Fang4<br>He2 | Similar to *fang* above, but also plucking with the right hand movement as indicated at the same time as the previous string is released. Produces one sound that should be harmonious or matching. |
| 罔 | 同聲<br>Tong2<br>Sheng1 | The two previously mentioned notes/movements should be played simultaneously, producing one sound. |
| 同 | 同起<br>Tong2<br>Qi3 | Similar to above, except applied to one plucked string, while another one (the formerly pressed string) is being brought up, producing one sound together. |

| | | |
|---|---|---|
| 唫 | 應合<br>Ying1<br>He2 | After playing a certain stopped note, slide up or down to match with the sound that is produced from an open note recorded before this symbol.<br>(e.g. A sound at 10th *hui* on the fourth string, then slides up to the 9th *hui* **just as** an open seventh string is played.) |
| *Appending Notation* | | |
| 取、慢 | 緊，慢<br>Jin3<br>man4 | "Tighten" and "Slacken", respectively. (Used for string tuning) |
| ○ | 句號<br>Ju4 Hao4 | Footstop. End of a musical phrase. |
| 合 | 入拍<br>Ru4 Pai1 | Play according to rhythm. (On beat, *alla tempo*) |
| 盒 | 入慢<br>Ru4<br>Man4 | Play section, slowed down. (*Ritardando*) |
| 杀 | 入剎/殺<br>Ru4 Sha1 | "(Re)Enter modal tone." The following section is performed in the tonic of the mode (for purpose of concluding a piece). |
| 乍<br>甪 | 再作<br>Zai4<br>Zuo4 | "(Perform) again." Repeat bracketed/implied section once more, totalling **two times**. |
| 二乍 | 二作<br>Er4 Zuo4 | "Two times." Repeat bracketed/implied section **once** more, totalling **two times.** Similarly, for 三作 (three times) etc., include the originally bracketed motions in the quotation mark 『 as one instance. |

| | | |
|---|---|---|
| 篗 | 從頭再作<br>Cong2<br>Tou2<br>Zai4<br>Zuo4 | Repeat from start. This is similar to the Italian term *"Da Capo"*. If in middle of a piece, refer to the start of the section instead of the whole piece. |
| 篗 | 從勾再作<br>Cong2<br>(Gou1)<br>Zai4<br>Zuo4 | Repeat from 『 (open quotation symbol – watch which direction it goes). This is similar to the Italian term *"Dal Signo"*. If multiple instances are used, be sure to check the direction of the quotation symbol to see which section is being repeated. At times, a Chinese character in a circle (for example, ⑭) may be used in pairs to bracket a musical phrase. |
| 雁 | 應<br>Ying4 | "Match." Denotes the 2 previous notes should produce a matching pitch and played in *legato* succession. |
| 省 | 少息<br>Shaao1<br>Xi1 | A brief pause. |
| 㿩 | 大息<br>Da4 Xi1 | A longer pause. |
| 奏 | 曲終<br>Zhong1<br>Qu3 | End of piece. Could also be written horizontally, [䌷]. Older manuscripts may have alternative characters like 操 (etude), 調 / 周 (mode), 意 (motif) instead of 曲 (tune), but the arrangement of the characters is the same. |

# Pitch and Temperament: Organizing Sounds to Tones

## Basic Concepts: Absolute and Relative Pitch

The main purpose of this book, an English-language work on a Chinese musical tradition, is to introduce the scholarly tradition of translation between the musical traditions, while avoiding the common imposing assumptions of one in the interpretation of the other. Explanations given in this chapter are introductory in nature, in order to let students familiarize themselves with basic musical terminology and concepts, and provide a gateway into further investigation if they so wish.

For those completely new to music, one must first understand that pitches, or how high a certain note of sound is, are expressed in one of two ways: By an *absolute* system that correlates a certain pitch with a fixed name, and a *relative* system that relates the pitches to a referent point from within the given passage of music (the "tonic"). This dual-system of pitch expression is common between both the Western and Chinese traditions; hence it is easy to find commensurate terminologies between the two languages.

## Absolute Pitch

In the Western tradition, the twelve tones are organized using seven Latin letters (ABCDEFG), with five of the tones expressed as an alteration of another, as either raised (sharp ♯) or lowered (flat ♭). Since C major (CDEFGAB) is the scale that expresses its natural scale without sharps or flats, C is often thought of as the fundamental note in establishing the pitches of the twelve tones. For the Chinese tradition, there are twelve unique names given to the twelve tones within the octave. The first and *fundamental* one that sets the precedent for all subsequent tones is known as the Yellow Bell, *Huangzhong*. Legend has it the Yellow Emperor ordered that this tone become the standard to measure sound, after having heard the sound of the phoenix's cries.

In both Western and Chinese history, the exact pitch of Huangzhong is a hotbed of academic contestation, but for the Chinese the stakes have critical political implications: Standards of measurement is directly tied with ritual, and subsequently the legitimacy of a ruling dynasty.

For the purpose of this book, the Huangzhong pitch is directly tied with the Western C pitch: This is done for two major reasons, the first being that this has been

英語琴統初階

the convention since the establishment of the first Chinese Republic in 1911. The second reason is that the pitch of Huangzhong of the bianzhong (orchestra bells) of Marquis Yi of Zeng, commissioned in 433 B.C.E. and unearthed in 1977 had its Huangzhong very close to the Western C2. The table below lists the names of the absolute pitches in relation to the Western pitch system, with Huangzhong starting from C:

The Twelve Absolute Pitches, starting from C (黃鐘 Huangzhong = 合 He):

| | | | | | | |
|---|---|---|---|---|---|---|
| Western | C | C♯/D♭ | D | D♯/E♭ | E | F |
| Chinese | 黃鐘 | 大呂 | 太簇 | 夾鐘 | 姑洗 | 仲呂 |
| Pinyin | Huangzhong | Dalü | Taicu | Jiazhong | Guxian | Zhonglü |
| Shorthand | ム | ㋮ | マ | ㊀ | 一 | 么 |
| Gongche | 合 | 下四 | 四 | 下一/乙 | 一/乙 | 上 |
| Pinyin | Ho/he | Xia-si | Si | Xia-yi | Yi | Shang |
| Western | F♯/G♭ | G | G♯/A♭ | A | A♯/B♭ | B |
| Chinese | 蕤賓 | 林鐘 | 夷則 | 南呂 | 無射 | 應鐘 |
| Pinyin | Ruibin | Linzhong | Yize | Nanlü | Wuyi | Yingzhong |
| Shorthand | ㄥ | 人 | ㋫ | フ | (り) | り |
| Gongche | 勾 | 尺 | 下工 | 工 | 下凡 | 凡 |
| Pinyin | Gou | Che | Xia-gong | Gong | Xia-fan | Fan |
| Western | C | c♯/d♭ | d | d♯/e♭ | | |
| Chinese | 黃鐘清 | 大呂清 | 太簇清 | 夾鐘清 | | |
| Pinyin | Huangzhong-qing | Dalü-qing | Taicu-qing | Jiazhong-qing | | |
| Shorthand | 久 | (ɡ) | ɡ | す | | |
| Gongche | 六 | 下五 | 五 | 高五 | | |
| Pinyin | Liu | Xia-wu | Wu | Gao-wu | | |

## Relative Pitch

Relative pitch, referred to as the solfège in English, is another system of referring to the pitches of the sound, but unlike the absolute pitch system uses the "key" or "mode" of the melody – usually the first note of a given passage – as the fundamental note to count from.

The Western solfège is usually credited to 11th century Italian musician Guido d'Arezzo, who accredited the seven sounds of the diatonic scale to the first syllables of the phrases in the hymn *Ut queant laxis* dedicated to St. John the Baptist, forming *Ut (do)-re-mi-fa-so-la-si*. Meanwhile the Chinese have various forms of "scales" in 5, 6, or 7 tone combinations. The fundamental names stem back to the five fundmental tones created in the cycle of fifths – *gong* (1), *shang* (2), *jue* (3), *zhi* (5), and *yu* (6). These names were first mentioned in the *Rituals of Zhou* but its origins apparently preceded the work. Since the five "proper" tones are the only undisputed notes in the various "scale" gamuts, conversely the sixth or seventh tone is referred to by different names in different systems. For example, in discussion to seven-tone scales used in *yanyue* or banquet music (i.e. Court music outside of Confucian sacrificial contexts), the *shang* scale uses *do-re-mi-fa-so-la-si*$^{b}$ where the last note of *si*-flat is referred by a unique name of *rün* (note ^). In the 1584 treatise *Complete Books of Music and Measurement* (*Yuelü Quanshu*), Zhu Zaiyu devised the names *zhong* ("middle") and *he* ("harmony") to refer to *fa*-sharp and *fa* respectively (note *).

For example, a tune that starts on F and follows its modal qualities would count F as "1" or "do" rather than "4" or "fa." American Chinese musicologist Rulan Chao Pian takes this one step further and counts "fa" as "1," and the pentatonic sounds 12356 are by default translated as "fa-so-la-do-re" (as opposed to what we'd otherwise write as 45612). While this has its advantages (to be explicated in the next chapter under "tuning"), this work, like most others, will remain on commensurating "do-re-mi-so-la" as "gong-shang-jue-zhi-yu" as 12356, upon consideration of starting from the most familiar fundamental tone from each tradition.

英語琴統初階

The Twelve Relative Tones, starting from do (the Five Primordial Sounds in grey):

| Solfege | Do | #do/♭re | Re | #re/♭mi | Mi | Fa (#mi) |
|---|---|---|---|---|---|---|
| Chinese | 宮 | 清宮 | 商 | 清商/嬰 | 角 | 清角/和* |
| Pinyin | Gong | Qinggong | Shang | Qingshang/Ying | Jue | Qingjue/he |

| Solfege | #fa/♭sol | Sol | #sol/♭la | La | #la/♭si | Si/Ti (♭do) |
|---|---|---|---|---|---|---|
| Chinese | 變徵/中 | 徵 | 變羽 | 羽 | 清羽/閏^ | 變宮/變 |
| Pinyin | Bianzhi/zhong | Zhi | Bianyu | Yu | Qingyu/rün | Biangong/Bian |

As we can see on the above chart, to build a heptatonic diatonic scale by adding the two tones after Jue on the Pythagorean cycle would involve adding two of the "bian-" or "qing-" non-pentatonic tones. Unlike Western heptatonic expression where fa (4) and si (7) have their own names, they are seen as a subordinate of the closest pentatonic tone ("raised Jue/#3" and "lowered Gong/♭1"). This logic effectively *reverses* Western practice of the sharp/flat cycle, as seen in the chart below:

| | | | | | | | | |
|---|---|---|---|---|---|---|---|---|
| Heptatonic (Western) | Solmization | | ♭1 | ♭5 | ♭2 | ♭6 | ♭3 | ♭7 |
| | Pitch | | ♭C | ♭G | ♭D | ♭A | ♭E | ♭B |
| Pentatonic (Eastern) | Pitch | | | | #C | #G | #D | #A |
| | Solmization | | | | #1 | #5 | #2 | #6 |
| Chinese | Pitch Name | | | | | | | |
| | Rel. Name | | | | Q-gong | Q-zhi | Q-shang | Q-Yu |
| | \\ | Start | here↓ | below | // | | | |
| Heptatonic (Western) | Solmization | 4 | 1 | 5 | 2 | 6 | 3 | 7 |
| | Pitch | F | C | G | D | A | E | B |
| Pentatonic (Eastern) | Pitch | #E | C | G | D | A | E | ♭C |
| | Solmization | #3 | 1 | 5 | 2 | 6 | 3 | ♭1 |
| Chinese | Pitch Name | | Huang | Lin | Tai | Nan | Gu | Ying |
| | Rel. Name | Q-Jue | Gong | Zhi | Shang | Yu | Jue | B-gong |
| | // | Start | here↑ | above | \\ | | | |
| Heptatonic (Western) | Solmization | #4 | #1 | #5 | #2 | #6 | #3 | #7 |
| | Pitch | #F | #C | #g | #D | #A | #E | #B |
| Pentatonic (Eastern) | Pitch | ♭G | ♭D | ♭A | ♭E | | | |
| | Solmization | ♭5 | ♭2 | ♭6 | ♭3 | | | |
| Chinese | Pitch Name | Rui | Da | Yi | Jia | Wu | Zhong | |
| | Rel. Name | B-zhi | B-shang | B-yu | B-jue | | | |

## Temperament: A Beginner's Brief History

While the earliest discovered musical instruments may present some form of organized series of tones, they were not systematized until the discovery of relationships between pitch and the instruments' lengths, quantified with the invention of measurement and rationalized through mathematics.

The human ear is receptive to ('likes') tones that often match up in its wavelength ('harmonious'), despite that they are different. Early sages discovered that this can be achieved by having two tones produced by similar instruments (say, two pipes of the same diameter or two strings of the same thickness and tension) but one is shorter or longer by a simple fraction of the other. As the simplest denominators, dividing tones by **twos and threes,** quickly gave birth to humanity's first organized tonal system, known as "Pythagorean tuning" in the Greek tradition, and "Sanfen Sunyi Lü" in the Chinese one. While both systems begin on the premise of multiplying and dividing by threes to generate **twelve individual tones**, the Pythagorean system starts from the **fundamental** (first tone) and only goes up by removing a third in one direction, and only adding on thirds in another, generating a spiral of tones spanning a wide range of octaves. Meanwhile, the Chinese system devised a formula to keep things within one octave, or the range between the length of the tone, and half of that.

While the pitch of a tone is often expressed as **frequency** today, refers to how fast the vibrations are beating and measured by number of cycles per second, it was difficult to observe, quantify, and measure such things without advanced instruments involving electricity. Instead, traditional pitch is visualized and quantified by the **length** of the body that sounded it – which is the reciprocal value of the former: The longer the length, the lower the pitch.

### Sanfen Sunyi Lü: Cycling within limits

We recognize the relationship of tones when dividing a length by halves (twos) and thirds, then we can quickly discover that twelve distinct tones, called *lü* or *lut* 律, can be created before

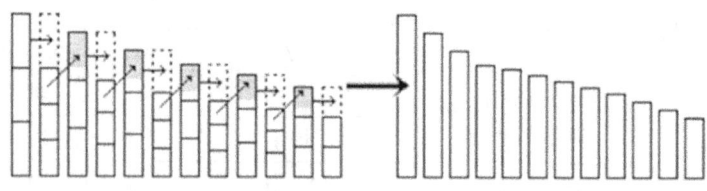

**Sanfen sunyi lü as a graphic, as according to the *Records of the Grand Historian (Shi Ji)*.**

they repeat themselves (with small differences – which we'll discuss below). When these twelve tones are created and rearranged in order by length, you'll notice that the

英語琴統初階

tones were created 7 lü apart when a third of the length is subtracted. Mathematically, this is expressed as $[original\ frequency] \times {}^2/_3$. On a string (such as the one on your qin), pressing it on the 9th *hui* (which is the distance marker for 2/3rds of the string's vibrating length) or compare two pitch pipes of the same diameter with one 2/3rds the length of the other. These are practical methods that will achieve this.

Take this new length and now *divide* it by two thirds, or measure and *add on* a third of that length. This will generate a tone 5 semitones or lü lower in pitch. On the qin, pressing on the 10th *hui* (the distance marker for 3/4ths of the string's length) *prior to* matching the standard string, and then releasing it, will add the remaining third onto the string.

The Chinese term, *sanfen sun-yi lü* 三分損益律, literally "Thrice divide (*san fen*), subtract (*sün*), and add (*yi*) temperament" describes the calculation process. As the Chinese count the original tone that you started off with are the distances between two tones, going up seven and down five semitones is iterated in Chinese as *shun-ba ni-liu* 順八逆六 ("progress eight, reverse six") instead.

## The Problem with Sanfen Sunyi and the Long Road of Temperament Studies

The problem with the twelve tones generated by the *sanfen sunyi* system is that upon returning to the supposed fundamental or base tone, instead of achieving a perfect ratio of **2:1** (or 2.00) where a perfect octave is achieved, such as playing an open string and its half length (7th *hui*), we have instead $2^{11} : 3^{-12}$ or $\frac{531441}{524288}$. This natural "imperfection" was recognized in writing as early as the Spring and Autumn period (~5c. B.C.E.), and while musicians and instrument makers had to adjust for the difference amongst the tones by intuitive "feel." There is no rational explanation of how that is to be done.

For centuries, mathematicians and musicians strived to devise a musical system that could fill or equalize the gap, known as a "comma", and reach 2:1 as close as possible, while using some expression of the 3:2 ratio or method.

The Chinese over the ages had several major approaches to solving this dilemma:

- by continuing the cycle to divide the octave into more tones with smaller steps,
- by adding more tones to account for the "extra tones" created in the comma, and
- by splitting the comma's difference and spreading them out amongst the twelve existing tones to "hide" it.

The first approach is credited to Han dynasty mathematician Jing Fang 京房, who devised a 60-tone temperament in the 1st century C.E.. Although it is futile to attempt to find a coinciding value between the powers of two (the octaves) and powers of three (the fifths) because they will never intersect, if we continue the *sanfen sun-yi* cycle, one would achieve values *very close* to the base tone from the 52nd permutation (53rd note) of the cycle onward: $\frac{177147}{176776}$ in his demonstrative thesis. This figure would be later precisely calculated by Dutch mathematician Nicholas Mercator and affirmed by William Holder in 1694 as $\frac{3^{53}}{2^{84}}$. In the 5th century C.E., astronomer and mathematician Qian Lezhi 錢樂之 attempted to refine the remaining 6 tones left over from Jing Fang's system. Qian expanded the sixty tone system six times to a 360 tone system, but did not discover a reasonably well-tempered balance. Modern mathematics proved that Qian's attempt had done *half* the work that was needed to achieve the next number of equidistant tones. By mirroring 308 of the 360 tones, but generated in the reverse direction (a move otherwise seen as an 'illegal move' by the classicists), Zhao Songguang published the completed 666-tone system in 1993.

The second approach of adding "extra tones" is actually a motley collection of distinctly different methods. The first comes with prioritizing performance in mind: Cai Yuanding proposed in the 12th century C.E. that one can avert dissonance by having instruments that can play the first 18 tones on Jing Fang's system – the 12 tones and 6 tones after that are "secondary/backup" tones that account for the Pythagorean comma. Another example is Emperor Kangxi's 14-tone scale in the Manchu Qing Empire, proposed in the imperial treatise *Lülü Zhengyi* 《律呂正義》 of 1713 and then expanded upon by his grandson Emperor Qianlong in 1746. Kangxi tried to create a set of tones that were equidistant when played heptatonically and matched perfectly in octaves. They also conform to traditional *sanfen sunyi* doctrine and have six yin and six yang tones. But instead he sacrificed the concept of *shun-ba ni-liu* ("progress eight, reverse six") and allowed himself to add two extra tones to the gamut. The result was fourteen tones in that actually go well beyond the natural octave. 20th century musicologist Yang Yinliu decried Kangxi's system as a failed rebuttal and misusage of Zhu Zaiyu's "New Temperament" described below. He intentionally did not credit and even denigrated Zhu's name to spite the academic and scientific value of the Ming prince's work. This was meant to elevate the the Manchu rulers' display of intellectual superiority. While

英語琴統初階

this system was mathematically flawed and unsound for the purpose of rounding the comma, modern scholars find new value in exploring this theory to understand received folk music in China today.

The third approach was to take the difference between the fundamental and the the comma, and "hide" them away to spread the comma equally among the twelve tones. The idea was first conceived by He Chengtian in 5th century C.E. to adjust the tones by lowering one twelfth of a comma for every jump in the cycle of fifths. While the concept of dividing the comma was novel, this approach over-compensates the later jumps in the cycle. Loosely inferring from He's idea, Zhu Zaiyu, in his 5000-page long compendium *Yuelü Quanshu* in 1584, Zhu divided the length between the fundamental and its octave counterpart successively by adjusting the natural *sanfen sunyi* tones. Zhu reduced each jump by a ratio of the twelfth root of two ($12\sqrt{2}$). But by forgoing the tradition of starting with the number 9 to define the fundamental length to start with, he calculated this work instead by the use of 2 (twice the length) and 1 (the fundamental note). The result was an unfamiliar, irrational, but unprecedently accurate figure for an equidistant set of tones. This theorem was allegedly transmitted to Europe by the Jesuit mission to Ming China, where it gained favour over time with lutenists and keyboard players. It is now the default temperament used in Western music, commonly referred to as the Twelve-tone Equal Temperament (12-tET).

The study of temperament is a shining hallmark of Chinese mathematics and physics. This is living proof of how Chinese science balanced both between theory and practicality. Despite the advances in theoretical models like Zhu Zaiyu's 12-tET, the seven-stringed guqin held fast to the simple 3:2 ratio of Just Intonation. Zhu's proposal was unfeasible (if not impossible) to tune by ear, and was made worse by the tuning system on the instrument, which is prone to constant string slippage and instability. Furthermore, offsetting the strings artificially like Zhu Zaiyu's system would make the harmonics lose their matching pitches when compared on multiple strings, and thereby lose a critical function and feature of qin musicking. Therefore, it is necessary to learn the quirks, attributes, and weaknesses of the more fundamental and older 'imperfect' temperament systems.

# Modality: Changing Modes & Tunings

Temperament deals with establishing a given pitch within the range of a quarter of a tone, and is usually mathematical and microscopic. After we have determined the finer points and established the twelve tones' exact pitches, we will make sense of the relationships between them within the more macroscopic, practical context of music. The more tones get exposited into a phrase of music, the more 'unstable' it gets. Not only due to the micro-discrepancies of the comma, the 'perfect ratio' relationships also get broken up into finer and finer intervals. Soon dissonance starts to occur between them. To determine the line between the threshold of 'tonal' or

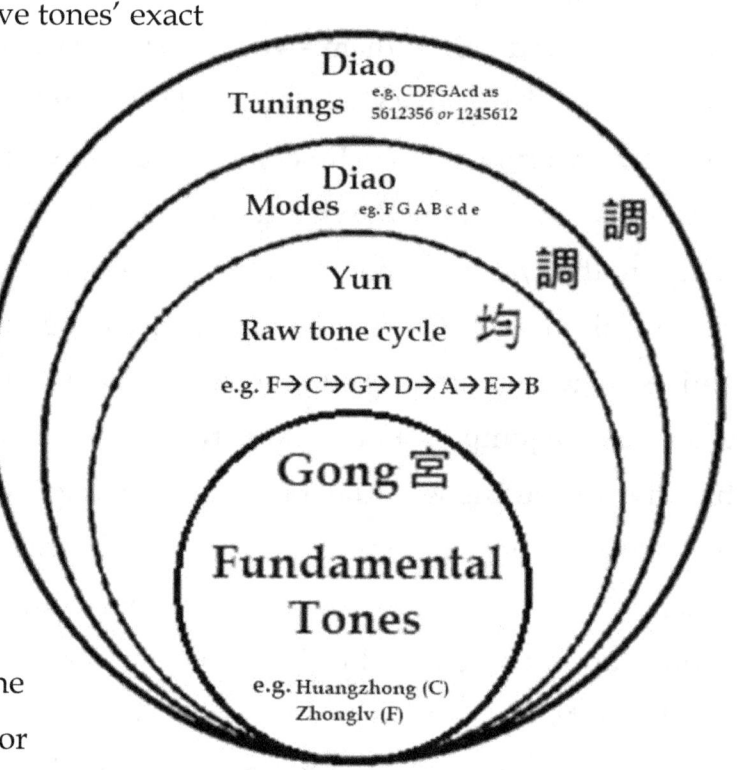

'beautiful-sounding' music and 'atonal' or 'dissonant/ corrupting/ugly' music has been a topic of not only mathematics, but also one of moral philosophy and metaphysics.

Nonetheless, there are three layers to the technical concepts of modality, each one building to the next: From establishing the pitches of the lü, comes the specific sequence in which the raw tones are generated, called Yun 均, and from Yun they are rearranged, organized, and classified into Diao 調 "modes". Through practical applications in which instruments are made and fine-tuned to play and represent those modes, there are "tunings", that confoundingly share the same character 調 Diào. As instruments (including the qin) reach beyond their home octave, any given tuning can also sound like another mode when played, by starting or focusing on another tone or another part of the instrument.

## Yün 均: Cycling Keys for strings of tones

Although written with the character 均 today is read *jün*, meaning "equal" or "equivalent," the *yün* reading is retained from the original character 韵/韻 when referring to the musical concept of modality. The character 韵/韻 is today instead

英語琴統初階

translated as "resonance" – the pure, lingering vowel/tone after the sound or *sheng* 聲 of the consonant that has been produced and passed.

While we may create the twelve tones from the *progress eight, retreat six*/cycle of fifths as a neutral and a thing-of-itself process, remember that due to the comma each resulting note drifts further and further away from the fundamental (by 2 cents). The idea is: If a musician created a new flute using a different base tone, or tuned a string starting from a different pitch, the same pitch's scale will sound different. The distance and discrepancy from the fundamental is different, too, as the timbre differences pitch is sounded from a different part of different instruments. Therefore, the Chinese take note of the *yün* fundamental seriously.

Yün sequences are named by its first, or fundamental tone, and move only forwards in fifths, as defined by the rules of *sanfen sunyi* cycling. For example:

Zhonglü (F) Yun is:       F → C → G → D → A → E → B.

Huangzhong (C) Yun is:   C → G → D → A → E → B → #F.

Do be careful, however, not to assume that simply by rearranging them to diatonic order would be equal to a mode or scale. Chinese music doesn't *necessarily* consider the key as the fundamental note ("tonal centre") as it was given simply because it is "the beginning" of the series. That piece of information lies instead in the next component, the mode.

## Mode: Arrangements of yun, two ways of expression

# Zhonglü (F) Yun 仲呂均 (F→C→G→D→A→E→B)

### rearranged diatonically AND
### tonic (starting) on the second note (C), therefore C-D-E-F-G-A-B

| C | 大調 Major | = | 黃鐘 Huangzhong(C) | (為)徵調 (as) Zhi |
|---|---|---|---|---|
| | | | Tonic [first tone played in scale] | Scale [Zhi modifying modal form from Tonic] |
| | | | OR | |
| | | | 仲呂 Zhonglü (F) | (之)徵調 ('s) Zhi |
| Key [mode applied into scale] | Tonic [first tone played in scale] | Scale [Taking key and defining intervals] | Mode [Major = Ionian = Zhi mode] | Key [First tone that generates the subsequent series. Only goes forwards in fifths.] | Tonic [Scale starts from the Zhi tone of the Key given, fitting all subsequent tones in Lydian form] |

Once we have a series of five to seven tones in a *yun*, we can rearrange them in diatonic, or sequential order from low to high. For example, F→C→G→D→A→E→B could be rearranged as C-D-E-F-G-A-B.

It is also possible to rearrange that diatonic arrangement to start from any other tone on that sequence, but keep the very same tones. Whether it is CDEFGAB or DEFGABC or ABCDEFG, they are all considered *scales* made of that original F *yun*, but by starting on a different part of the series the nature or *mode* is different because the distance from one note to the next (measured in lü/semitones) are each unique. When this is possible starting on all twelve fundamental tones, one would end up with 60 pentatonic (5 modes per yun) and 84 heptatonic (7 modes per yun) variations. Ultimately, these 60 or 84 scales are rearrangements of the same 12 tones. Some will sound very similar to others. Some start on the same tone and are only one tone off from the next, while others share the same modal pattern but start on a different tone.

Western common practice today has adopted to only refer to specific scales using the terms "major" and "minor" (with connotations for referring to two modes in the latter, when ascending or descending). In Chinese practice, aside from having five

英語琴統初階

major modal forms (represented by starting on each of the Five Primordial Tones), there are two major ways to refer to a scale: They refer to the role of the *tonic* or first tone in the scale, or refer to the *modal form* of the scale. While it may be a mouthful to say, the Chinese system makes explicit each concept, and allows for every detail to be customizable for every need.

| 太簇商調 // "Taicu Shang Mode" | | | | | | | |
|---|---|---|---|---|---|---|---|
| (Relative) | Gong 1 | Shang 2 | Jue 3 | Qingjue 4 | Zhi 5 | Yu 6 | Qingyu ♭7 |
| "Taicu **as** Shang" *Taicu wei shang* 太簇 為 商 (tonic-centered, relative mode) | 太簇 Tai cu **D** | 姑洗 Gu xian **E** | 蕤賓 Rui bin **#F** | 林鐘 Lin zhong **G** | 南呂 Nan lü **A** | 應鐘 Ying zhong **B** | 黃鐘 Huang zhong **C** |
| "Taicu's Shang" *Taicu zhi shang* 太簇 之 商 (mode-centered, relative tonic) | 姑洗 Gu xian **E** | 蕤賓 Rui bin **#F** | 林鐘 Lin zhong **G** | 南呂 Nan lü **A** | 應鐘 Ying zhong **B** | 黃鐘 Huang zhong **C** | 太簇 Tai cu **D** |
| (Absolute) | Gong 1 | Shang 2 | Jue 3 | Bianzhi #4 | Zhi 5 | Yu 6 | Biangong 7 |

Like the concept of "absolute pitch" versus "relative pitch", the modes on various tones can be organized and considered in "absolute" and "relative" systems – however, whether the mode's key, or the tonic of the scale become the measuring standard of this 'absolute', the answer may be exactly the opposite from each other. Therefore, in this case it is better to be acquainted with these two systems as it is known in Chinese: *Wei-diao* 為調 and *zhi-diao* 之調 modal systems.

## Wei-diao 為調: the Tonic-centered classical orthodoxy used by the guqin

| One Yun, Seven Modes: 1 = tonic/starting note (wei-diao 為調 "as mode" system) | | | | | | | | |
|---|---|---|---|---|---|---|---|---|
| **Zhonglü Yun** | **F** | **C** | **G** | **D** | **A** | **E** | **B** | **Diatonic scale** |
| **Relative name** | Gong | Zhi | Shang | Yu | Jue | Bian | Zhong | |
| F as gong (Ping-diao) | 1 | 5 | 2 | 6 | 3 | 7 | ♯4 | F,G,A,B,C,D,E |
| C as zhi (Se-diao) | 4 | 1 | 5 | 2 | 6 | 3 | 7 | C,D,E,F,G,A,B |
| G as shang (Qing-diao) | ♭7 | 4 | 1 | 5 | 2 | 6 | 3 | G,A,B,C,D,E,F |
| D as yu (Ce-diao) | ♭3 | ♭7 | 4 | 1 | 5 | 2 | 6 | D,E,F,G,A,B,C |
| A as jue (Chu-diao) | ♭6 | ♭3 | ♭7 | 4 | 1 | 5 | 2 | A,B,C,D,E,F,G |
| (E as biangong) | ♭2 | ♭6 | ♭3 | ♭7 | 4 | 1 | 5 | E,F,G,A,B,C,D |
| (B as bianzhi) | ♭5 | ♭2 | ♭6 | ♭3 | ♭7 | 4 | 1 | B,C,D,E,F,G,A |

The Han Chinese indigenous system for referring to modes and scales is the *Wei-diao* "as mode" system. After stating the *yun*, a pitch name is referred "as" the starting note of a scale under the specified modal form. For example, "F as gong" and "C as zhi" would share the same *yun* key (that being F), but the player would play the pentatonic scale starting from the specified tone. From the Han period on, three of these modal scales held particular importance as instruments like the qin and dizi flute could play these scales in its entirety without adjusting for accidental sharps or flats. This system was later theoretically expanded to all five tones, although the first three still hold higher importance due to their natural sequentialness.

| One Yun, Seven Modes: 1 = the specified yun key (wei-diao 為調 "as mode" system) | | | | | | | | | | | | |
|---|---|---|---|---|---|---|---|---|---|---|---|---|
| **e.g. Zhonglü (F) Yun →** | | **F** | | **G** | | **A** | **B♭** | **B** | **C** | | **D** | | **E** | **(F)** |
| Gong [mode of F] | Lydian | 1 | | 2 | | 3 | | ♯4 | 5 | | 6 | | 7 | 1 |
| Shang [...] | Mixolydian | 1 | | 2 | | 3 | 4 | | 5 | | 6 | ♭7 | | 1 |
| Jue | Aeolian (Minor) | 1 | | 2 | ♭3 | 4 | | | 5 | ♭6 | | ♭7 | | 1 |
| (Bian-zhi) | Locrian | 1 | ♭2 | | ♭3 | 4 | | ♭5 | | ♭6 | | ♭7 | | 1 |
| Zhi | Ionian (Major) | 1 | | 2 | | 3 | 4 | | 5 | | 6 | | 7 | 1 |
| Yu | Dorian | 1 | | 2 | ♭3 | 4 | | | 5 | | 6 | ♭7 | | 1 |
| (Bian-gong/Runjue) | Phrygian | 1 | ♭2 | | ♭3 | 4 | | | 5 | ♭6 | | ♭7 | | 1 |

英語琴統初階

The strength of using the *wei-diao* system is its practical straightforwardness on a pre-tuned instrument, such as a woodwind or even on a guqin. One can easily play the corresponding scale simply by starting on the given tonic: For example, on a standard tuning qin (which is Zhonglü/F *yun*), one can play *most* of the tones of a given mode on open strings – everything on the gong scale (starting from F, string III), 4 out of 5 tones on the Zhi scale and 3 out of 5 on the Shang scale. For these two scales, those tones are not found on the gong scale, they are found either on the skipped holes on the woodwind, or are played as pressed tones on the qin.

The downside to this system is that to the unaccustomed, thinking about a scale from its relative tonic, rather than the fundamental of the key (the gong) can be outright strange. Much of the time, the *yün* may not even be mentioned, so the player may have to reverse-engineer the mode to figure out the actual key to figure out the tones being used. But aside from that, this system provides an intuitive way to understand, at a glance, both the instrument in its natural tuning, as well as the obvious pentatonic tones that will be subsequently played.

## *Zhi-diao* 之調: western import, re-exported eastward

In the year Kaihuang 3 or 583CE, the Sui court adopted a heptatonic, 84-mode system as the official modal theory for the cycling of the twelve tones from the former Kuchean court musician, Sujiva. Although the Sui fell in mere decades after that to the Tang, this musical system proliferated and stuck with the scholarly and musician class for contemporary music. As traditional Confucian temple music was seen as sacred knowledge, Korean and Japanese emissaries and students were not privy to learning it. Instead, they absorbed the popular folk and its court banquet counterpart to become its own court music, where the system persists to this day.

Compared to the *wei-diao* system, *zhi-diao* modal systems operate in reverse logic: Rather than state the starting tone and

| Zhonglü Yun Tones, rearranged into seven diatonic scales, 1=relative Gong (tonic) of each scale | | | | | | | |
|---|---|---|---|---|---|---|---|
| | **F** | **G** | **A** | **B** | **C** | **D** | **E** |
| F as Gong | 1 | 2 | 3 | ♯4 | 5 | 6 | 7 |
| G as Shang | ♭7 | 1 | 2 | 3 | 4 | 5 | 6 |
| A as Jue | ♭6 | ♭7 | 1 | 2 | ♭3 | 4 | 5 |
| (B as Bianzhi) | ♭5 | ♭6 | ♭7 | 1 | ♭2 | ♭3 | 4 |
| C as Zhi | 4 | 5 | 6 | 7 | 1 | 2 | 3 |
| D as Yu | ♭3 | 4 | 5 | 6 | ♭7 | 1 | 2 |
| (E as biangong) | ♭2 | ♭3 | 4 | 5 | ♭6 | ♭7 | 1 |

then the modal form, *zhi-diao* always operate on gong diao or Lydian scale, where the yun is also the tonic. For example, "gong mode of F 仲呂之宮" and "zhi mode of F 仲呂之徵" would both be based on Zhonglü or F yun (FCGDAEB→FGABCDE), but would start on different tones according to the specified mode. In the examples, above, the Gong scale would start on F, and the Zhi scale on C.

| Seven Diao, One (Gong/Lydian) Mode: 1 = the specified *yun* key (*zhi-diao* 之調 "mode of" system) | | | | | | | | | | | | | |
|---|---|---|---|---|---|---|---|---|---|---|---|---|---|
| **e.g. *Zhonglü* (F) Yun →** | C | | D | | E | F | #F | G | | A | | B | (C) |
| Lower Zhi Mode | 1 | | 2 | | 3 | | #4 | 5 | | 6 | | 7 | 1 |
| Lower Yu Mode | | 7 | 1 | | 2 | | 3 | | #4 | 5 | | 6 | |
| Biangong-Runjue Mode | | 6 | | 7 | 1 | | 2 | | 3 | | #4 | 5 | |
| **Zhengsheng (Gong) Mode** | 5 | | 6 | | 7 | 1 | | 2 | | 3 | | #4 | 5 |
| Qingshang Mode | | #4 | 5 | | 6 | | 7 | 1 | | 2 | | 3 | |
| Qingjue Mode | | 3 | | #4 | 5 | | 6 | | 7 | 1 | | 2 | |
| Bianzhi | 7 | | 1 | | 2 | | 3 | | #4 | 5 | | 6 | 7 |

Due to the legacy of Tang conservative scholars holding fast to the qin and its traditional musicological systems; from the rapidly changing folk and banquet music scene, the qin's tunings are worked around *wei-diao* system. The singular exception is Wuxue Shanfang Qinpu 悟雪山房琴譜 (1832) by Cantonese qin player Wong King-Sing (Huang Jingxing) 黃景星, who organized his manuscript in the *zhi-diao* system. He referred to the tunes not by their common tuning names, but by their *yun,* and spelled out the pitches string by string if necessary.

英語琴統初階

## Conversion between *Wei-diao* and *Zhi-diao*

There are two ways to think about and convert between the two systems, one using the circle of fifths diagram and one without.

Since we know that the *gong* (Lydian) mode is always used in *zhi-diao* parlance, in the absence of the diagram, the same can be done by counting the number of semitones (lü) going clockwise from *gong* to the said tone (for *wei* to *zhi*) and from said tone to *gong* (for *zhi* to *wei*) and apply the distance accordingly.

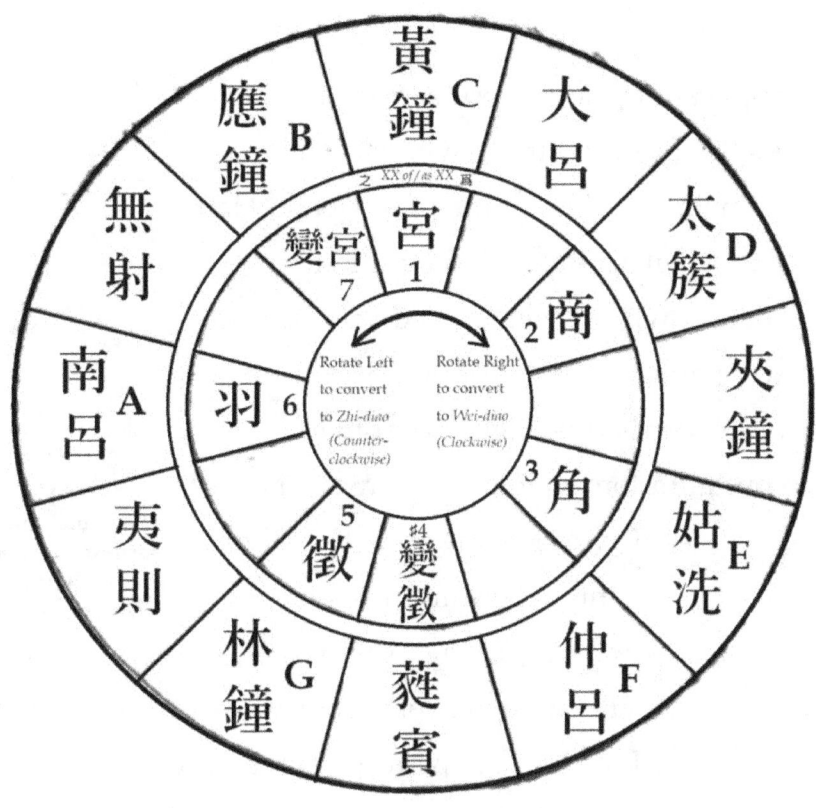

Let's try an example from each direction:

- Linzhong (G)'s Yu 林鐘之羽: Since there are 9 semitones from *gong* to *yu*, the *wei-diao* name would be "Guxian (E) as Yu 姑洗爲羽."

- Guxian (E) as Yu 姑洗爲羽: Since there are 3 semitones from Yu to Gong, the *zhi-diao* name would be "Linzhong's Yu 林鐘之羽."

Similarly, you can use the chart by rotating the relative pitch inner circle until *gong* aligns with the *zhi-diao* pitch indicated, and find the corresponding *wei-diao* counterpart with the pitch names showing the starting tone. Conversely, aligning the relative *wei-diao* tone (in this example, Yu) to the pitch in question and then trace to the corresponding *gong* pitch you would find the *zhi-diao* equivalent. This is why *zhi-diao* is also known as "left-rotating *zuo-xuan* 左旋" while *wei-diao* is called "right-rotating *you-xuan* 右旋".

# Tuning – Thinking modality practically and flexibly

String tunings are the physical application and representation of modes. As the Qin was strung with various number of strings in the pre-Qin and Han periods, it stabilized around the 4th century with seven, and the open strings were tuned pentatonically. Seven strings has several advantages over other configurations in the pentatonic context:

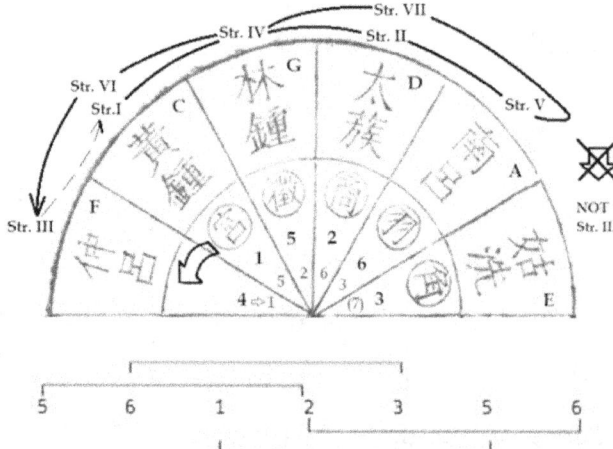

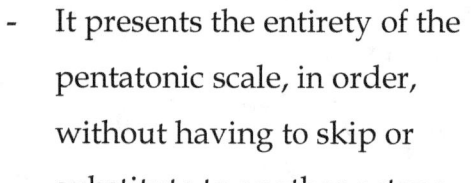

The square brackets show where the fifths (pairs using harmonics) match. Seven strings are the only ones where the top half and the bottom half both have 2 pairs, whereas more or less strings would be lopsided.

- It presents the entirety of the pentatonic scale, in order, without having to skip or substitute to another octave – even after some degree of modulation.

- It is the most perfectly symmetrical distribution of said tones: any more or less strings, and one would be left with with a major third between any of the bracketed pairs of strings.

- The pentatonic cycle is able to "cycle back" to the fundamental tone in **one** direction, without having to stop and start again in another direction, or to reuse the same strings and backtrack on fifths.

It is possible to create a plethora of modal scales under these rules. Depending on the source, tunings go by multiple names or references. However, they can all be summed up in two major categories: **Internal tunings**, and **external tunings**, where the latter can be further divided into another three types. But first, let's take a look at where we start off, with the how and why standard tuning comes to be today.

## Standard Tuning – The default setting of the strings

The Zhonglü as Gong (Lydian on F) on third string tuning is the formal name of the standard tuning that all other tunings are based and measured from. This tuning leverages the advantages of the seven-string layout mentioned above. It can play the pentatonic scale in the gong-centered 56123 and gong-leading 12356 configurations with ease; either by starting on string I or string III.

英語琴統初階

Throughout history, there are actually two (and a half) major models of what "standard" is perceived to be. According to Prof. Ding Jiyuan (1991)[1], those are:

| Mode | Pitches (Relative & Absolute) | Proponents/Pundits for the system |
|---|---|---|
| *Zhonglv Yun* [*'s/*之] Zhi mode | 56 123 56 CDFGAcd | Jiang Kui 姜夔 (Southern Song, 12~13c.) Yang Zhan 楊瓚 (S. Song, 13c.) Xu Li 徐理 (S. Song, 13 c.) Chen Minzi 陳敏子 (Yuan, 14c.) |
| *Huangzhong Yun* Zhi mode | 56 123 56 GACDEGA | Zhu Zaiyu 朱載堉 (Ming, 16c.) Wang Binlu 王賓魯 (Qing, 19~20c.) |
| *Huangzhong Yun* Gong mode | 12 356 12 CDEGAcd | Nie Congyi 聶崇義 (N. Song, 10c.) Cao Tingdong 曹庭棟 (Qing, 18c.) Wang Xuan 汪紱 (Qing 18c.) |

Like many other string instruments, the most effective and accurate method to tune a qin is by comparing halves and thirds using the harmonic overtones on two strings: by touching lightly on one spot of the string to produce a high frequency, which can then be matched with the supposed matching string and position. Western lutes and bowed strings usually have the third-length and half-length harmonics on adjacent strings that cause each string to be a dominant (or seven semitones) apart. However, the qin (among other East Asian horizontal zithers) makes full use of this relation by rearranging the strings to produce a sequential gamut.

To set the modern standard tuning (*zheng-diao* 正調), use a pitch pipe, tuning fork, or electronic tuner to set either the first string as C (two octaves lower from middle) or the third string as F. This is optional: If you are unable to tighten a certain string any higher, you use that tone as the standard instead. For a number of reasons, we may want to tune the instrument lower from this standard. This may include personal preference, the older age of an instrument, to avoid peculiarities like buzzing or ringing resonance, or the use of some silk strings. Many players prefer setting their instruments a tone or two lower from the above description when playing solo.

Tuning pieces (such as *Xianweng Cao* and the following harmonic tuning exercise) and beginner etudes all work around the principle of a single string used as standard.

---

[1] Ding Jiyuan 丁紀園. "Lue Lun Guqin de Wuyin Zhengdiao yu Shier-lv Xuangong Xian fa"

Then we can compare it with an equivalent pitch on a different string. This book strongly recommends the student to manually fine-tune the instrument with the harmonic method described on the following page, over the *sanfen sunyi* or Pythagorean temperament, rather than rely on an external tuner. This is due to discrepancies in the copying process, or due to the tuner's measurement in 12-tET. For adjustments toward Just Intonation temperament, use stopped and open string pairs instead. For specific instructions, refer to the footnote in Xianweng Cao, contained in Repertoire A.

Tuning revolves around comparing the dominant (*zhi*, "so") pitch of a string with the tonic (*gong*, "do") of another. The dominant sound can be produced by:

- Stopped notes, on the 9th *hui*
- Harmonic notes, on the 5th or 9th *hui*

Whereas the tonic sounds can be produced by:

- Open strings
- Stopped notes, on the 7th or 4th *hui*
- Harmonic notes, on the 10th, 7th, or 4th *hui* (12th and 2nd also work, but are not usually used except for precision)

## Tuning by Harmonics

To better understand these basic traits of the instrument, we can now tune the instrument by matching pitches on different strings, criss-crossing on either side of the dominant position.

1. First, select either 9th or 5th *hui*. The 5th *hui* is preferred by some for its closer range from the player's eyesight and clearer sound, but the 9th are used by others for familiarity of muscle memory.

2. A harmonic note on a given string at 9th/5th *hui* is equivalent to the pitch of the lower tonic harmonic, 3 strings down ("2 strings in the middle"). This relation is referred to in this book as 'Set A'. (For example, string IV at 9th/5th hui = string VII at 7th *hui*)

3. A harmonic note on a given string at 9th/5th *hui* is equivalent to the pitch of the higher tonic harmonic, 2 strings up ("1 string in the middle"). This relation is referred to in this book as 'Set B'. (For example, string IV at 9th/5th *hui* = string II at 10th/4th *hui*)

4. After setting a certain string's set pitch (e.g. 1st = C), locate Set A positions (e.g. string I @ 5th = string IV @ 7th) and play the two strings in rapid succession, with the tuned string first. The objective is to have both strings sound together and compare their pitches.

5. Using the tuning peg on the right, tighten or loosen the un-tuned string until the harmonic pair sounds as similar as possible. Fine tuning is possible by nudging the fly-knot on the bridge as well.

6. Using the newly tuned string, locate Set B positions (e.g. string IV @ 5th = string II @ 4th) and match the pitches using the previous techniques.

7. Using this newly tuned string, return to Set A and tune. Criss-cross using Sets A and B until all seven strings are tuned.

8. Be aware of the *gong-jue* ("do-mi") relation: The pair (on Set B) do not match, and have to be skipped over. An approximate equivalent can be found 1 *hui* away from the centre (e.g. 4th/3rd *hui*, or 10th/11th *hui*). 10th/4th *hui* on string III and 9th/5th *hui* on string V (on standard tuning) is an example of this relation.

9. Don't be afraid to test strings that were previously calibrated! Cross-checking weeds out ear-tuning imperfections and strings slipping on their own. Play all seven open strings at the end to check one more time.

10. If your ear can detect the smallest beating of a tone difference - you will find that after cycling through most of the strings, the latest tone you have tuned will be higher than the previous ones when you cross-check. That's the the Pythagorean comma at work and you'll never make everything perfect, so don't sweat striving for every pair to precisely match up. **Don't sweat it, and move on.**

For quick reference and a substantial score where this is demonstrated, see the following page.

# 泛音調絃法例 Harmonic Tuning Method Exemplar

Arranged by Juni Yeung

Standard Tuning 正調

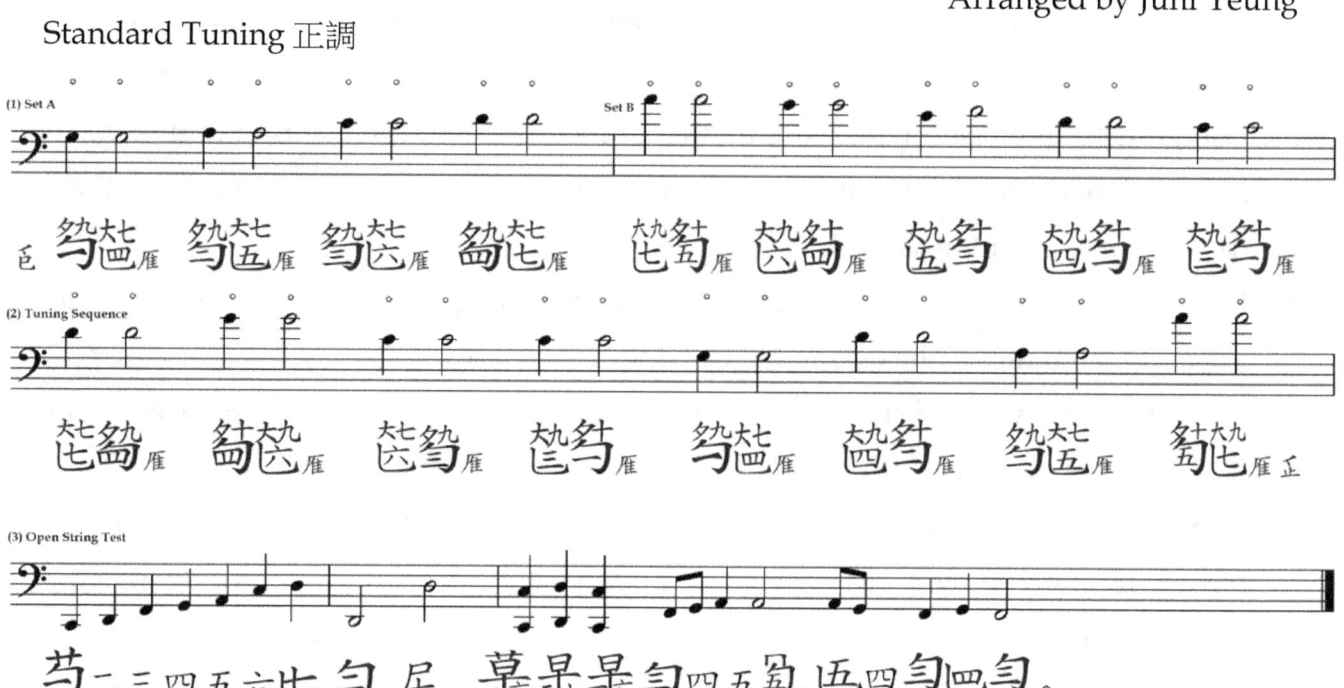

The tuning exercise starts on the second line, in this example starting on the 7th string. Starting on any given string would work, as long as you alternate between Set A and B (shown on the first line) – one can freely play a "snakes and ladders" progression as shown in the following chart below, until all strings are sufficiently considered in-tune:

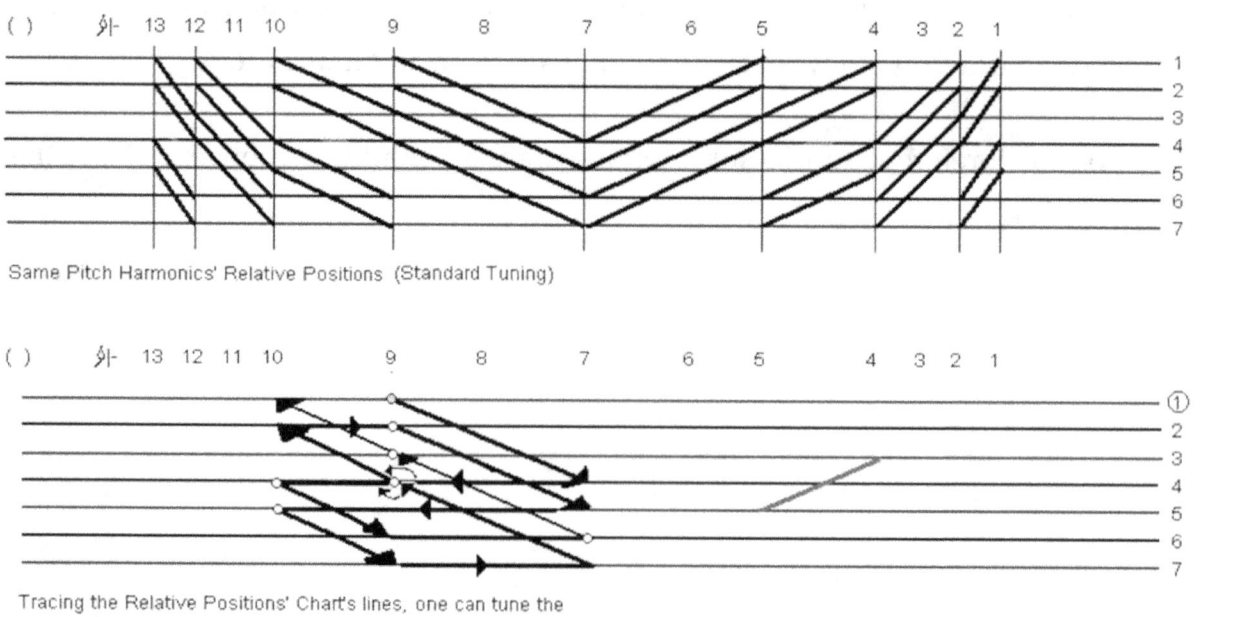

Same Pitch Harmonics' Relative Positions (Standard Tuning)

Tracing the Relative Positions' Chart's lines, one can tune the Standard tuning with ease.

66

英語琴統初階

# A Mental Checklist

1. The first string: Is it tight enough to produce a clear tone with no buzzing, but not over-tight so that other strings won't be too tight?
2. Using this string, will I be playing Set A, or Set B?
   a. Which strings am I playing?
   b. Using this set, which string is the standard? Which is getting tuned?
      i. Play the standard ("the right one") first!
3. Play the pair clearly.
   a. **Don't think now** – hands on the tuning pegs right after you play them!
   b. **Now listen** - Is the standard note higher than the other note? Lower? By how much?
   c. **Then tune** – Am I turning the right tuning peg? Am I turning it enough to make a difference? (About 1 full twist per semitone, varies per instrument).
4. Do the strings now sound the same? Am I even playing on the right positions?
   a. **If they do** - move on to the next pair on the other Set. If you were on Set A, go Set B. If you were on Set B, go Set A.
   b. **Still seems off** – Keep twisting for big differences. Push the fly-knot if it's a tad too low, or press down on the string with your right hand fingers where you play to pull the string a bit.
   c. **Can't tell by ear** – Try putting your hand on the wood and *feel* the hum. A near-exact match would produce regularly pulsating "waves", while an exact match would only produce a barely recognizable smooth hum on the surface.
   - **If you can't tell whether it's higher or lower** - just experiment by going one way. Worst thing to do is freeze. Try to imitate those two pitches with your voice, listening closely to match the instrument. Notice if your vocal cords need to tighten or loosen in the change from the first to the next sound.
5. If you come back to a pair you have tuned before, play them again ("cross-checking") – you may find that you're slowly going up higher and higher because of the Pythagorean system. Adjust *lower* when necessary – it may even go backwards once.
6. Have I gone through all the strings yet, with at least a cross-check or two?
   a. I did - Play through all seven open strings and they should sound good!
   b. Not sure - Play through them all anyway, and see if any one of them are off.

## Nei-diao 內調 (Internal Tunings): Same tuning, different modes

On Standard Tuning, one can easily play any of the pentatonic scales without having to change any string tunings. If a given piece of music uses all of the open strings, one can deduce that the music is probably in one of the first three modes (in cycle of fifths jumps - gong, shang, and zhi). It would be even more indicative if certain pressed notes play pitches that are unique to that specific mode, or start and stop the piece on the tonic of that mode. For example, a piece in Shang or Zhi modes would avoid using Jue tones (3) and will tend to use press that string.

To understand what constitutes "a gong *diao*" differs according to the manuscript or the school of thinking, however. For example, pre-19th century manuscripts consider 'gong *diao*' as pieces beginning with the gong *string* rather than the gong *pitch*, and this duality continues to this day. The following table presents how the 1425 manuscript *Shenqi Mipu*《神奇秘譜》interprets internal *diao* on standard tuning:

| Standard Tuning (CDFGAcd) | | | | |
|---|---|---|---|---|
| Mode | Solmization (main sequence highlighted) | Main String | Phrases tend to end on this tone (and string number) | Frequently occurring tones (and string number) |
| Gong | 56**123**56 | 3rd | 1 (3rd string) | 5 (6th string) |
| Shang | **12456**12 | 1st/6th | 1 (1st/6th) | 2 (2nd/7th),5 (4th) |
| Jue | 561**235**6 | 3rd | 1 (3rd) | 3 (5th), 6 (2nd/7th) |
| Zhi[2] | 1245612 | 4th | 5 (4th) | 2 (2nd/7th) |
| Yu | 5**612356** | 2nd/7th | 6 (2nd/7th) | 3 (5th) |
| Shang-Jue | **12456**12 | 1st | 1 (1st/6th) | 3 (*pressed* 2nd), 6 (5th) |

The first five qin strings were named "gong (宮), shang (商), jue (角), zhi (徵), yu (羽)"after the sounds of the pentatonic scale, but in practice the strings were actually tuned to zhi-yu-gong-shang-jue. With the standardization of the qin to seven strings and the perfection of its tuning system from that depends on open and stopped strings for harmonic overtones, a debate for which is the 'standard tuning' began. Ban Gu (ca.

---

[2] Pentatonically speaking, Zhi mode is modally the same as Gong mode. Historical manuscripts classify zhi-mode as pieces that start with/focus on zhi string under this category. See essay on following page and John Thompson. "Some Issues in Historically Informed Qin Performance," http://www.silkqin.com/08anal/hip.htm#zhidiao.

英語琴統初階

32~92 C.E.) wrote in the *Han Records* that the qin sounds were "gong/shang/jue/zhi/yu/shaogong/shaoshang." Qing exegesis scholars in the 17th to 19th centuries cited this conflict in argument that the *gong* tone should be on the first string that bears its namesake. Then others argued that since antiquity, *gong* sound has always been on the third string. Prof. Ding Chengyun's (2001)[3] rationale was that both were correct, depending on the period in question: Back when the qin was only five strings, the respective strings may have played the respective tones, but as the number of strings increased, the advantages of starting from zhi (as explained in the previous section), which was already the default tuning of the 25-stringed se, became prevalent, and matched the Guanzi's account that the zhi and yu lengths were longer than gong itself.

81  108  72  96  64

Gong  Zhi  Shang  Yu  Jue

**Guanzi's pitches featured a lower zhi and yu. (Guanzi: Diyuan Chapter 58)**

The mode of the current standard tuning, assumes that the first string is tuned to Huangzhong or C, and the seven strings would be CDFGAcd. Conventions would indicate that the pentatonic scale begins on the third string (on F pitch). In other words, the scale is first considered as "'so-'la-do-re-mi-so-la" or 5612356 rather than "do-re-fa-so-la-do-re" or 1245612, because 'fa' or 4 is not one of the pentatonic sounds – the first five tones going up on the Cycle of Fifths (or in Chinese terms, 'downwards-generated' by the *sunyi* cycle).

In retrospect, the first-string tonic system would mean that in order to fit with the standard pentatonic scale (do-re-mi-so-la, or 12356), the strings will have to be tuned to CDEGAcd. This can be done by lowering the third string by one semitone (one '*lü*'), so that the tonic or gong string will be on the first instead of the third.

Many players today instead opt to play pieces in this system using Standard Tuning, avoid playing its open string, and lower their pressed notes by one position whenever a supposedly changed string is involved. This is called *jiediao* 借調 or "Borrowing another tuning"or *cenong* 則弄 "side transposition." As Zhu Zaiyu wrote in his 1584 treatise *Lülü Jingyi* 《律呂精義》 , just because a pentatonic system is established (*li-ti* 立體 "establish-body") in such a way does not mean its application

---

[3] Ding Chengyun. "Qindiao Suyuan: Lun Guqin Zhengdiao Tiaoxian Fa," Shanghai: *Yinyue Yishu* (2001:4) 40-43.

(*wei-yong* 為用 "as use") is fixed on its given gong. It can be rotated in its use anytime when playing.

| Standard Tuning | 7-string Example | Gong Sound (Str.III) | Zhi Sound (Str.I/VI) | Shang Sound (Str.IV) | Yu Sound (Str.II/VII) | Jue Sound (Str.V) |
|---|---|---|---|---|---|---|
| **[Start Str.I] Application (Se-diao)** | [12]X5612 | [Qingjue] | Gong | Zhi | Shang | Yu |
| **[...Str.III] Established (Ping-diao)** | [56]12356 | Gong | Zhi | Shang | Yu | Jue |
| **[...Str.II] Application (Qing-diao)** | [23]56X23 | Zhi | Shang | Yu | Jue | [Qingyu] |

## *Wai-diao* 外調 (External Tunings) – Modulating System & Nomenclature

As we see from the modes chart in the previous section, Standard Tuning allows for a great degree of flexibility in performing the pentatonic modes. But this often sacrifices of its mediant or range (the mode starts from the edge of the instrument and cannot go lower/higher). This is when gamut will have to be retuned and the *gong* repositioned onto another string.

The natural *gong* or tonic of any given string tuning (not the mode!) usually can be conveniently identified on the guqin as the one that matches with the open string sound 2 strings down (otherwise expressed as "1 string in the middle") while pressing slightly above the 11th *hui* rather than the 10th. This is because the 10th *hui* or ¾ the length of the instrument will generate a natural perfect fourth or qing-jue (4), one semitone higher than jue pitch. Conversely, just as pressing 9th *hui* will generate a natural perfect fifth, doing so on the jue string will generate a bian-gong (7), one semitone short of returning to *gong* pitch. The same results can be produced using the same positions with harmonics, two octaves higher.

英語琴統初階

These pressed qing-jue and bian-gong sounds are the "hidden" notes of the heptatonic scale on a given tuning, and are essential for changing the tuning of the instrument and hence assign it a new key by a process called *Xuan'gong Zhuandiao* 旋宮轉調. Literally "rotate the gong and change the tuning," by either **loosening the gong sound string to become jue** (慢宮為角 *man'gong wei jue*), or **tightening the jue sound string to become gong** (緊角為宮 *jin-jue wei gong*), we **modulate** both the *yün* and the starting pitch.

There are also two types of *wai-diao*, or "external tunings." The first are **perfect** modulation tunings, where utilizing the cycle of fifths to raise or lower certain strings in order, a perfect pentatonic scale with no 'accidental' tones is presented. For example, by raising the fifth string by one lü, the unmatching pair on Set B harmonics is moved from strings III and V to V and VII, and the mode now starts on Wuyi (♭B) rather than Zhonglü (F). The next perfect modulation would then raise strings II *and* VII, as they represent the same tone.

Similarly in the other direction, we could also choose to have String I as *gong*, by lowering String III by one lü from standard tuning to make the scale CDEGAcd (1235612), with the first five notes suggesting the pentatonic scale. The next modulation

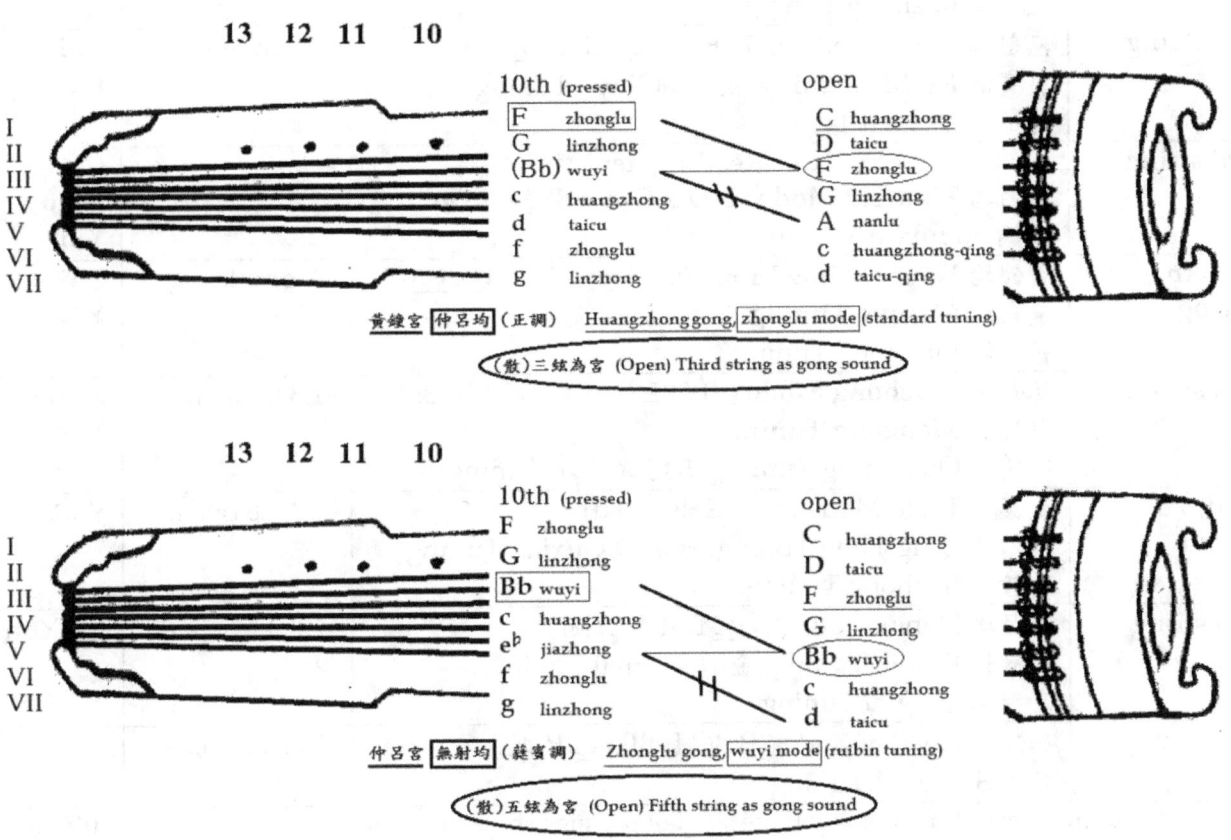

would lower strings I and VI as they share the same pitch. Using this cycle, it is possible to cycle through all eleven tones as the fundamental tone and play its pentatonic sounds using the seven strings, although the location and order of the five sounds are varied. Although every modulation starts on a different pitch, there are in practice only five modally unique scales. Given the qin is a relative-pitch instrument when played solo, similar modal qualities can stand in for each its counterparts starting on other pitches. The twelve tunings are listed in the chart below, with **the five common "proper" modes** in bold:

| Gong string | Mode (key) Name / Tuning Name | Strings altered | Notes |
|---|---|---|---|
| 5th string | 應鐘均 Yingzhong Mode (♭D ♭E ♭G ♭A <u>B</u> ♭D ♭E) " <br> 蕤賓調 Ruibin Tuning | +5 two *lü* <br> +1,2,3,4,6,7 one *lü* | |
| 3rd string | 蕤賓均 Ruibin Mode (♭D ♭E <u>♭G</u> ♭A ♭B ♭D ♭E) <br> 正調 Standard Tuning | +1,2,3,4,5,6,7 one *lü* | |
| 1st/6th string | 大呂均 Dalü Mode (<u>♭D</u> ♭E F ♭A ♭B <u>♭D</u> ♭E) ' <br> (黃鐘調 Huangzhong Tuning) | +1,2,4,5,6,7 one *lü* | Jue Diao |
| 4th string | 夷則均 Yize Mode (C ♭E F <u>♭A</u> ♭B c ♭e) * <br> 慢宮調 Mangong Tuning <br> 泉鳴調 Quanming Tuning, 夷則調 Yize Tuning, | +2,4,5,7 one *lü* | Yu Diao |
| **2nd/7th string** | **夾鐘均 Jiazhong Mode (C ♭<u>E</u> F G ♭B c ♭<u>e</u>) 6123561**^ <br> **清商調 Qingshang Tuning**, 姑洗調 Guxian Tuning, <br> 夾鐘調 Jiazhong Tuning | **+2,5,7 one *lü*** | **Shang Diao** |
| **5th string** | **無射均 Wuyi Mode (C D F G ♭<u>B</u> c d) 2356123**" <br> **蕤賓調 Ruibin Tuning**, 金羽調 Jinyu Tuning, <br> 清羽調 Qingyu Tuning | **+5, one *lü*** | **Zhi Diao** |
| **3rd string** | **>>>** Start Reading here **<<<** <br> **仲呂均 Zhonglü Mode (C D F G A c d) <u>5612356</u>** <br> **正調 Standard Tuning** | -------- | **Gong Diao / Yün** |
| **1st/6th string** | **黃鐘均 Huangzhong Mode (C D <u>E</u> G A c d)<u>1235612</u>** ' <br> **慢角調 Manjue Tuning** <br> 林鐘調 Linzhong Tuning | **-3, one *lü*** | **Zhi Yün** |
| **4th string** | **林鐘均 Linzhong Mode ('<u>B</u> D E G A <u>B</u> d) 3561235*** <br> **慢宮調 Mangong Tuning**, <br> 泉鳴調 Quanming Tuning, 夷則調 Yize Tuning | **-1,3,6 one *lü*** | **Shang Yün** |
| 2nd/7th string | 太簇均 Taicu Mode ('B D E ♯F A B d) ^ <br> 清商調 Qingshang Tuning, 姑洗調 Guxian Tuning, <br> 夾鐘調 Jiazhong Tuning | -1,3,4,6 one *lü* | Yu Yün |
| 5th string | 南呂均 Nanlü Mode ('B ♯<u>C</u> E ♯F A B ♯c) " <br> 蕤賓調 Ruibin Tuning, 金羽調 Jinyu Tuning, <br> 清羽調 Qingyu Tuning | -1,2,3,4,6,7 one *lü* | Jue Yün |
| 3rd string | 姑洗均 Guxian Mode ('B ♯C E ♯F ♯<u>G</u> B ♯C) <br> 正調 Standard Tuning | -1,2,3,4,5,6,7 one *lü* | |

' " * ^ The tuning methods marked by these symbol pairings share the same mode, but start on a different pitch due to the direction of the transition.

In Edo (17th and 18th c.) Japan, qin scholarship by Confucians such as Ogyuu Sorai (~1722) and Yamagata Daini (1763) considers The Five Tunings as the prescribed method of naturally playing the five primordial modes, superceding using internal tunings and playing them transposed with pressed notes as with Chinese common understanding. The Sorai school categorizes the modes observed by starting on either the first or second string into Yang and Yin modes respectively, thereby centreing the perspective of the modes on the leading tone. This identification method greatly differs from the Chinese teaching that looks for the *gong* leading string on a given tuning to play the *gong* scale, which illustrates the differences in the Chinese *zhi-diao* mindset from the Japanese *wei-diao* perspective. This model is astoundingly similar to Wang Binlu's modal system in his *Mei'an Qinpu*, but Wang preserves the Zhonglü yun standard tuning as the Gong mode, whereas the slackened third tuning is called a Zhi mode.

| Category | 陽 律 Yang Lut (Starts on Str.I) | | 陽動 ◉ 陰靜 | | 陰 呂 Yin Lü (Starts Str.II) | |
|---|---|---|---|---|---|---|
| **The 5 Tonics** | 商音 Shang 2 | 徵音 Zhi 5 | 宮音 Gong 1 | | 角音 Jue 3 | 羽音 Yu 6 |
| **Japanese Modes (Japanese/ Chinese readings)** | 側調 Soku-chou/ Ce-diao (2) 45♭712 4 (or (3)561235) | 瑟調 Shitsu-chou/ Se-diao (5)6 123 56 | 平調 Hyou-jou/ Ping-diao | 大石調 Taishiki-chou/ Dashi-diao | 楚調 Sou-chou/ Chu-diao 2(3) 56 123 | 清調 Sei-chou/ Qing-diao 5(♭7) 12 45♭7 (or 6123 561) |
| | | | (1)23 56 12 / 1(2)3 5612 | | | |
| **Guqin Tunings** (Strings altered [in Roman numerals]) | 緩宮 (泉鳴)調 Man'gong (Quanming) Tuning (I,III,VI, -1) B D E G A B d (II, IV, V, VII +1) C ♭E F ♭A♭B C♭E | 正調 Zheng (Standard) Tuning (---) C D F G A C D | 緩角調 Manjue Tuning (III, -1) C D E G A C D | | 緊羽 (蕤賓)調 Jinyu (Ruibin) Tuning (V, +1) C D F G♯A C D | 清商調 Qingshang Tuning (II, V, VII, +1) C ♭E F G♭B C♭E (I, III, IV, VI -1) B D E F# A b d |

The second type of external tuning goes in the other direction, where two strings repeat the same sound, or forego one of the pentatonic tones. This type of tuning is an emulation of a raised standard scale by two semitones (from CDFGACD → DEGABDE) devised by the Han to Wei court, but folk and scholarly practice unbound by the requirements of absolute pitch simply adapted the intervals instead. The resulting scales were then known as Qing, Ping, and Shang scales, also known as the "as gong, as zhi, as shang" scales in Tang and later periods.

| Gong string | Tuning Name | Strings changed | Missing string from closest perfect tuning |
|---|---|---|---|
| 1st | 慢商調 Manshang Tuning (C C F G A c d) | -2 two lü, match 1st | 2nd by +2 lü to standard on Zhonglü mode |
| 1st/5th | 黃鐘調 Huangzhong Tuning 無射調 Wuyi Tuning 復古調 Fugu Tuning ('♭B D F G ♭B c d) or (CEGAcde) | +5 one lü, -1 two lü | 1st by +3 lü to *Ruibin* on Wuyi mode |
| 2nd/7th | 碧玉調 Biyu Tuning (B D ♭G ♭G A B d) (in 1525 manuscript) | -1,4,6 one lü +3 one lü, match 4th. **(theoretically +2,5,7 one lü, +3 two lü)** | 3rd by -2 lü to *Qingshang* on Taicu Mode **(Secondary method: on Jiazhong Mode)** |
| 1st/6th | 間弦調 Jianxian Tuning (C D E G ♭B c d) | +5 one lü –3 one lü | 3rd by +1 lü to *Ruibin* on Wuyi Mode, or 5th by -1 lü to *Manjue* on Huangzhong Mode |
| 1st/5th | 離憂調 Liyou Tuning ('♭B C F G ♭B c d) | +5 one lü -1,2 two lü | 1st and 2nd by +2 lü to *Ruibin* on Wuyi Mode |
| 4th | 泉鳴調 Quanming Tuning **2561**235 ('A D E G A B d) (in 1525 manuscript) | -3, 6 one lü -1 three lü | 1st by two lü to (*Linzhong* Mode) |

Technically an extension of the second type of tunings above, but going beyond the Qing/Ping/Se scales and into the "Chu" and "Ce" (or, 'as Jue' and 'as Yu') as well, is the third group of external tunings, listed below. If you intentionally change one string (usually strings I/VI or II/VII) but leave another unadjusted, it creates two simultaneous effects: Now the new tuning becomes ambiguous. It can have one or two possible places that can be considered *gong*, and the unadjusted string will become a non-pentatonic *bian* tone (4 and 7) on the open strings. In other words, by rotating the location of the gong sound followed by altering additional strings to change the modal form, these hexatonic tunings provide great flexibility that can be interpreted in multiple ways.

英語琴統初階

| Gong string | Tuning Name | Strings changed | Missing string from closest perfect tuning |
|---|---|---|---|
| 3rd | 玉女調 **Yunü Tuning** <u>7235</u>612 / ('B D E G A c d) <u>571</u>♭34♭67 | -1,3 one lü | 6th by -1 lü to *Quanming* on Linzhong Mode |
| 2nd/7th or 1st | 側商調 **Ceshang Tuning** ♭7123561 or (C D E ♭G A B d) <u>123</u>♯4672 | -3,4,6 one lü | 1st by -1 lü to *Qingshang* on Taicu Mode |
| 1st | 泉鳴調 **Quanming Tuning** 12♯45♭71♭3 (C D ♭G G ♭B c ♭e) (in 1618 manuscript) | +3, 5, 7 one lü | --- |
| 2nd or 5th | 淒涼調 **Qiliang Tuning** <u>2456</u>123 or 楚商調 **Chushang Tuning** <u>6123</u>567 (C ♭E F G ♭B c d) | +2,5 one lü | 7th by +1 lü to *Qingshang* on Jiazhong Mode |
| 4th or 1st | 無媒調 **Wumei Tuning** <u>1235</u>672/<u>4561</u>235 慢角調 **Manjue Tuning** (C D E G A B d) | -3,6 one lü | 1st by -1 lü to *Quanming* on Linzhong Mode |

There are 35 unique irregular tunings with 37 names in surviving handbooks. They have conflicting instructions on their specifications and usage. The charts in this book are by no means exhaustive, but include most of the ones used in pieces played or studied today.

Despite the complex and sometimes confusing nomenclature, players today only mention the *diao* or tuning system for the purpose of setting up for performance, especially when calling for a non-standard setting. However, if you understand the *yun* system it will provide insight into analyzing the music as a composition, as well the historical manuscripts and how pieces are sorted within them.

## Tuning in Ensembles and with Electronic Tuners

For students who are uncertain of their aural capabilities to determine if two given strings are producing the same pitch, if you purchase an electronic tuner or tuner app with automatic pitch detection this may help. However, modern tuners using 12-tET will be ineffective if followed too closely and try to exactly match the harmonic overtones. The higher the pitch used, the more inaccurate the tuner will read, with the machine insisting on a "correct" pitch that is lower than the naturally produced harmonics.

Some instruments have secondary vibration frequencies produced by resonance with other strings, or with the cavity. They are so noticeable that some electronic tuners detect both pitches and the indicator jumps back and forth between the two. So, set your tuners to detect pitches in Pythagorean temperament. However, many teachers will prefer to train their students to tune by ear as a basic aptitude requirement.

The guqin is tuned to absolute pitch when playing in harmony with another instrument or a group of instruments, but it is not confined to this during solo play. Practice tuning with both another instrument and on its own in order to train your flexibility for listening to the same tune in different keys or pitches, as well as for speed and accuracy in the tuning process. The common way of matching the qin to another instrument is by matching the third string to the given concert F or fifth string to the concert A, and then tuning the other strings according to the standard harmonic tuning method.

Keep in mind, however, that the qin is inherently using just intonation, and will not match up entirely to a 12-tET instrument. Knowing this, smooth out any commonly-used tone in the working range as needed – this is an art that can only be perfected by practice and creative adaptation.

The following essay provides further reading on the history and examples of how this confusion between string names, pitch names, and doctrinization played out, and evolves to conversations on Chinese musical knowledge unto today.

## _Ruibin_ Tuning: A Misplaced Name for the Tightened 5th String Tuning

by 南風 Nanfeng

(陳磊 Chen Lei, 2005)

"_Wuyi_ mode tuning" refers to a tuning with the seven strings tuned to _Huangzhong, Taicu, Zhonglü, Linzhong, Wuyi, Qing-Huangzhong_ pitches (equivalent to the modern C,D,F,G,♯A,c,d), and is named so because of the Wuyi (♯A or ♭B) on its fifth string as the Gong (tonic) sound. Wuyi mode tuning has many other names in guqin history, such as "_Ruibin_ (蕤賓) tuning", "_Zhonglü_ (仲呂) tuning", "_Zhi_ (徵) tuning", "_Jinyu_ (金羽, golden yu) tuning", "_Qingyu_ (清羽) tuning", etc. This essay will attempt to investigate the legitimacy of these aliases.

Using the twelve tones' (十二律, lü) and the word 'mode' (yun 均) as the label is a relatively reasonable method in identifying and naming the un-transposed mode. The 'scientific' aspect of this nomenclature is that the name contains the name of the mode's pitch, allowing the reader to directly relate the name to its pitch. But "Wuyi mode tuning (with its tonic pitch at Bb)"being called *"Ruibin Diao/Tuning"*, *"Zhonglü Tuning"* etc. not only cannot show where the pitch is, but can also cause misunderstanding to the person reading the score, thinking that the tuning is in a *Ruibin* (#F) or *Zhonglü* (F) key or mode. What's more important, is that when the tuning is used to explain the interpretation of the pitch and the transpositions of the guqin pieces, these alternative names or aliases become even more difficult to explain themselves.

Here are two examples: in Zha Fuxi's *Dongting Qiusi* (洞庭秋思 In Vol.III of the Classic Guqin recordings), although the strings are set to *Zhonglü* mode tuning (CDFGAcd), the melody in the first section did not use the F mode (à la tonic/*gong* on 3rd string, 1=F), but is actually side-transposed to *Linzhong* mode (tonic/gong on 4th string, 1=G) in performance. The second section then shifts to *Wuyi* mode (1=♭B). Or, in *Wuxue-Shanfang Qinpu*'s 《悟雪山房琴譜》 *Azure Rivulet and Flowing Stream* (*Bijian Liuchuan*, 碧澗流泉), although it says the strings are set to *"Zhonglü* mode tuning", the 6th section is actually a side-transposition to *Huangzhong* (C) mode, and the one after that onto *Wuyi* ( ♭ B) mode. If we don't use *"Huangzhong Yun/*mode", *"Wuyi Yun"*and so forth proper mode nomenclature, not only will we confuse ourselves with modal names' relations with the piece itself, we can't even say much for the functionality of traditional jargon to explain modality, and students won't even know where to begin to learn about pieces and their mode transpositions. *"Ruibin Tuning, Zhi tuning…"*and other names cannot properly and clearly describe these guqin pieces' modality changes.

The first five names in the *Gong, Shang, Jue, Zhi, Yu, Wen, Wu* (宮、商、角、徵、羽、文、武) refers to the order of the guqin strings (in similitude to *jia, yi, bing, ding, wu* 甲乙丙丁戊 used for order of precedence in Chinese), and not the pitches (i.e. "Do, Re, Mi, So La"). This reason works well for explaining tunings such as *"Manshang* Tuning 慢商調" (lit. Loosen-Shang Tuning), in which the 2nd string (Shang) is loosened two semitones (or in proper Chinese terminology, *lü*). As for *"Wuyi* mode tuning" being called *"Ruibin* Tuning", *"Zhonglü* Tuning", *"Zhi* Tuning" etc., it does not share similar reasons.

*Wuyi* mode tuning being named as *"Zhi* Diao/Tuning" originated with Wang Tan's 王坦 thesis *Qinzhi* 《琴旨》 in the Qing Dynasty, where he used the third string as the basis of all tunings' names. Since *Zhonglü* (F) mode's tonic (Gong) is on the third string, it is called *"Gong* Tuning". In *Huangzhong* mode tuning, the third string is a mediant (*Jue*), it is called "Jue Tuning". As for *Wuyi*, the third string is the dominant

Standards of the Guqin

77

(*Zhi*), hence named "*Zhi* Tuning". But in reality, *Guxian* (E) and *Zhonglü* mode's third string are both tonics, so they should be in theory both called "*Gong* Tunings". This obviously is unreasonable, and is easily mixed up with other modes – too casual of an arrangement.

*Wuyi* mode tuning being named as "*Zhonglü* Tuning" originated from Wang Binlu 王賓魯 of the Zhucheng school 諸城派, who suggested that the third string of the guqin in standard tuning should be *Huangzhong* (C), and the fifth string after tightening would be *Zhonglü* (F), hence the name. This is because the starting point of the mode itself is different; therefore it has no tradition or reasonable logic backing it.

As for the other two names "*Jinyu* Tuning" and "*Qingyu* Tuning", it is probable that because it is tightening the *Yu* (5th) string, the words "*Jin1* 金" and "*Qing1* 清" were passed down (as a mistake, or perhaps to euphemize) instead of the original word "to tighten (緊, *jin3*)", a close homonym to the two.

If the reason why *Wuyi* mode tuning being called "*Zhonglü* Tuning" because the starting point is different is still excusable, then because *Ruibin* Tuning's name has absolutely no relationship with the *Ruibin* (♯F) pitch, it is absolutely unprovable. As for the name "*Ruibin* Tuning", *Xilutang Qintong* in the Ming Dynasty gives a point of view: "Taking the *Zhonglü* string and tightening the 5th, letting its 11th hui match the (open) seventh, is what we call *Ruibin* Diao today. The *Ruibin* (tuning) actually has its own proper modality, and by (calling) *Wuyi* as *Ruibin*, is just a colloquial (俗, can also be interpreted as 'vulgar') name."

The Chinese Music Dictionary contains a precise definition on the issue of improper naming of modes with other pitch names: "[The issue is caused by the reasons of] having a different starting point for Gong-shang or modes, in addition to improper passing down of tradition. For example, tightening the fifth string being called "*Qingyu Diao*", "*Jinyu Diao*", or "*Ruibin Diao*" and so forth."

Using the names of pitches that cannot describe the mode's actual modality makes the name no more than just a decoration, and is suspect of being 'dilettante'.

(Translated by Juni L. Yeung, 2005.)

英語琴統初階

# Maintaining Your Instrument

## The Body

Qin players often talk about the material, maker, and origin of their instruments: not only is there a sense of pride in the handcraftsmanship, but also serious consideration is given to the longevity (or simply survival) of the instrument itself against the natural elements.

Natural tree lacquer requires a balanced humidity to cure and dry, is considerably hard, and is resistant to water and corrosion. However, the generally dry conditions of North American climates and its central-heated indoors in winter are death spells to the instrument, especially for those of the "southern" or Sichuan subtropical Chinese origins. Enquire with your shop dealer or maker about the climate of manufacture, and avoid prolonged exposure to wind, direct sunlight, air vents, and direct water contact. Wiping the wood with **pure tung oil** (commonly found in hardware stores) is a classic method of preserving the surface, as well as an effective de-dusting and polishing method.

Adverse climates and an improper way of storage (i.e. laying on playing position for prolonged periods) may cause structural warping over time. Instruments should be hung upside down on a wall when not being used, using a secure hook attached firmly to the *fengzhao* (Phoenix swamp, see picture). The wall should be far from air vents or windows, to prevent warm or cold winds from directly or leaking towards the instrument.

If conditions cannot allow for such arrangements, store your instrument in a lined cloth bag (usually comes with instrument) and hard case, allowing it to "stand" on its side or upside down.

Light, localized cracking on the lacquer from age and prolonged playing is highly prized by players. Such patterns (called *duanwen* 斷紋) are elegantly named, such as "flowing water 流水紋", "snake belly 蛇腹紋", or "ox hair 牛毛紋". They do not (and should not) affect performance or tone quality in a negative way. Large cracks or faults at connecting parts, the sides, or near the Dragon gums usually do negatively impact on performance, and the lacquer should be chipped out and reapplied, with any structural repair work done in between. Some qin makers may offer replacement instruments, while others may charge for repair work.

## Strings

Regardless if it is nylon, nylon-metal, or silk, strings should be loosened from the tuning peg side when not in play. While the string tension on qins are considerably less than other string instruments (especially bridged ones, like the zheng), it causes the wax or glue (on nylon coiling) that binds the string to lose integrity, while changing the habit of the material to become accustomed with the new length, therefore loosening it. This is especially evident on traditional silk strings.

The general rule is: loosen strings after play, before travel, and for prolonged storage.

Strings accumulate dust and dirt from time and playing. Playing on dirty strings (and fingerboard) causes friction and might injure your fingertips or even hands. For nylon strings, use a damp cloth to wipe the surface board and pat dry afterwards, while the string should be scrubbed down by clamping a damp cloth or alcohol wipe around a string and running it back and forth on the length of the string for several times. For silk, use a dry cloth and reapply string glue afterwards.

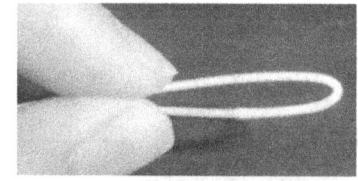

When a string is broken, it should be taken down in reverse order of how it was put up, before replacing it with a fresh string or section.

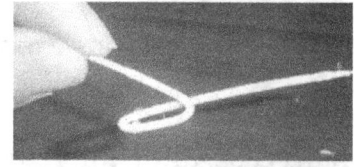

All images in the stringing tutorial are courtesy of Charles Rupert Tsua of LYQS and his "Treatise to Tying the Fly-knot" series.

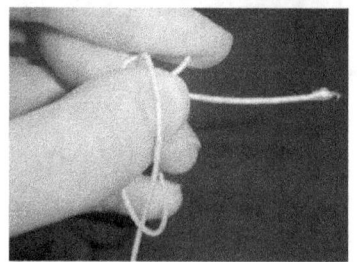

## Tying the Fly-knot

It is important to first determine which end of the string is the head: on silk strings, there is a longer section of reinforced wax that signifies the end, and a metal eye protruding from the nylon wrap on the ends of metal ones.

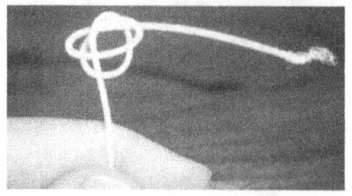

You want the fly-knot to sit between the reinforced head and the string material itself. Begin by bending a loop near the end of the silk wrapper, hold with left hand. Use your

英語琴統初階

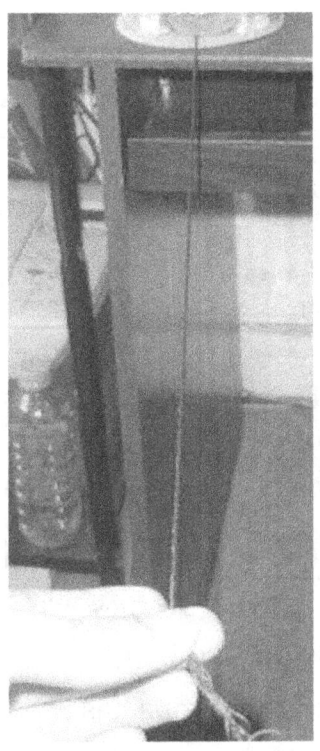

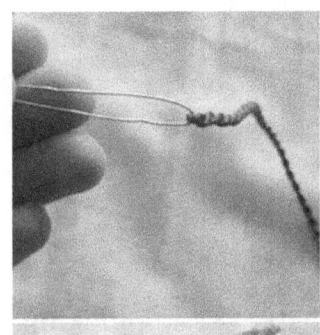

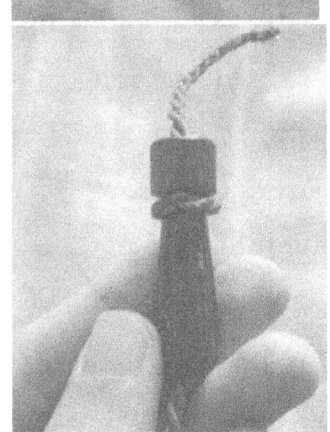

right hand to form another loop with the incoming string and put it over the first loop, clamping down in the middle of the two bends. This forms two small "fly-wings". Tuck the majority of the string under instead of over these fly-wings to secure it, and then tighten the arrangement with the help of a second person or a small hole in the wall to tug against, before slipping the knot between the rongkou silk cord and then pulling and fixing the string on the other end of the instrument.

## The Rongkou String Cord

The string cord is made by twisting strands of strong, relatively inelastic silk (embroidery) thread together. Each cord is about 9 to 11" when assembled. The colour of the thread should match with the colour of the instrument. Avoid bright colours.

To begin, prepare 20~30 strands of thread, about 30" long (50" if you want tassels), gather together and secure one end on a heavy object while twisting the other end with your palms in an **anti-clockwise** direction. The more you twist, the finer and stiffer the cord will be. When satisfied with the tension, pinch the end and fold the cord together in half. It should naturally spiral and twist its own way to become a thicker cord.

Picking out between the middle of the cord (now the other end), use a small paper clip to help hook it through the tuning pe.g. After poking through, use the hook to pull the string out in the middle from the side hole, then loop the cord around the neck of the peg after twisting it once anti-clockwise. This is essential to keep the cord from slipping on the peg.

After the peg setup is complete, use the hook to lead the cord through the string holes by the bridge. Poke the string and let the fly knot rest on the cord. This setup should sit in the middle or on the forward edge of the bridge (adjust the cord by tugging the loop on the peg accordingly) before the actual stringing process begins.

## Stringing the Instrument

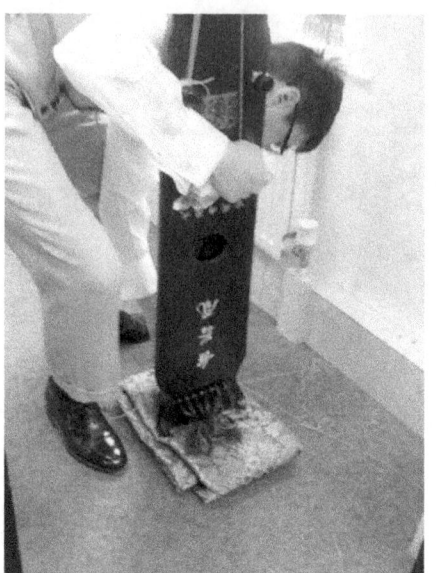

After the fly knot is secured into the cord, pull the string across the surface board and around the dragon's gums (if there are grooves designed for the string, use it). Before winding the string onto the goose feet, here are a few things to remember:

- Strings 1 to 4 go on the outer foot, and 5 to 7 on the inner.

- Strings are traditionally put on in this order: 1, 5; 2, 3, 4; 6, 7.

- Wrap the end of the string around a thick folded towel as a handle to pull on. Some claim wrapping the string around their fingers (with 3 layers of gardening gloves) gives more dexterity, but one has to bear with the strangling pain when pulling.

- Place the qin bag or a carpet under the qin. Do not tilt the instrument towards the bottom-board side (peg protector 'legs' may pop out).

- Have another person hold the instrument still if need be.

As you pull down, you should adjust your energy to make the pitch reach within a tone from its intended pitch. Maintain the tension as you loop around the goose feet (from inside outwards), staying as close to the bottom board as possible. Keep plucking the string to check if it is staying in tune (if it loosened, restart). You should be able to relax after the third loop, where you slip the string behind the incoming string, sandwiching it with the bottom board, but **do not pull with more strength after looping around the feet once**, for all the tension will grind the string into the feet instead and it may snap there. Still not letting go, circle around the goose feet until the string is almost used up, and finish by pulling it tight with pliers if required.

After stringing is complete, pull on the string away from the surface board to tighten both ends. Then, adjust to the proper pitch with the tuning pegs. Repeat for the other six strings. Use relative tuning between all strings for suitable tension across all strings and the instrument itself, as modern electric tuners use pitches that may be too high for some and in a temperament unsuitable for playing between harmonics and pressed notes.

英語琴統初階

# 'Unorthodox' Methods to Dealing with Lesser-Quality Instruments

Often new students settling for cheap instruments will come across specimens made in an 'unorthodox' or even unprofessional way. Problems may range from the 13 marker positions placed awkwardly and not able to produce harmonics, to the bridge being too high and pressing down strings becoming dangerous to the hand. Here are a few common features of modern-day poor quality replicas, and ways to temporarily fix or avoid them:

- String height: "A finger by the bridge, a business card by the tail". If there's significantly more room than that, it is too high. Avoid this instrument at all costs.

- Paint or artificial lacquer: Chemical paint and varnish sticks to the hand and makes it difficult to slide. Tung oil is the traditional cleaner and varnish on lacquered surfaces to keep the board slippery and protected, but waiting for it to dry may take time. Therefore, wiping Vaseline or even baby oil onto the surface board can partially counter the problem (baby oil makes strings harder to slide on, in turn – do not get the oil into the strings!) Talcum powder on silk strings, and guitar Finger-Ease may also work for some. In worse-case scenarios (to the qin or person), a bandage to the left thumb keeps the show going on.

- Harmonic markers (*hui*) are out of place: Prepare some black and white nail varnish. Blot out the old ones. Redraw the markers based on the calculation method written in the "Construction" chapter.

- Buzzing sounds with open string: Find the funny spot by trying stopped notes on all positions on the board. If it is 10th *hui* or below, elevate the string with a toothpick, bit of string, or folded paper by the dragon's gums. Checking the strings on the underside and wrapping tissue around the ends of the string may also help.

- Buzzing sound on a pressed position: If it can't be solved with the above, check for cracks around the said position. Avoid the position by dragging the string to one side, or fix with filling or lacquer rework.

- Buzzing ring on harmonic: Check if there are cracks on the instrument, or if strings are overlapping on the side or under the instrument; objects around the instrument or on the table may reverberate. Otherwise, adjust entire instrument's tuning slightly to avoid that frequency on that string.

- Broken parts: Unless it's the peg protector 'legs', take it for repairs immediately. Always have spare strings and *rongkou* twisted cord, and if you can afford it, spare tuning pegs and even goose feet.

# Traditional Aesthetics for Guqin Music

The guqin has been tied with the Yin-Yang School of thought from the earliest records of history as the representative of silk (plucked string) instruments, as well as the symbol of the five sounds on each of its strings. By determining which string (or tone) dictates the melody, one can determine the subject of the message the musician is trying to convey. For example, in anecdotes of Master Wen of Zheng (Shi Wen 師文) and Master Kuang of Jin (Shi Kuang 師曠), both cautioned their kings not to listen to music in *shang* pitch (and later the *Jue* and *Zhi* pitch), as this caused season-changing chaos. True to their word, their states fell after they were forced to play anyway. This relation between tone quality and the rest of nature is a backbone of Chinese musical philosophy, and as much as later composers denied such fantastical tales and refused to believe it, the system is still often cited in full at the preface or as part of music theory in manuscripts.

A turning point in Chinese music came when Xi Kang (or Ji Kang, 嵇康, 223-262 C.E.) wrote two major essays: The *Qin Fu*《琴賦》, praising that no instrument can produce music as transcendent as the qin; and the essay *Sheng Wu Ai Le Lun*《聲無哀樂論》, or "On Absence of Sentiments in Music", suggesting that the previously mentioned relation between sound and emotions and other external factors is a purely artificial construct, hence moot. Xi himself noted at the end of the essay that there was no way to thoroughly discard the notion of music being emotionally provoking, and called for listeners to seek internally for more intrinsic reasons of sentiments and decadence rather than putting the blame on music.

After Xi's era came over two centuries of chaos, as the Chinese empire was broken up by foreign barbarian invasions. When the Sui and Tang dynasties created the cosmopolitan culture of the Second Chinese Empire, Chinese court music (as played by Masters Wen and Kuang) fell largely out of favour for foreign tunes. Poet Liu Changqing 劉長卿 (709-786? C.E.) lamented in the poem *Playing Qin*《彈琴》:

冷冷七絃上，*On the rang-ranging of the seven icy strings,*

靜聽松風寒。*I silently listen to the image of cold wind whistling by the pines.*

英語琴統初階

*古調雖自愛，* Although ancient tunes are my passion,

*今人多不彈。* Most do not play them in this time of mine. (Transl. Juni Yeung)

A major change in guqin culture during the Second Empire is the instrument becoming less a part of the ritual orchestra and more a solo instrument, preferred by the literati and Daoist and Buddhist clergy. Scholars praised the instrument as the sole defender of "ancient rituals and music", although Song Dynasty court music under Emperor Taizong made attempts at changes and innovations in its genre, including the inclusion of 1, 3, 5, 7, and 9-stringed qins in ritual and temple orchestras, they all ultimately worked within the same pentatonic tuning system. Because of the lack of functional difference despite the variation, lashback from the empowered scholar-official class vocalized by the Daizhao (court specialist) for the qin Zhu Wenji 朱文濟 made sure that such changes were summarily dismissed and its influences never went past the palace walls. This power play as well as several other similar events in the Song court asserted the dominance of discourse by the literati class, which brought about the rise of accessible written music culminated in the scholars chronicling a *Qin History* 《琴史》 by Zhu Changwen 朱長文 that for the first time, firmly categorized the instrument and its music as a field of study on its own, with its lineage of sages, movers, and innovators.

Sometime in the 10th Century, a person named Cao Rou 曹柔 devised a system of writing guqin music that reduced an entire sentence of words into one compact symbol – *jianzipu* 減字譜. This system has greatly encouraged written records of pieces and demystification of the exclusive master-disciple oral tradition. It has also greatly legitimized it as a scholarly study rather than artisanship of lowly musical "workers". Versions of the *jianzipu* system of various degrees of simplifying the original Chinese characters were devised and classified by Zhao Yeli 趙耶利 and Chen Chuo 陳拙 from previous centuries. Zhao's system was used in many earlier surviving scores such as the *Shenqi Mipu*, while Chen's system is the set commonly recognized and used today.

This "elegant" scholar versus "vulgar" musician dichotomy escalated and conflicted from the Song Dynasty until mid-20th Century, with the scholar-players criticizing professional players and their complex pieces as "the deviant music of Zheng and Wei" (implying the notion 'empire-breaking'), believing that guqin composition and performance should focus on the notion of "great music is sparse with sound 大音希聲". Professional players and sympathizers of alternative traditions countered with the rebuttal that scholars overlooked the importance of proper theoretical knowledge when learning music - especially as elite as the guqin, which carries the burden of transmitting the remnants of the earliest Chinese tradition.

During the height of the Ming Dynasty, the scholarly tradition won the majority voice in dictating the principles of "elegant art", including painting, calligraphy and qin. Two famous essays listing the qualities of guqin performance are essential reading for any qin student even now – The Sixteen Methods of Qin Sounds (*Qinsheng Shiliu Fa* 《琴聲十六法》) by Leng Xian 冷謙, and the more famous *Xishan Qinkuang* 《谿山琴況》 by Xu Shangying 徐上瀛.

The *Xishan Qinkuang* 24 qualities of qin performance are: *harmony 和, serenity 靜, clarity 清, distance 遠, antiquity 古, unadornedness 澹, tranquility 恬, transcendance 逸, elegance 雅, beauty 麗, brightness 亮, lustre 采, cleanliness 潔, moisture 潤, roundedness 圓, firmness 堅, grandeur 宏, fine-detailed 細, smoothness 溜, vigour 健, lightness 輕, heaviness 重, slowness 遲, and rapidity 速.*

Of these qualities, four are particularly highlighted and praised as the key qualities of the highest degree of refinement: Purity, harmony, un-desiring, and elegance. Minor variation with words from homonym switches or popular sayings exist, which adds in features such as intricacy 微, and blandness 淡 also had a significant effect to guqin music as a "profound and meditative" music of "few sounds" today.

Ever since the literary inquisitions of Kangxi 康熙 and Qianlong 乾隆 by the Manchu Qing regime in the late 17th to early 18th century, the way how pieces are composed and manuscripts compiled have greatly changed. Complex right hand movements and similar left hand movements are broken down into simpler denominators, with finger positions now written in an "exact" decimal (*huifen*) system rather than shorthand that denotes "between xx and xx position" (*huiwei* system). Feeling the threat of Western powers and sweeping social corruption, conservative qin players after the First Opium War (1842) felt that "decadent" and "lascivious" music had contributed to the downfall of China. They felt that in order to rectify the *qi* life-force of the empire, the music must comprise the five proper tones – and they set out a movement to "correct" pieces which contained heptatonic notes to anhemitonic-pentatonic ones. Coupled with the promulgation of Kangxi and Qianlong's revision to the imperial standard of tonal studies compendium *Lülü Zhengyi* 《律呂正義》, Zhu Zaiyu 朱載堉's 12-tone equal temperament (which Western music adopts today) was denounced as flawed and false, replacing it with a practically dysfunctional 14-tone scale based on collating two 7-tone equidistant scales together. This spurred on a wave of pentatonic musical forms with a unique "off-color" flavour that still lingers on today in Southern Chinese folk traditions such as Beiguan woodwinds, as well as Fujian and Cantonese opera. For the guqin, the orthodoxy and repertoire of written music underwent significant revisionism eliminating non-pentatonic tones, but also used more pressed notes adjusted to a slightly lower Just Intoned pitch, similar to the 7-tone systems theorized by the Qing court and experimented in folk music. When Ming dynasty scores were re-discovered and re-examined in the 1970 to 80's, performers and listeners alike were surprised by the deliberate use of heptatonic progression and non-pentatonic sounds, breaking the three centuries-old stereotype of Chinese music as a "strictly pentatonic" one.

During the Chinese Cultural Revolution in the 1960's, besides the abrupt termination of research that had begun a few years earlier, the instrument (and the artisanship for creating its parts) came under threat of losing its tradition. Since the *qin* was an instrument for the court and later the literati (aka. 'landlord' class), it was considered one of the prime targets for destruction. Students and teachers alike had to switch over to other instruments. Even after the Revolution, there was unease with the instrument's image and there were attempts at 'converting' the instrument to give it more 'modern appeal'. Examples include adapting the qin to use 'modern' nylon-wrapped metal strings for a brighter sound suited to large public performances. Tunes were transposed from other instruments and some new tunes for promoting the Revolutionary cause were played. The most visible legacy of this era include Li Xiangting's compositions *Three Gorges Boat Song* (*Sanxia Chuange* 三峽船歌) and *Building a Road in a Blizzard* (*Fengxue Zhulu* 風雪築路), as well as Gong Yi's *Song of a Plum Garden* (*Meiyuan Yin* 梅園吟), *Spring Wind* (*Chun Feng* 春風) and *Loulan Verse* (*Loulan San* 樓蘭散) with daring style and technique borrowed from other instruments like the pipa, guzheng, and ruan, and borrowing musical themes from the People's Republic's inner Asian frontier and its Turkic indigenes' traditions.

With the onset of modern reform, guqin aesthetics went in two directions: one is to retrace its lost heritage from studying surviving handbooks and resurrecting obscure pieces back into performance via the dapu interpretation process, while the other looks beyond its cultural borders to seek interaction and collaboration with international music traditions. Today, we see Chinese citizens aspiring to live the scholastic life of the literati enjoying qin played in private studies and upper-class teahouses. High school and university students pick it up as an extracurricular activity or a way to reconnect to their roots despite their busy lives. Musicians like Li Xiangting, among others, are experimenting with fusion music and improvisation, and promoting the qin's recuperative properties in the meditation and spa music fields. Musicians from China and beyond have attempted (some quite successfully) new methods of construction (such as new lacquer and wood types, electric pickups and amplification, and new tuning devices), as well as using the qin in popular music. In Guangzhou, a local techno-metal band known as The Swamp (*Zhaoze* 沼澤樂隊) is comprised of guitarist, bass, drums, and electrically-amplified qin with sustain pedals. A Singapore group uses several qin tuned to different tunings and arranged on a rack as an alternative to a synthesizer. With the age of the computer, there are various attempts at digitizing *jianzipu* into a new method for storing the score, and ultimately for digital playback. With the boom of Chinese computer users and the onset of the Internet, qin culture has entered an explosive new environment and development direction into the 21st Century.

英語琴統初階

# Further Reading: *Fuqin Jue* (Rules of Qin-Strumming)

By Wang Zhi, in *Xilutang Qintong* (1525), Folio IV; Translated by Juni Yeung

When playing the qin, regardless of whether there are people nearby, one must play as if facing your elders. Placing the qin to the front of you, the body must be upright, your energies and spirits at peace and settled.

Collect your heart and cut off all worries, focus on your emotions and intentions.

Fingers do not give false strikes, and strings do not give false rings.

One does not look at the right hand, but only listen to its sounds.

The eyes do not look elsewhere, nor the ears listen to anything else.

When the heart does not think other thoughts, that is when one achieves the meaning of the qin. It is essential to recognize the sentencing and phrasing of rhythm, while there mustn't be too many pauses or stops. Li Mian [Tang era, 717-788CE] noted, "*Yin [vibratos]* and stops are well-measured, while slowness and speed are orderly. Hurriedly, but not messy. Leisurely, but not stopping. Neither hurriedly or leisurely, like drifting clouds and flowing water. This is the crucial essence."

Use of fingers must include both flesh and nail, in order to give a crisp sound. Too much nail and the sound is scorched. Too much flesh and the tone is convoluted. Both left and right hands cannot over-exaggerate.

There are three types of sound on the qin: First is *san* (open), second is *an* (pressed), third is *fan* (harmonics). Each pluck is like breaking the strings but the fingers pluck shallowly. Pressing the strings into the wood are to be firm but strength cannot be seen. *Fan* sounds are to be played near the bridge, lightly touching the string where the *hui* marker is with a brief point [of the fingertip], and its sound shall be clear and rounded.

If the body wavers and the neck twists often, pandering left and right, looking up and down, or if the facial expressions change, it is as if one is ashamed.

Or, if one's eyesight scurries about, panting in with heavy breath, without regulation in advances and retreats, with a lax spirit or form, it will reflect itself in form of sound. Although the fingerings are right, the resonances of the sound will be messy and it cannot conform to the Five [proper] Sounds.

Not tuning the strings properly, playing heavily when it should be played lightly, or playing quick when it should be slow – all of these are major diseases [faults] to playing.

The rule of playing the qin, is to be simple and clean. It is not in asking for one as a person to be calm, but in one's hands. The throbbing of the fingers is called being raucous, while being concise, lightly-treading on a steady pace is called being calm.

It is unnecessary to wobble the [left] finger outside of the sound. Let the proper sound be harmonious and smooth, and that will be good.

For the Junzi [Superior Person] of antiquity creates [regulates] to the causes of matters, he attenuates himself to pleasuring the mind, or describes his heart with irony, or expresses his lone resentment to transmit his ambitions. Hence it [i.e. the music] is able to focus the essence of sincerity, and move the spirits and gods.

One may only know three or five etudes, but refine it to the limits of excellence. However students of our day, perceive ability by sheer quantity. Hence the idiom "Sheer quantity leads to lack of quality. Quality leads to less quantity." May the Junzi who understands true sound [i.e. friends] pay attention to this.

Here we have the rules of playing qin. What is difficult to procure are the scores to the music, for they must be requested to be passed down from the masters. Furthermore,

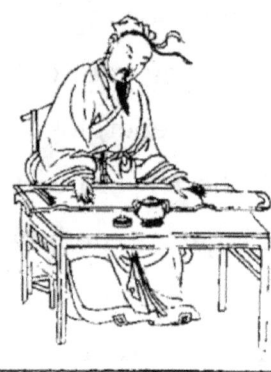

撫琴勢

英語琴統初階

fingerings and rhythm cannot be exhaustively detailed in the work of writing, so when facing a manuscript to play, we often only get its sound, but its profound intricacies in tempo and rhythm are forgone. This is like having rough measuring tools – you have the drawn shapes, but it lacks the precision that fine tools give.

In more prosaic terms, any given piece can be roughly divided into three sections: First slow, then tense, and finally slack. From slow to tense to stop forms the motif to a piece of music.

Often times there are indications of "do two times from mark." (從勾二作, 从冂乍) Play through it plainly the first time, to finish off the motif from the last sentence. Pause, and in the second play-through, play it strongly. From playing strong and then easing gradually and finishing with a powerful strike-in, forms the continuation to the sounds afterward. One must make the front and back relate with each other, clearly differentiating the beginning from the end.

Another example is the "Perform three times with spaced *gou*." (三作間勾, i.e. *Da-jiangou* 大旳) First play the two sounds, pause, then respond to the previous section with four sounds, and finish off with one powerful strike-in.

A nine-tone long chain (*chang-suo*, 镺) involves playing two sounds, pause, and finish off with seven strong notes. This induces rise and fall at the front and back, connecting the motifs by arteries and veins, leaving its resonance drifting as if fading but still slowly progressing, and then a jolt at the end.

From slow to tense, and from tense to leisurely, if control of fastness and slowness is appropriate, and *yin* [vibratos] and stops do not lose their degree, then naturally the strings will resonate with clear rings. Sounds should preferably be clear, aim for simple and calm, and must not be messy. This is how an elegant, antiquated motif of profound emptiness is.

And this is why the intricacies are so hard to attain for manuscripts then and now. So for those self-studying the qin, and have yet to receive transmission from a master, it is best to focus your mind and dedication and ponder on these words. Follow the fingerings according to the manuscript to the hands, meticulously and slowly, accumulate one sound onto the next, section unto section. After days and months of practice, the heart and intention will connect, and the hands will automatically do its job. Then, you will naturally attain mastery as the ancients have.

As proverb has it: "When practice is perfected, it is the same." [*Doctrine of the Mean*, 20]  The act of strumming the qin is precious in its accumulated progress, as prolonged experience leads to expertise. If one is eager and greedy for more, wanting for speed leads to one unable to arrive at the destination and all is then for naught, which must be avoided. I shall leave the essay on this note for students of the future to read, to dispel their anxious doubts.

英語琴統初階

# A Brief on early 21st Century Guqin Culture

## China

Since UNESCO's recognition of the music as a piece of Cultural or Intangible Heritage in 2003, the instrument has gone through a worldwide fad for learning this once elite practice closely related to personal refinement and transcendence. Despite the official narrative claiming that the number of guqin players are constantly on the decline (such as during the

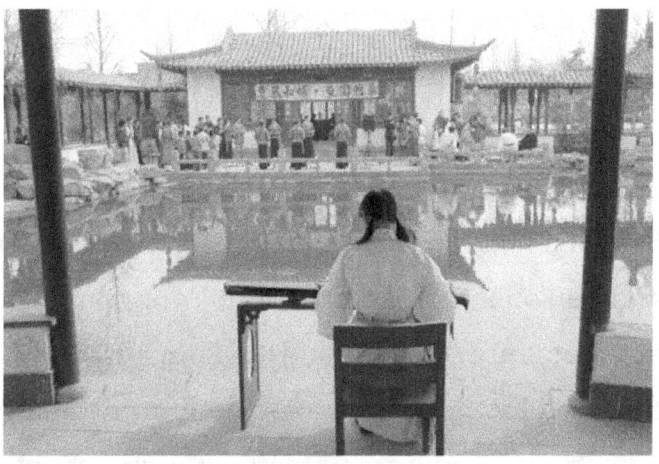

**Dongyuan Gathering in Sanzichan Teahouse, Shimen, Hebei Province, on March 19, 2006.**

Opening Ceremonies of the XXIX Olympiad in Beijing 2008, reporters were given statistics that less than 50 players remain), a new generation of young cultural enthusiasts and students are keeping the torch alive, if not burning brighter with new innovations and research results.

China has been taking an active stance in promoting the instrument and the tradition, while applying a modern conservatory examination and grading system across the nation. Despite large amounts of disagreements and protest, an examination level repertoire was first released in late 2003, and the first examinations were held in major cities across China in 2004. Examinations are held twice yearly, with recognition issued by the Beijing Central Conservatory of Music and Beijing Guqin Yanjiuhui (Research association). The Level 10 recognition can be counted as bonus credits towards the National High School Examination System, used for the Chinese tertiary education application. This places the guqin on equal stature alongside with other instruments, Chinese or Western, in the education system.

The guqin used as an instrument of public competition has been attempted as early as 2002, and many instructors claimed that it was sacrilege to the non-competitive nature of the literati tradition. Their worries were proven especially valid when animosity between competitors (in person or online) materialized into the stuff of tabloid headers, creating the environment of "smoke and miasma" that traditional guqin practitioners fear the most. To this end, there is still a significant portion of players who advise their disciples and students in aversion of competitions and the official examinations.

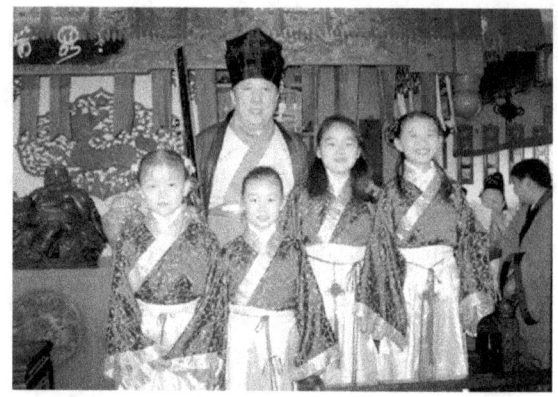

**Beijing guqin and Pipa teacher Yang Qing and students in Hanfu, at a local gathering in early 2005.**

Modern guqin culture is also often related to the Hanfu Restoration Movement, which advocates wearing traditional Han Chinese dress to raise ethnic awareness and from it a heightened appreciation for classic arts and personal moral refinement. Young hanfu advocates are often pursue the Four Scholarly Arts, the first of which is the qin, followed by *Weiqi/Igo*, brush calligraphy, and painting. Increasingly during elegant gatherings people are witnessing participants dressed in the traditional y-shaped cross collar and wide sleeves of the scholarly robe and wearing tall caps, thus seeking to promote China as a broad and accepting culture, while maintaining a 5,000-year old tradition of the Mean and Middle Way.

Anthropologists have repeatedly taken note of the recent mass production of qin instruments with lavish tonewoods excavated from old buildings and tombs, modularized large classes with young children scuffled by their parents, and commercialized, performance-heavy salon culture closely tied with the bourgeois and even nouveau-riches consumerism, as a side effect of China's rapid global economic rise, with varying attitudes and opinions. Skeptics such as Maria Siumi Tam and Hongyan Nan (2010)[4] denounce the new culture as a denigration of the old, a youth fad of Chinese anachronisms, a symptom of anxiety to modern Chinese nationalism, and as a debauchery to the traditional arts by debasing it into a commodity in the market, tainting it with the vulgarity of opportunistic investment and speculation. Meanwhile, Omid Burgin (2014)[5] celebrates the phenomenon as the vitality of the traditional art adjusting to a rapidly changing socio-economic environment, as the qin amongst other Chinese cultural items has increased market supply and quality, as new producers compete to create better instruments and components both aesthetically and in

---

[4] Tam, Siumi Maria 譚少薇 and Nan, Hongyan 南鴻雁. "To Where is the Guqin Going? Chinese Contemporary Tradition of Guqin, Consumerism, and Literati Recognition" (《古琴往何處去？中國當代的古琴傳習，消費主義與文人認同》), in Lau Chor-Wah 劉楚華, *Essays on Qin Studies: Traditions of the Guqin and its Human Ecology* (《琴學論集：古琴傳承與人文生態》). Hong Kong: Cosmos Books, 2010. pp.171-194.
[5] Bürgin, Omid. "Representations of Guqin in China Today: From Recurrent Nostalgia, Cultural Etiquette to Revival Movements," in *Music in China Today: Ancient Traditions, Contemporary Trends* by Bernhard Hannekin and Tiago de Oliviera Pinto. Berlin: Verlag für Wissenschaft und Bildung, 2017. pp 75-110.

英語琴統初階

performance, and this is clearly visible from an instrument made in the 1990's from one just one decade later.

## Europe and North America

The Internet is the key source of general information, new theories, and intercourse between the global communities of players, who have organized themselves in major cities to share their music and

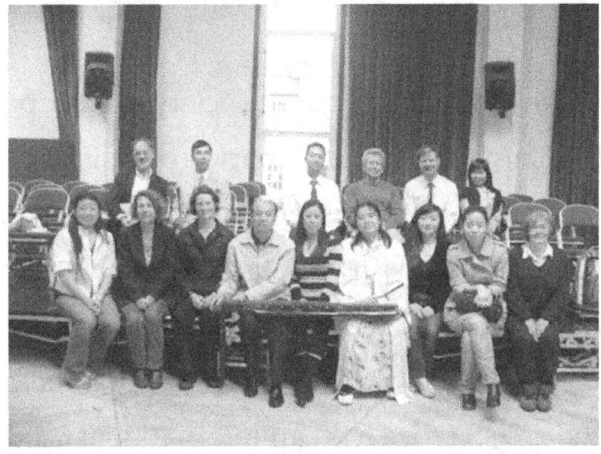

The author (First row, 4th from right) with Zeng Chengwei (1st row, 4th from left) and Cheng Yu (front row, centre) and members of the LYQS in AMC Summer School gathering, July-August 2009.

insights with fellow players. The Internet has also allowed easier access to the older archives stored in libraries around the world to be widely available for audience and researchers alike.

There have been various attempts on the digitization of guqin tablature, but no widely recognizable consumer-based program is yet available. CAD-edited prints or scanned hand-copies, coupled with a five-line or number-staff are still the standard today.

Toronto is one of the most active guqin communities in North America, sharing the buzz with New York, Seattle, San Francisco and Vancouver. Other active communities outside the Chinese geographical area include England, Spain, Germany, Singapore, and from the mid-2010s onward, Japan. The most prominent society in

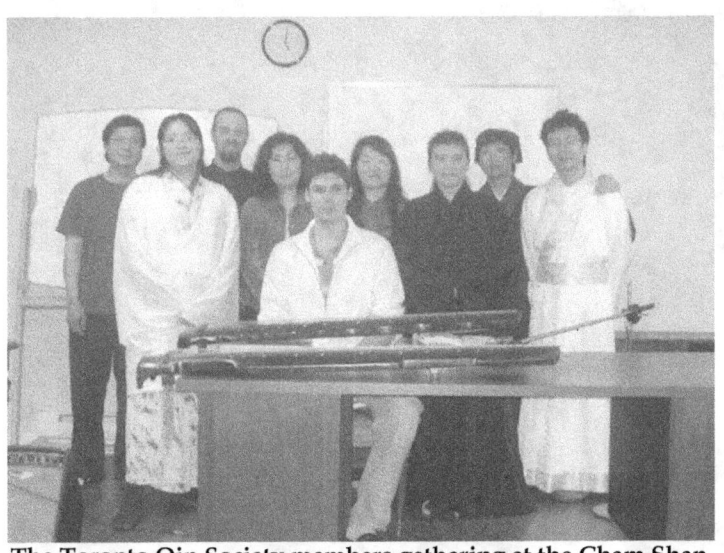

The Toronto Qin Society members gathering at the Cham Shan Buddhist Temple, June 2009.

community involvement is the North American Guqin Association (NAGA), operating in the San Francisco Bay Area. Its greatest achievement was the recognition of "Guqin Day" on June 19 in Milpitas, CA. Meanwhile, New York Qin Society (NYQS) retains the scholarly tradition by incorporating meditation and the Scholarly Arts in practice in a peer-based circle. While there is no formal qin society, Seattle (and its satellite Bellevue) also has an active and growing community of players.

Standards of the Guqin

The largest guqin society in Europe is the London Youlan Qin Society (LYQS). Similar to the North American Guqin Association, they hold regular gatherings and do some work in qin essay translation and piece interpretations. They have also collaborated with various NPOs such as the Asian Music Circuit (AMC) and academic institutions such as the Royal Academy of Music, SOAS, and Goldsmiths to invite masters from China to instruct students in weeklong summer camps. In 2018 and 2023, the LYQS twice held an international academic conference on the guqin and qin studies alongside its annual summer school program, attracting scholars from Brazil, Canada, China, Italy, Netherlands, and Taiwan, to advance knowledge, technologies, and theories in the field.

Outside of Britain, there are small groups across the entire Western Europe and Sweden. A feature of the European community is the amount of original research on the guqin, as well as translations of less-studied manuscripts published in various languages, including Catalan and Swedish. In 2009, the 14th International CHIME conference in Brussels, Belgium offered a platform for exploring the present and future of the qin communities around the world and online, as digital media for the qin extends from mere display into the realm of interactivity and virtual realities.

A major difference in the nature of modern guqin societies in the West with China is its legal identity. In China, guqin societies are usually physically attached to a

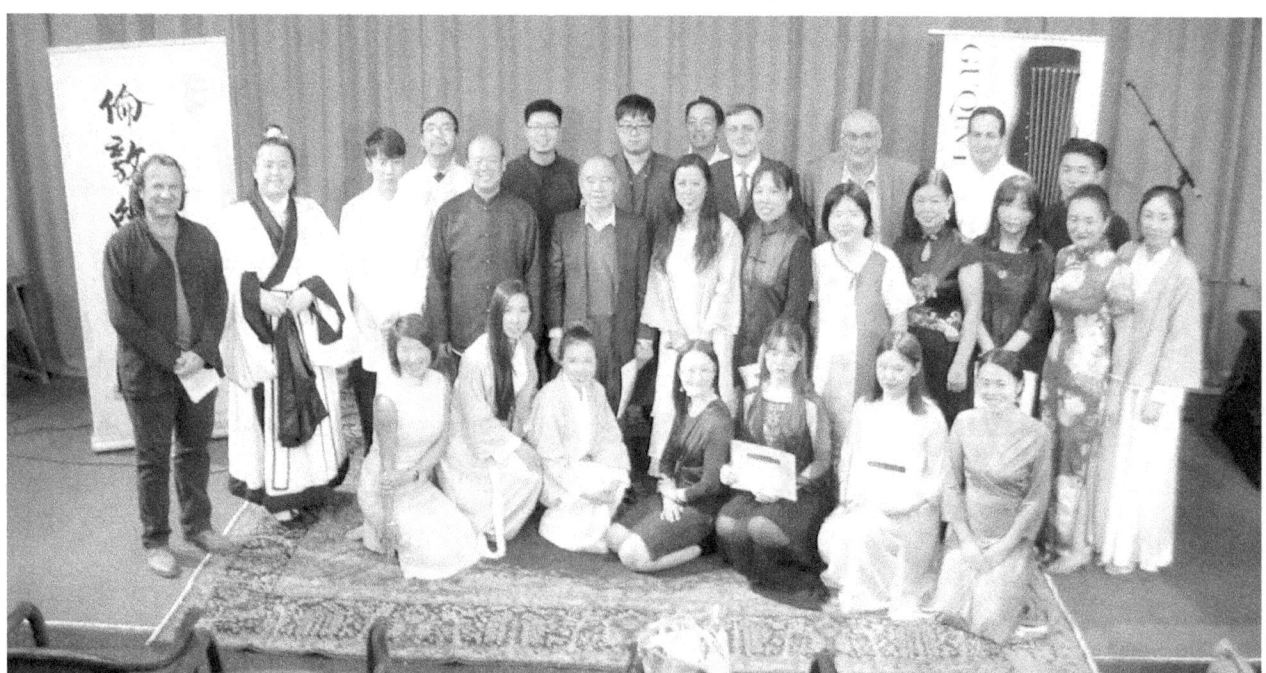

**LYQS Grand Yaji after the first International Guqin Conference at the School of Oriental and African Studies (SOAS) in August 2018. Chinese masters Zeng Chengwei (2nd row, 4th from left) and Li Xiangting (same, 5th from left) were featured guests at the proceedings.**

英語琴統初階

physical space, usually a tea and music salon or academic institution, where regular lessons and gatherings are held on a regular basis. In the West, however, while some societies may have affiliations or partnerships with other organizations such as universities or NGOs, many societies are unregistered organizations administrated by an individual or a small collective of organizers – the form that used to be prevalent in China.

# Towards a Computerized Dapu Process: A History

Dapu is the analytical reinterpretation of a written passage of guqin tablature manuscript, translating it from a written piece of music. According to the *Zhongguo Yinyue Cidian* (Chinese Musical Dictionary), *dapu* is "a term referring to the process of playing out a qin melody from a qin manuscript. Since qin manuscripts do not directly record musical notes but only string positions and fingerings, as well having a considerable flexibility in rhythm interpretation, *dapu*'ers must be familiar with conventions in and performance technique to deduct the melodies' progression, and then to recreate it. Its aim is to reproduce the state in which it was originally performed – since most surviving pieces are lost in practice, one must undergo the *dapu* process to restore the music." (p.64)

The traditional guqin manuscript system was conceived by Cao Rou presumably around the 10th century C.E.. It supplemented the musician as a reminder for fingering technique in case of forgetfulness, assuming that the melody and rhythm are already impressioned into the player's mind. As primarily an oral tradition, students studying under a master would not have to encounter the *dapu* process as melodies would have been passed from performance imitation, without drawing from a written medium. John Thompson posits that the tradition of learning guqin pieces directly from a book, without aid of a teacher or another musician transmitting a predetermined rhythm was nonetheless existent and popular.

Much of the discussion on dapu in guqin circles and academia discuss on whether the act of dapu is an "archaeological" rediscovery of an 'authentic original' performance through surmising or deducing missing elements required in musical performances from the imperfect information on existing tablature, versus a form of original artistic creation by the contemporary guqin artist derived from the historical text. Regardless of where artists may lie on this spectrum, the process of dapu remains the same.

Technically, sight-reading an original text for musical performance is possible and crudely fits into the definition of dapu as translation from text to performance, and its credibility and authenticity may be verified through various kinds of audio/visual recording devices. However, as a scholarly tradition, the legitimacy of the translation is recognized only through the quantifiable, empirical medium of the text – in other words, while the common definition iterates dapu's ultimate purpose is for the music to

英語琴統初階

'transcend' or 'liberate' from the textual realm into the aural one, in reality it never escapes this plane of existence but rather becomes increasingly confined by the empirical scrutiny of increasingly meticulous annotation and establishment of parameters.

Hence, dapu in the modern sense means the meticulous recording or revising of necessary components to guqin music, which involves the use of *jianzipu* tablature, as well as another system that records pitch and rhythm. The common method involves three major steps:

1. rewriting the tablature in compatible layout with the score for the pitch and rhythm (typically from vertical layout to horizontal layout, when dealing with historical sources),

2. determine the number of sounds and correlate the characters to each of its pitches according to tuning, accounting for any mode changes should a solfege-based recording system (e.g. jianpu) is used, and

3. assign and record the tempo and rhythm of the performance, based on the dapu'er's deliberation.

At any point during these three steps, the dapu'er also has to make decisions and be held accountable for discrepancies and changes between the source text and the new score, whether they'd be intentional or accidental. For example, one may discover that a cadenza may not end in a typical matching paired interval but one pentatonic tone apart, that can be easily corrected by using the subsequent string. The artist will then have to deliberate on whether that is intentionally required by the piece, or if it is a misprint due to error in its transmission (such as a scribal

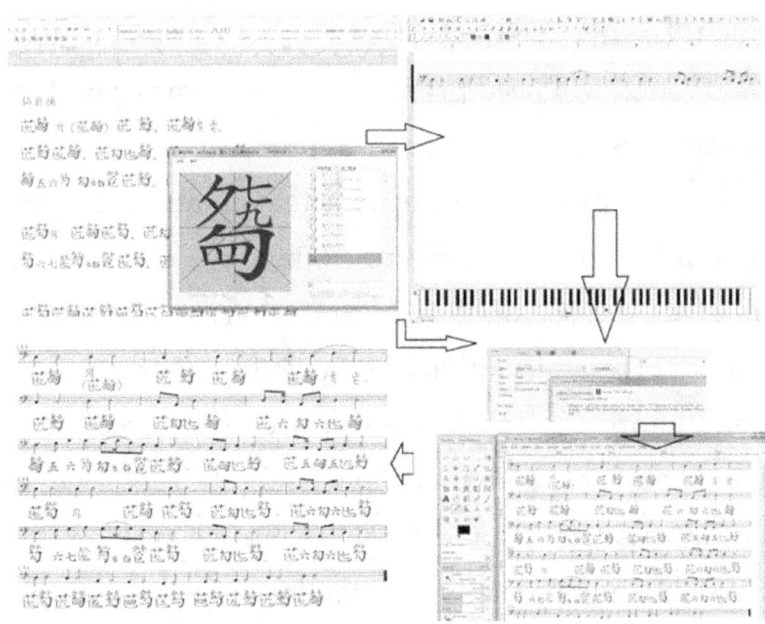

A flowchart of how the scores are produced in Standards of the Guqin. The final product is a PNG image.

mistake or faulty photocopying). If such a deliberation is made, regardless of whether an actual change is made from the original text – it is also up to the dapu'er to record such changes in writing to be held accountable for future reference and scrutiny.

Even in the early 21st century, dapu for the most part is a manual process – scores are written and rewritten by hand, and the pitches linked up by hours of tedious cross-referencing with the instrument's pitch charts. Although publisher-grade scores now involve computer-assisted drawing, the musical work itself remains unchanged. Taking my work *Standards of the Guqin* as example, the tablature is rewritten digitally by a database of prearranged vector images of strokes that resemble *parts of* jianzipu that are formed together by entries that group them together, as well as separately creating the five-line staff music using a market-available typing and output program for such purpose.

To date, there is no available software (commercial or open-sourced) that can perform this task because the technology to digitize *jianzipu* itself is young and tentative. With the exception of *Guangling Shenqi* developed by guanglingsan.com, all other projects struggle along how to account for all possible variations, much less categorize and designate a dynamic input system. Once that logistical issue is resolved, the next logical step is for the computer software to parse the text as a generated sound and pitch. To effectively actualize this, the computer-generated *jianzipu* previously mentioned will need profiles of each character with a breakdown of the necessary parameters for the computer to process.

A typical parsing of an actual notation character will follow this heuristic: First, determine the current tuning of the piece. Based on the pitches of the open strings, all given pressed or harmonic positions are extrapolated from there, and it reduces the chance of miscalculation or inflexibility to external tuning. Next, determine if the left hand information is an open, pressed, or harmonic note. Once these pieces of information are gathered, a pitch (and type of tone) can be derived, but it would be up to the musician to mold the notes into a sensible piece of music by the addition of rhythm, and optionally annotations on performance style. When the missing elements are edited into the new score, a computerized printout or rendition will forego the need of another manual rewrite for spacing and cleanliness as notes are automatically spaced and formatted to the page.

英語琴統初階

Currently, some experimental projects in China also explore in developing a 'fuzzy AI' in allowing the computer to determine the missing rhythms and other stylistic treatments – in other words, to fully automate the process. This objective is no smaller than developing an independent thinking computer that can freely compose a musical masterpiece, and belongs to a different category from the scope of developing a digital guqin manuscript archive and *dapu* assistant mechanism. Another pursuit is in Optical Character Recognition (OCR) technology integration with guqin tablature to allow speedy archive and digitization of the classic texts, which may speed up the process greatly as compared to data entry using existing techniques (i.e. typing characters in long form).

Further reading:

Zhou Changyue. *Guqin Yishu de jiqi yanyi* (Mechanical interpretation of the art of guqin). Beijing: China Science Publishing. 2013. Table of Contents available at http://www.baiyue-music.com/song_con.php?idept=2&isdept=7&pk=2470&page=

Chang Hong. "MIDI Guqin yanzou: Kexue yu yishu de chuangxin jiehe (MIDI Guqin performance: A culmination of science and artistic innovation)," People.com.cn, snapshot backup at http://swannbb.blogspot.ca/2015/01/digital-guqin-at-beginning-chen.html. Last accessed September 17, 2015.

Zhang Yingxue. "ChinAR," http://www.yingxuetzt.com/#!project01/c1mqf. Last accessed September 17, 2015.

(This article was originally published on Toronto Guqin Society's blog on September 17, 2015.)

# An Introduction to the Repertoire

In this book, music scores are written on the five-line staff, horizontally from left to right, denoting the pitch, tempo, and time value of notes. Below the staff, positional markings and fingerings in the commonly-recognized simplified characters tablature system (*jianzipu*) are used. The five-line staff system presents the musical contours and a general idea of rhythm in the piece, supplementing missing elements from the *jianzipu* system. Syncopated *rubato* or *diédang* are mimicked to the best of ability but its intricacies may be absent on paper, hence all time value are approximate and should not be used as an absolute standard to a metronome.

To emphasize free interpretation and meter in the music, no time signature is given under the five-line staff system, and bar-lines are used to express musical phrasing as suggested by the *jianzipu* and the writers' interpretation, as opposed to representing regulated bar and meter. All single tones are combined into one note to represent its time value, abandoning the use of connected ties. Sliding movements are denoted with slurs, and harmonics have a degree (°) symbol on top or below the cipher note.

In most cases, vibratos and glissandos are represented by arrows and lines denoting a general pattern of amplitude, length, strength, and degree of repetition. The time value of these modifications is included in the previous note. However, there are cases when full cipher representations are written, emphasizing the detail of how the movement is to be executed.

The repertoire in this book is categorized into four sections. The repertoires A and B are shorter preludes (*yín*) and etudes (*cào*) selected for the beginner to learn while studying various fingering techniques taught in the earlier chapters, while repertoire C are larger pieces with more complex motifs, and are more suitable as main performance pieces at recitals and gatherings. Repertoire B are pieces that require retuning from the standard tuning (called "external tunings"), and are clearly marked in the introduction page prior to the score. Repertoire D is a written exercise to interpret original scores, and the final product is written by the student's own hand.

This book only provides a skeletal repertoire for critical skill development, **so it is highly recommended** that every student should also purchase the two-volume First Edition or three-volume Third Edition of the *Guqin Quji* to expand their playing list. Bibliographical information on these books is available under the reading list section.

英語琴統初階

(This page left intentionally blank)

**General Study Notes**

# REPERTOIRE A

♫

# STANDARD TUNING ETUDES

XIANWENG CAO

LIANGXIAO YIN

QIUFENG CE

ZHAO YIN

GUAN SHAN YUE

LIU SHANG

英語琴統初階

# Xianweng Cao

*Etude to the Transcendent Venerable One* is traditionally the introductory piece for a guqin student, after having learned basic left and right hand movements mo 抹, tiao 挑, gou 勾, ti 剔 for the right hand, and pressing properly with the thumb and ring finger on the left hand along with simple slides and a pickup movement (Tao-qi 掐起).

Melodically, the piece serves two purposes: the student learns the pattern of positions on adjacent strings that give perfect unison pitches; and also how to

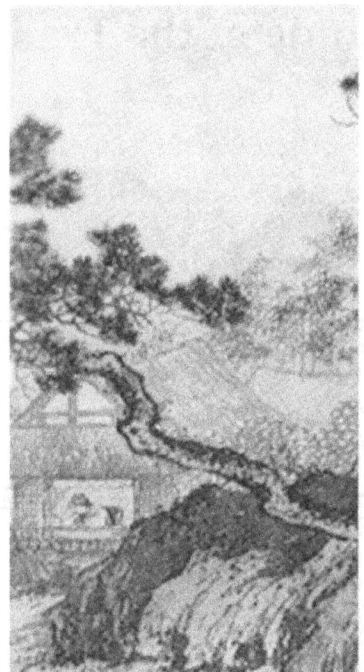
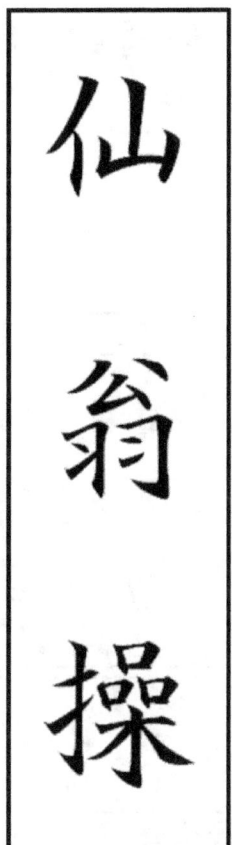

**Tang Yin (1470-1523), "Dreaming of Immortality in a Thatched Cottage" (section), Freer Art Collection.**

correct the strings by tuning and cross-checking using this piece.

The piece got its name from the continual matching tones sounding similar to the words "Xian Weng (仙翁)". This piece is also related to the story of a famous Daoist named Chen Tuan 陳搏 (courtesy name Xiyi 希夷), who was known to hide in the deep mountains, away from strife and chaos in the world, and sleep for hundreds of years. However, given the nature of the piece's composition and arrangement, it is not to be classified as a religious Daoist piece.

# 仙翁操 Etude of the Transcendent Venerable One

Original score by John Thompson 唐世璋
from transmission by Sun Yuqin 孫毓芹
Reinterpreted score by Juni Yeung

Standard Tuning 正調

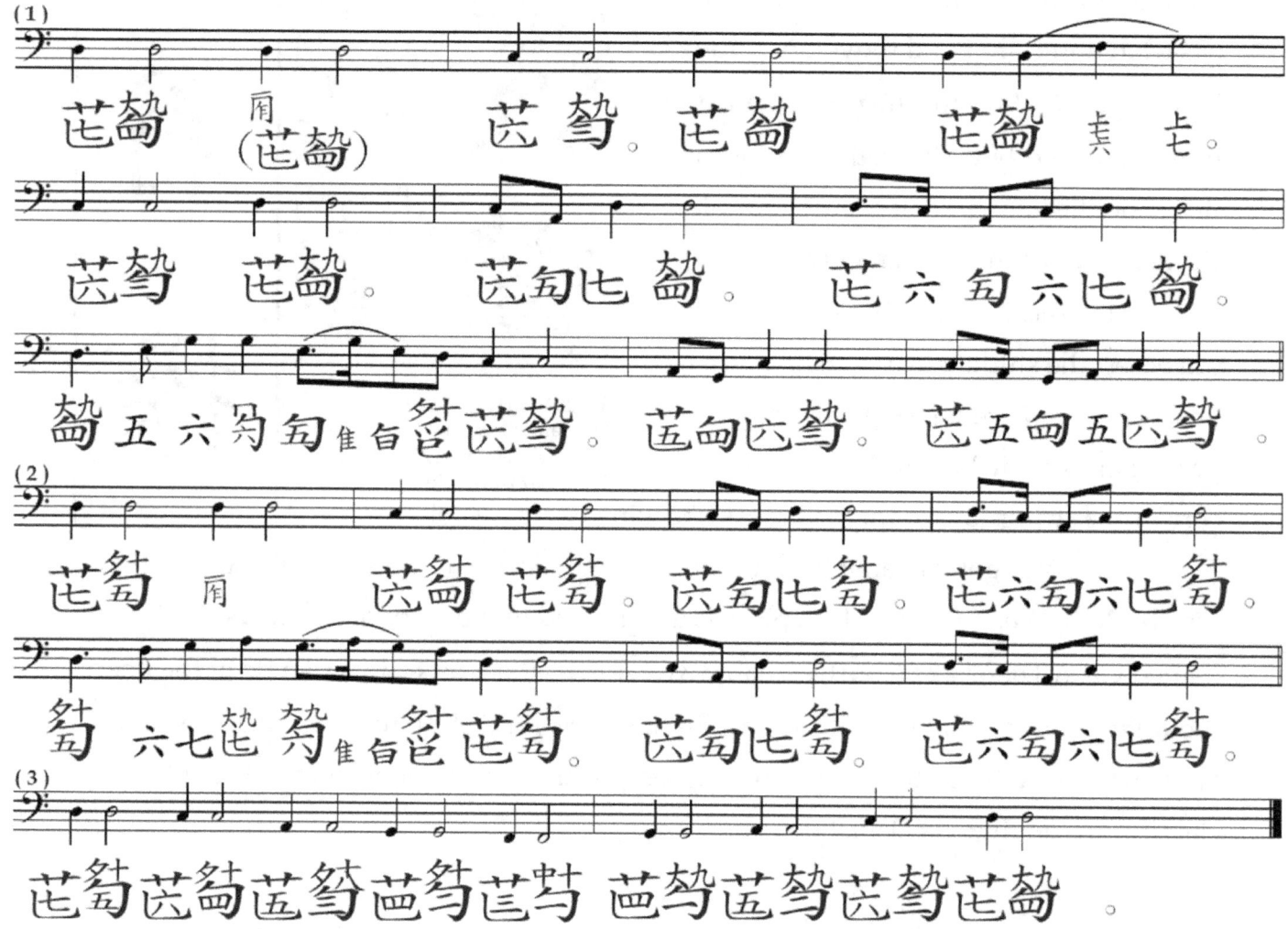

## Tuning with Xianweng Cao

The words "Xian Weng 仙翁" require the speaker (regardless of dialect) to pronounce the two syllables in an elevated, long and even tone. To have the guqin player sing this word over and over while playing this helps with listening to the strings for off-key pitches. Section 1 of the piece shows exemplars of Set A tuning applied in stopped 9th hui and open notes, while Section 2 shows exemplars of Set B tuning applied with stopped 10th hui and open notes. Intertwining use of Set A and B (playing each bar of section 1 and 2 in parallel) to tune strings is an effective method.
Section 3 makes a concise summary of all the possible combinations in both tuning sets.

## Lesson Pointers:

- Am I following the fingerings by the book? Are the sounds clear and distinct? Am I keeping a steady rhythm?
  - **Look up symbols that you're unsure of in the index, and copy them here.**
  - The first tone in a sliding note has time value too – don't start sliding up until you've given it its deserved time value.
  - Even for the "easy sections", like a chain of open string notes, it is important not to rush.
- Do I notice that on a tuned qin, there are fixed pairs of movements (open, pressed strings, or harmonics) that give the same pitch?
  - Two strings in the middle (e.g. String 7 and 4), upper string pressed on 9th *hui*.
  - One string in the middle (e.g. String 7 and 5), upper string pressed on 10th *hui*.
  - Matching sounds tend to finish off phrases.
- On line 3: Barring multiple strings (pressed): Do I only press on the strings that are to be sounded, while covering the others reasonably well to be pressed down at any given time?
- Do I notice that instead of the 10th *hui*, I need to press on position 10.8 when matching the fifth string?

英語琴統初階

# Liangxiao Yin

*Prelude to a Fair Evening* is a popular and mandatory piece for any beginning guqin student to learn. Soft and meditative, it shares the same opening theme with another song also associated with pleasant evenings – *Wuye Ti*《烏夜啼》.

Occurring in over 30 manuscripts and handbooks, the most popular version today is from the Wuzhizhai Qinpu of 1722, coupled with Guan Pinghu's recorded performance in the 1960's, which this version is based off of.

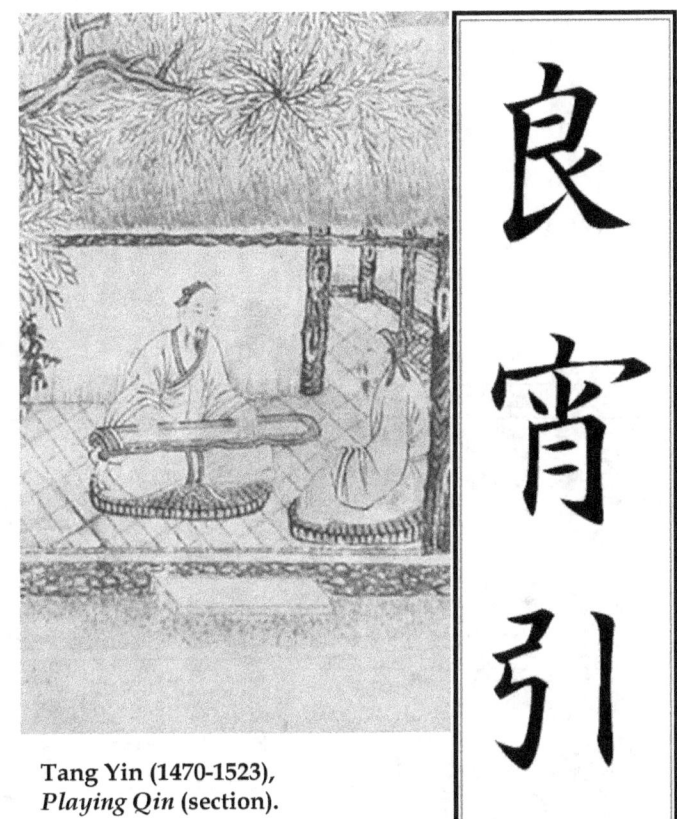

**Tang Yin (1470-1523),**
*Playing Qin* **(section).**

In this piece you will begin to combine and utilize all forms of playing techniques for left and right hand, of which to note are the following:

➤ Right hand:

厂 *Li* (index finger grazing forward one or more strings)

囚 *Yan* (thumb hammering down onto position as ring finger is pressed)

令 *Lun* ("wheel" with ring, middle, index finger forward)

𥥤 *Shuang-tan* (middle AND index finger plucking forward with force)

➤ Left hand:

Harmonics (巳 start, 正 stop),

隹/上 *jin/shang* (advance/up), 艮/下 (retreat/down), 自 (return)

𠂒 *Yin* 丂 *Nao/rou* (different types of vibrato; refer to fingering index)

卜 *Chuo* (Slide up to position), 氵 *Zhu* (Slide down to position)

應合 *Ying-he* (pluck the next indicated open string as you slide to the position)

➤ Special characters:
曰 *Da-yuan* (pause, then do the two aforementioned notes two more times)
省 *Shao-xi* (brief pause)

# 良宵引 Prelude to a Fair Evening

From Guqin Quji (1962), Wuzhizhai Qinpu (1722)
Score by Wang Di with modifications by Juni Yeung
正調 Standard Tuning

Lento 慢起

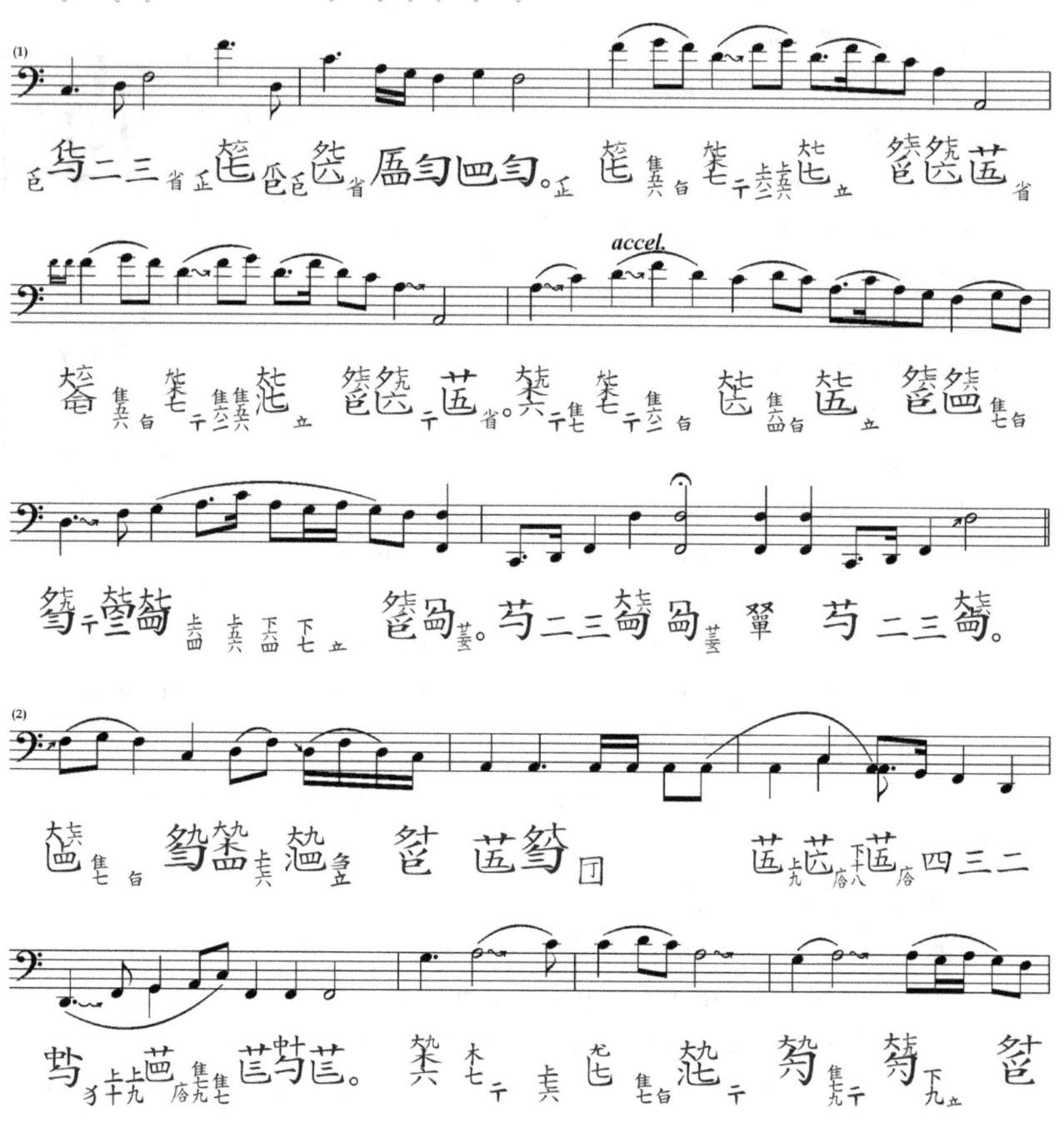

英語琴統初階

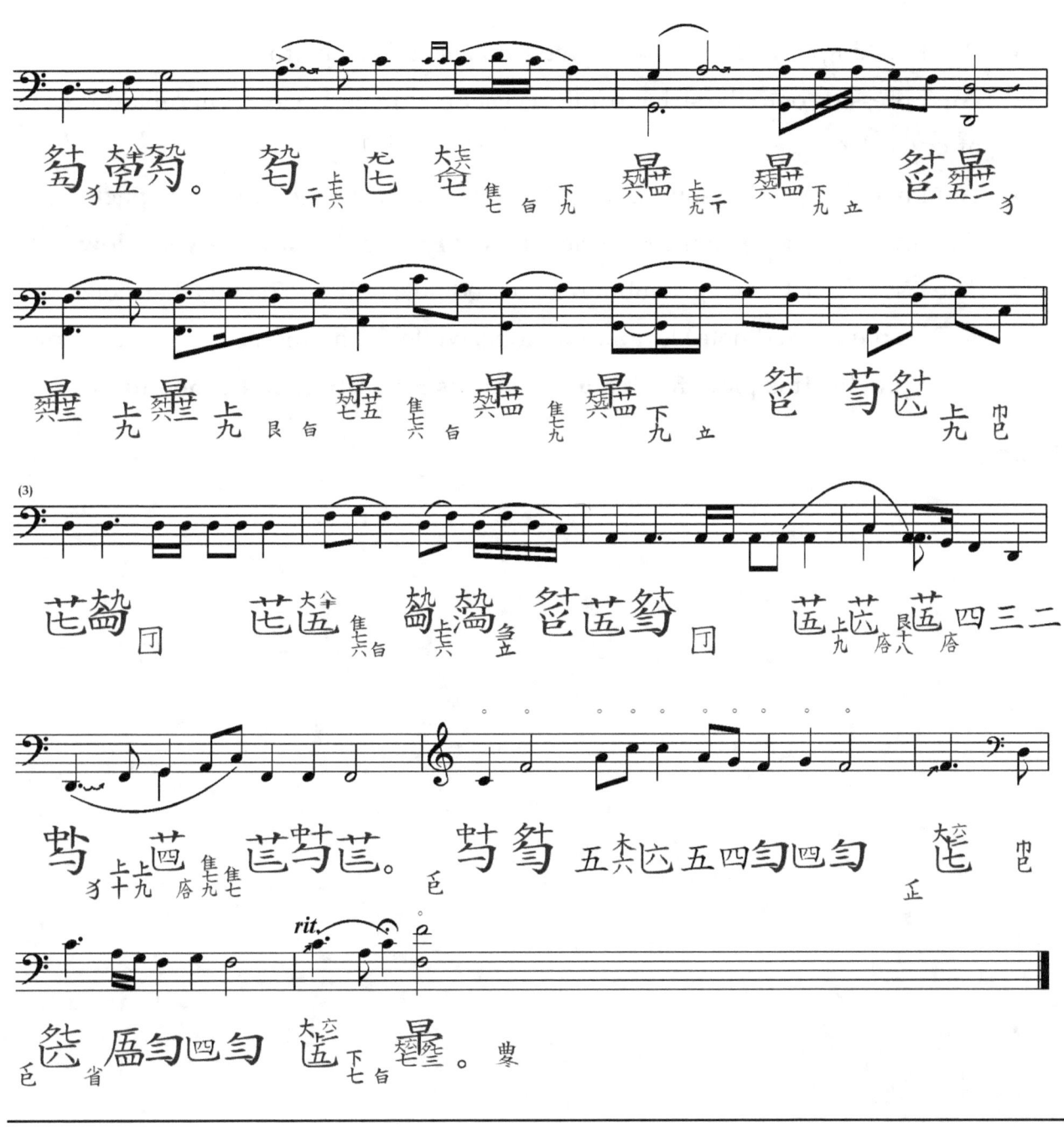

## Lesson Pointers

- Am I making clear the difference between *yin* and *nao* performances?
- Am I pressing onto the string firmly as I slide? Am I still clearly audible afterwards?
- Am I matching up the sounds at *ying-he*, and do they sound the same pitch?
- Are my *Lun* (wheel) giving off 3 clear notes? **Practice to play this very slowly.**
- The last note of the song combines a pressed note (VII @ 6.2) and a harmonic (III @ 7). Is the pressed note clear and on-tone, while the harmonic is clear and long?
- **Am I playing this piece feeling unrushed, as if strolling in the moonlight?**

## Notes

英語琴統初階

# Qiufeng Ce

A qin song made immortal in the early 20th century Mei'an Qinpu, *Ode to the Autumn Wind* is a verse written by Li Bo.

Because of its simple lyrics and direct transcription onto the qin, meaning that the singer and instrument both play the same melody, it is a popular beginner's piece to practice both playing technique and vocal accompaniment. This is not true for all qin songs, however, as earlier repertoire (such as *Three Variations of the Yang Pass Theme* and *Moon Over the Mountain Pass*) proved that multiple syllables can fit on less obvious movements on the music.

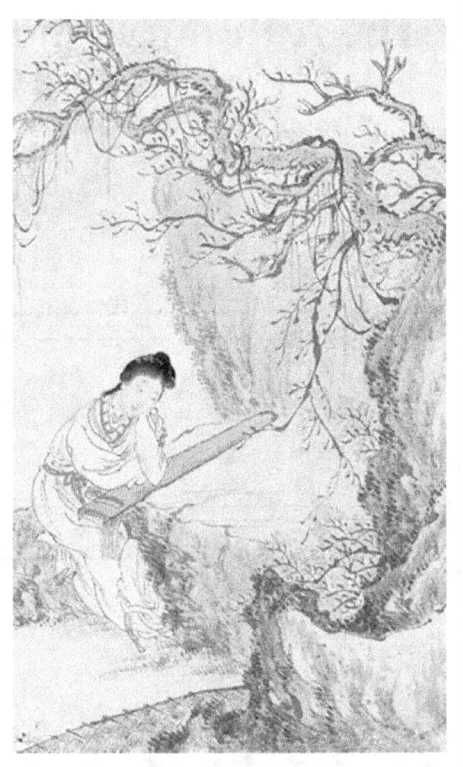

Pan Zhenyong (1852-1921)
*Stopping from Qin Playing.*
(Section)

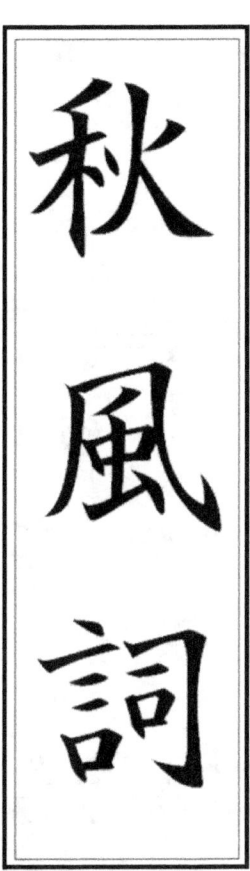

秋風清、秋月明、

落葉聚還散、寒鴉棲復驚。

相親相見知何日？此時此夜難為情。

入我相思門、知我相思苦。

長相思兮長相憶、短相思兮無窮極。

早知如此絆人心、何如當初莫相識、

何如當初莫相識！

*Fresh autumn breeze, bright autumn moon.*
*Falling leaves collect and scatter, winter ravens roost and flutter.*
*When, my love, will we meet again? Now tonight I feel only sorrow.*
*Enter my longing gates, know my longing pains.*
*Distant longing evoke distant memories, short longings have no end.*
*Had I known it so entangling, how I wish we never met,*
*How I wish we never met!*

*(Juni Yeung Translation)*

## 秋風詞 Ode to the Autumn Wind

From Guqin Quji (1962), Mei'an Qinpu (1931)
Score by Xu Jian, based on performance by Wang Ji-Ru
Modified by Juni Yeung

正調 Standard Tuning

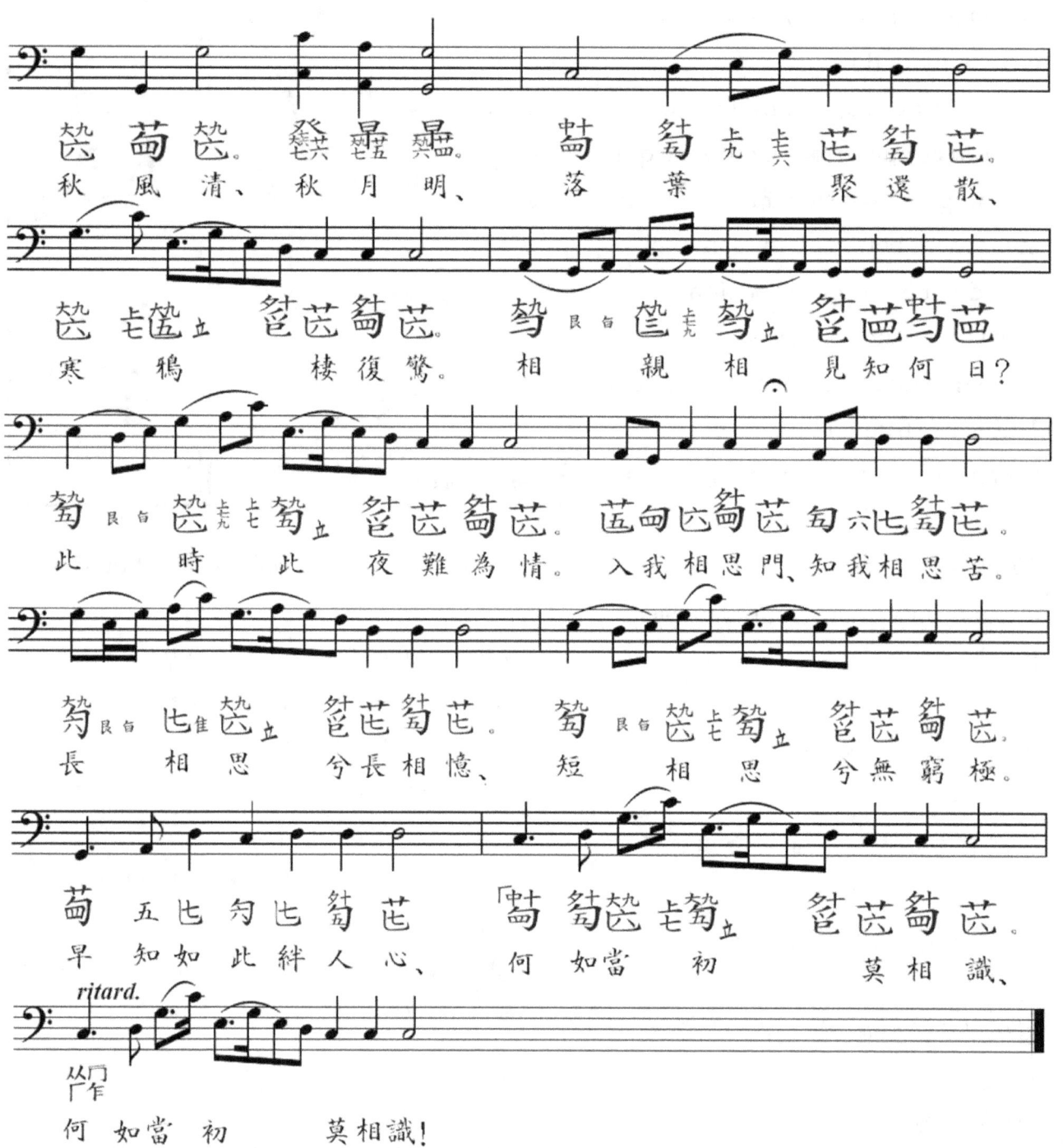

英語琴統初階

## Lesson Pointers

- The majority of new techniques are applied in the first line of the piece.
    - Make sure that the second bar is to be played at the same tempo as the first, despite having much more complex fingering.
    - Try practicing those 3 notes with only the pressed string first, at positions 7.6 and 9 on String VII, then 9 on VI.
- Don't forget any of the matching sounds at the end of phrases!
- Although easy to play, don't speed up playing the open-string heavy phrases.

# Zhao Yin

According to the *Shenqi Mipu* (1425), *Seeking Seclusion* is a piece attributed to early Jin 晉 (3rd c. C.E.) scholar-official Zuo Si 左思. He was known to have kept brushes and paper all around his house to catch whatever idea came up for a poem, and was known for his majestic use of diction. However, he had no ambitions for civil service, preferring a reclusive life of poetic leisure. An earlier poem titled "Summons for a Recluse" in the Chu Lyrics, attributed to Liu An 劉安, Prince Huainan 淮南王 of

Tang Yin (1470-1523), "Dreaming of Immortality in a Thatched Cottage" (section), Freer Art Collection.

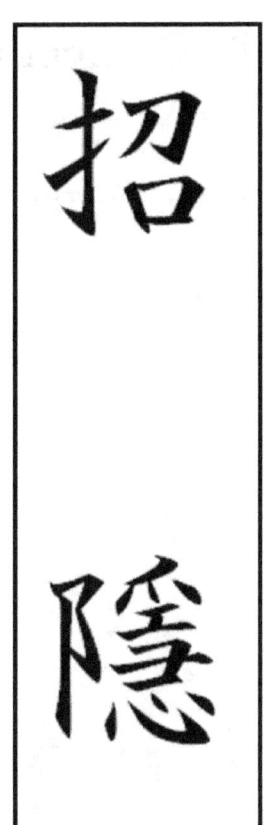

Western Han (2nd c. B.C.E.), implies that the invitation of a secluded sage back into the world to bring order. However, neither the *Shenqi Mipu* nor its later historical supplement *Qin Shi* (both by Zhu Quan, Prince Ning of Ming) makes a mention of this. Given the similarities between Zhu and Liu's status, refinement, and political situations (both lived precariously in the time of powerful Emperors who ascended to an unsteady throne), this piece would have been either a sincere call to renounce the world, or probably a cover declaration to avoid the suspicions and rumours of the Emperor and the

court.

# 招隱 Seeking Seclusion

Original from Shenqi Mipu (1425)
Score by Juni Yeung
Standard Tuning 正調

Grazioso 優悠地

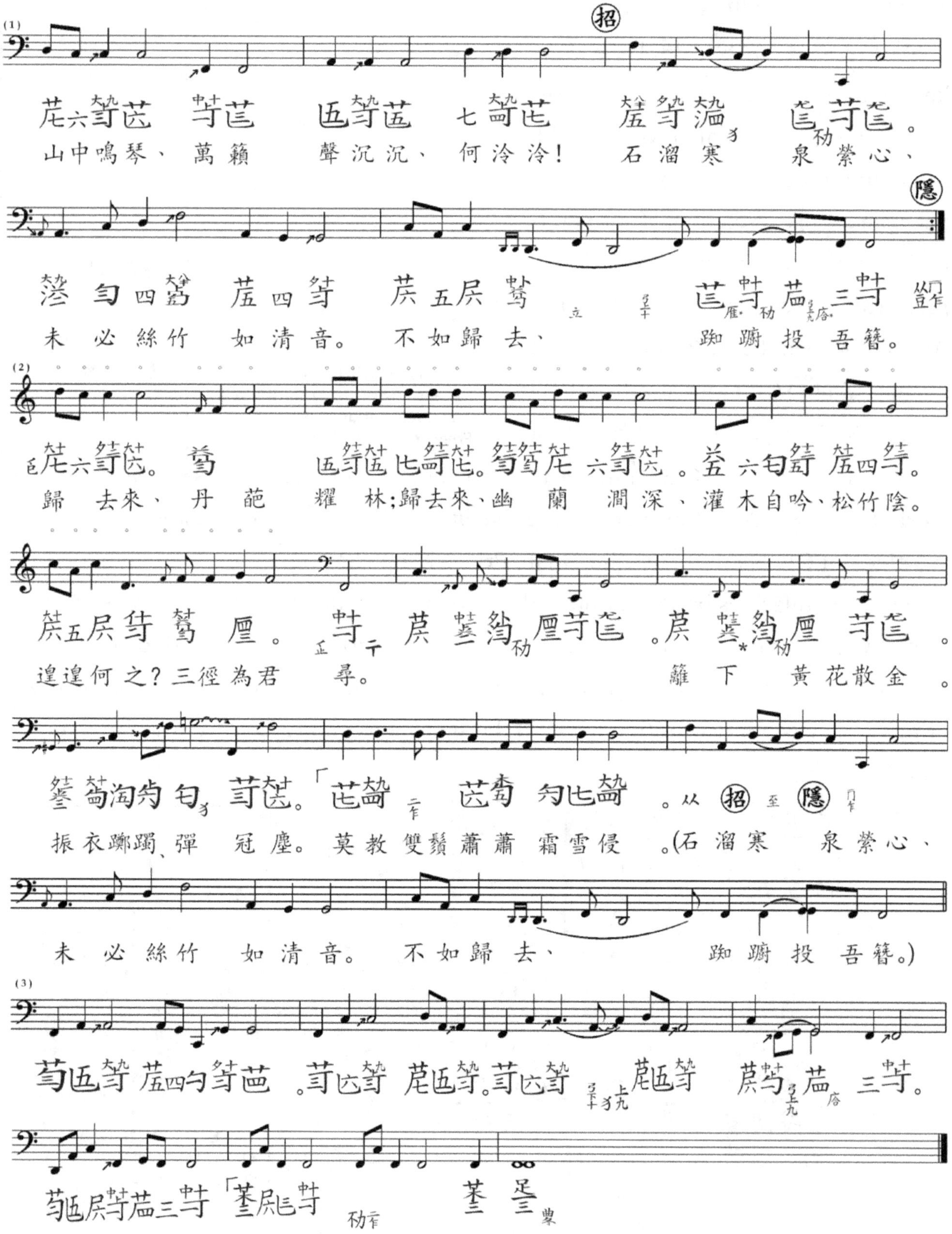

招

隱

山中鳴琴、萬籟　聲沉沉、何泠泠！石溜寒　泉縈心、

未必絲竹　如清音。不如歸去、　踟躕投吾簪。

歸去來、丹萏　耀林;歸去來、幽蘭澗深、灌木自吟、松竹陰。

遑遑何之?三徑為君尋。　籬下　黃花散金。

振衣踟躕、彈冠塵。莫教雙鬢蕭蕭霜雪侵。(石溜寒　泉縈心、

未必絲竹　如清音。不如歸去、　踟躕投吾簪。)

118　英語琴統初階

## Notes

* (LH): A 應 (match/echo) and 應合 has been added for disambiguation.

* (RH): Several positions have been changed, while retaining the string used.

## Lesson Pointers

- Am I using the right hand ring finger as directed, instead of replacing it with the middle finger?

- Am I playing the *Chuo* 綽 and *Zhu* 注 movements? Am I giving about a half-tone's distance sliding up or down before stopping for the majority of the time on the noted pitch?

- Am I giving ample representation for *Yin* 吟 and *Nao* 猱? Are the impressions of the two movements, such as directions and time value, clearly separate from each other?
    - Make *Nao* more stretched out, and make sure it goes in one direction above or below the original sound.
    - *Yin* should go above and below the given pitch, and shouldn't take up too much time, so that it disrupts the flow of the phrase.

- Am I playing the "Collide" (*Zhuang* 撞; looks like "立") correctly?
    - The main sound has a little more time compared to the 'spiking' movement that proceeds after it, to which the left hand focuses more energy pressing when going back down.

- Can I read the score reasonably ahead of time, to accommodate for more complex sequences?
    - Become familiar with how traditional scores handle section markers and repeats.
    - Make your own notes on the page – complex repeats can have you searching for the start of the section, disrupting performance.

# <u>Notes</u>

英語琴統初階

# Guanshan Yue

*Moon over the Mountain Pass* is a popular modern qin adaptation to a Tang dynasty poem of the same name by Li Bo (李白 Li Bai). The original poem is arranged and sung in the following melody, with the melody a relatively modern composition created much after the poem's original creation. The structure of the melody and integration with the poem bears the main feature of one note per one sung character, but technical flairs like the use of *lunzhi* ('wheel' movement) also show traces of the guqin's recent influences by Chinese folk and Western musical styles. The original poem goes:

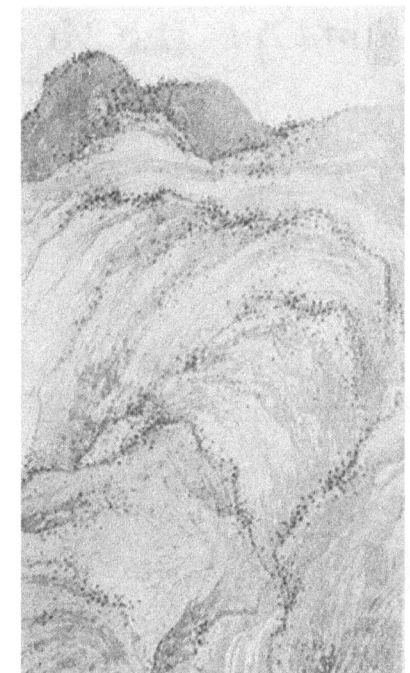

Tang Yin (1470-1523), "Dreaming of Immortality in a Thatched Cottage" (section), Freer Art Collection.

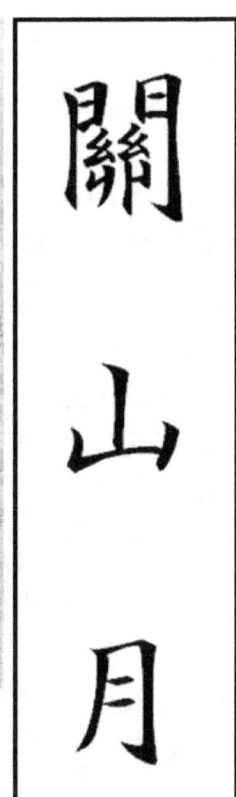

明月出天山，蒼茫雲海間。長風幾萬里，吹度玉門關。
漢下白登道，胡窺青海灣。由來征戰地，不見有人還。
戍客望邊色，思歸多苦顏。高樓當此夜，歎息未應閑。

*The bright moon lifts from the Mountain of Heaven*

*In an infinite haze of cloud and sea,*

*And the wind, that has come a thousand miles,*

*Beats at the Jade Pass battlements....*

*China marches its men down Baideng Road*

*While Tartar troops peer across blue waters of the bay....*

*And since not one battle famous in history*

*Sent all its fighters back again,*

*The soldiers turn round, looking toward the border,*

*And think of home, with wistful eyes,*

*And of those tonight in the upper chambers*

*Who toss and sigh and cannot rest. (Bynner Version Translation)*

# 關山月 Moon Over the Mountain Pass

From Mei'an Qinpu (1931) and Guqin Quji (1962)
Score and modifications by Juni Yeung

Standard Tuning 正調
Allegretto con brio 輕快有力

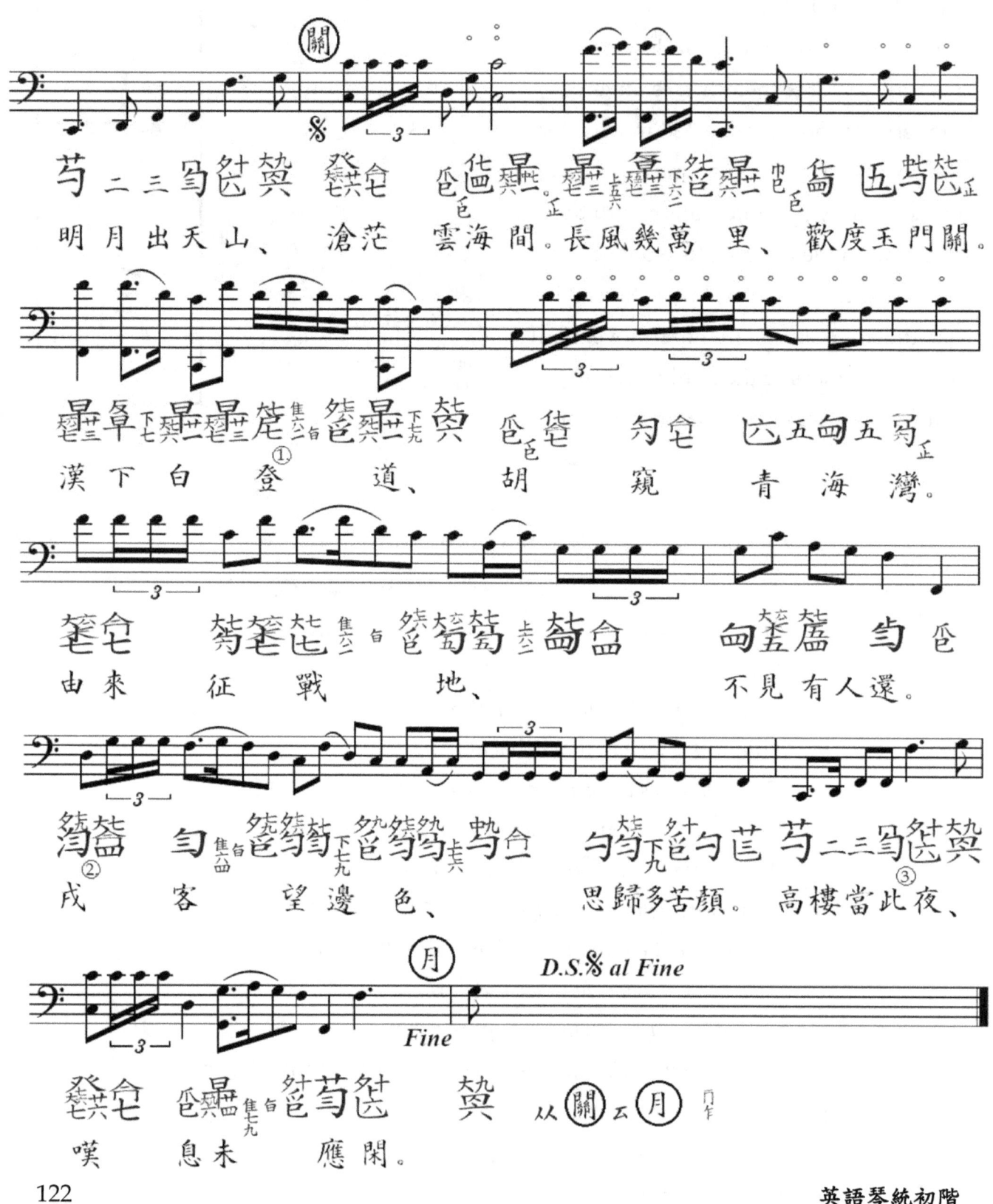

明月出天山、　滄茫　雲海間。長風幾萬里、　歡度玉門關。

漢下白登　道、　胡　窺　青海灣。

由來　征戰　地、　　　不見　有人還。

戌　客　望邊　色、　　思歸多苦顏。高樓當此夜、

嘆　息未　應閑。

英語琴統初階

① ③: Additions made by the score writer that were previously not included in the source document.

②: Originally left thumb on *hui* 7 of String II.

## Lesson Pointers

- Can I play this piece well slowly or quickly, with equal control over technique?
    - Can I maintain fluidity of the melody (i.e. not breaking up or stopping) while making the jumps from one position to another far away, without sounding pretentious or awkward?
    - Does my wheel movement (*lunzhi*, 輪指) give three crisp sounds of equal speed, without sounding crammed together? Can I do this when the melody is slower? Faster?
    - Can I press on the middle strings clearly, without interfering with open strings?
    - Am I pressing on the right spots between two hui? Do the sounds match the open matching sound?
- Can I handle more complex information in the score when sight reading at full speed? Can I grasp a way to assume the other half of the information in context just by looking at one part of a symbol?
    - Know your matching positions! Grasp only key parts: read the left hand position, assume others from logic or experience.

# <u>Notes</u>

英語琴統初階

# Liu Shang

According to the account given by Wang Zhi 汪芝 in the *Xilutang Qintong* manuscript, *Flowing Goblet* is a piece that describes the famous spring elegant gathering of Year 9 of *Yonghe* in the Western Jin dynasty (晉永和九年 353CE) immortalized by the casual cursive calligraphy of master Wang Xizhi 王羲之.

The "Flowing Goblet" refers to a drinking game where a goblet filled with wine is set adrift downstream, where participants sat on the

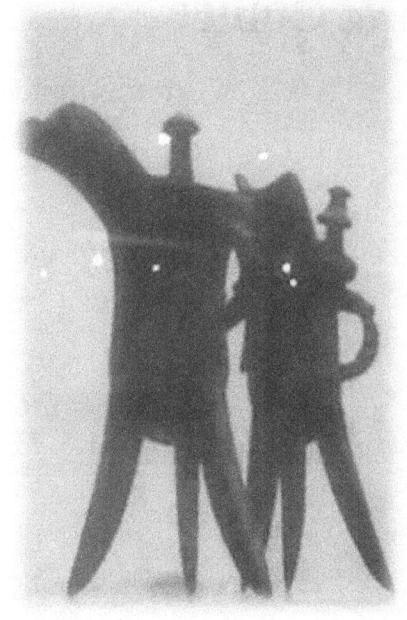
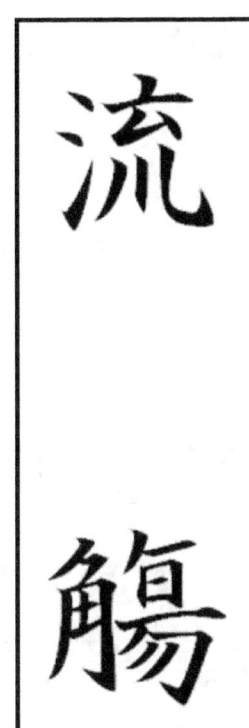

*Jue* wine goblets circa Eastern Zhou Dynasty, on display at the Royal Ontario Museum, Toronto, Canada.

riverbank and created poems on the spot, should the goblet stop in front of them. Those who could not finish a poem would be penalized by drinking the wine.

The joyous theme in this description contrasts somewhat with other accounts of this piece in other manuscripts, under the name Jiu Kuang 酒狂 *Drunken Madness*, where the context refers to Ruan Ji 阮籍 (slightly earlier in the same period) using extreme drunkenness and drug usage to avoid suspicion and service in the newly-founded Jin regime, founded under a political coup against the Wei state of the Cao house by the Sima clan 司馬氏.

Players of this version can attempt some contrast in the theme by accentuating the 'imperfect' phrase endings, as well as the whole harmonic section at the end of the piece, absent in other manuscripts and versions.

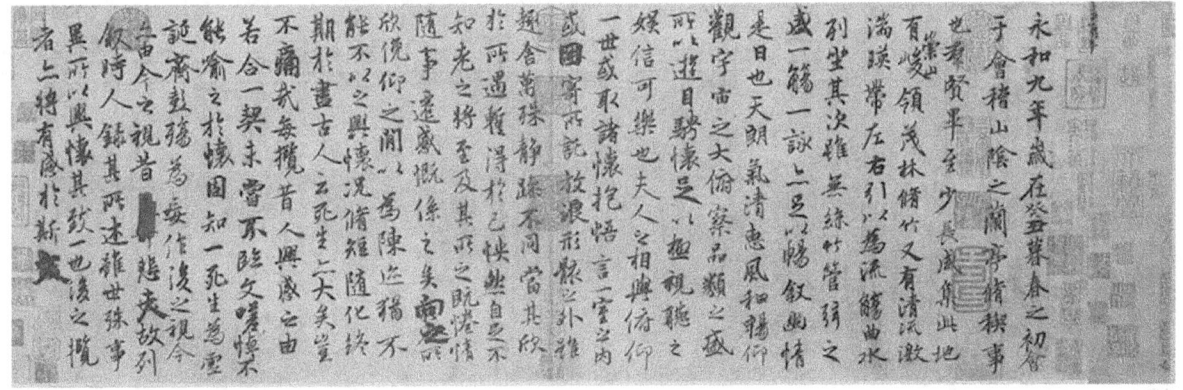

# 流觴 Flowing Goblet

As transcribed from Xilutang Qintong 西麓堂琴統 (1525)
Score by Juni Yeung
Standard Tuning 正調

Animato bruscamente 突然而生動

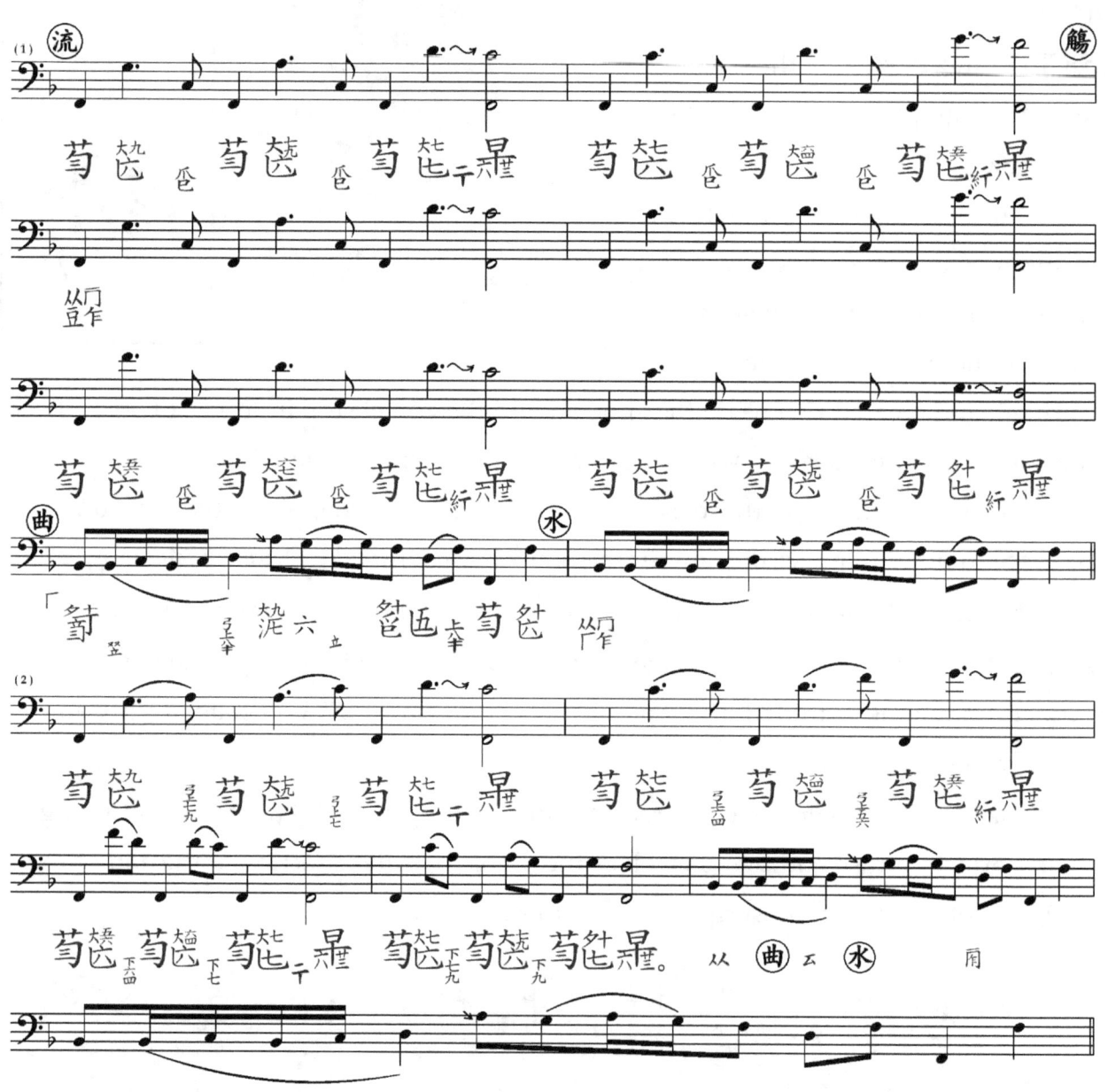

英語琴統初階

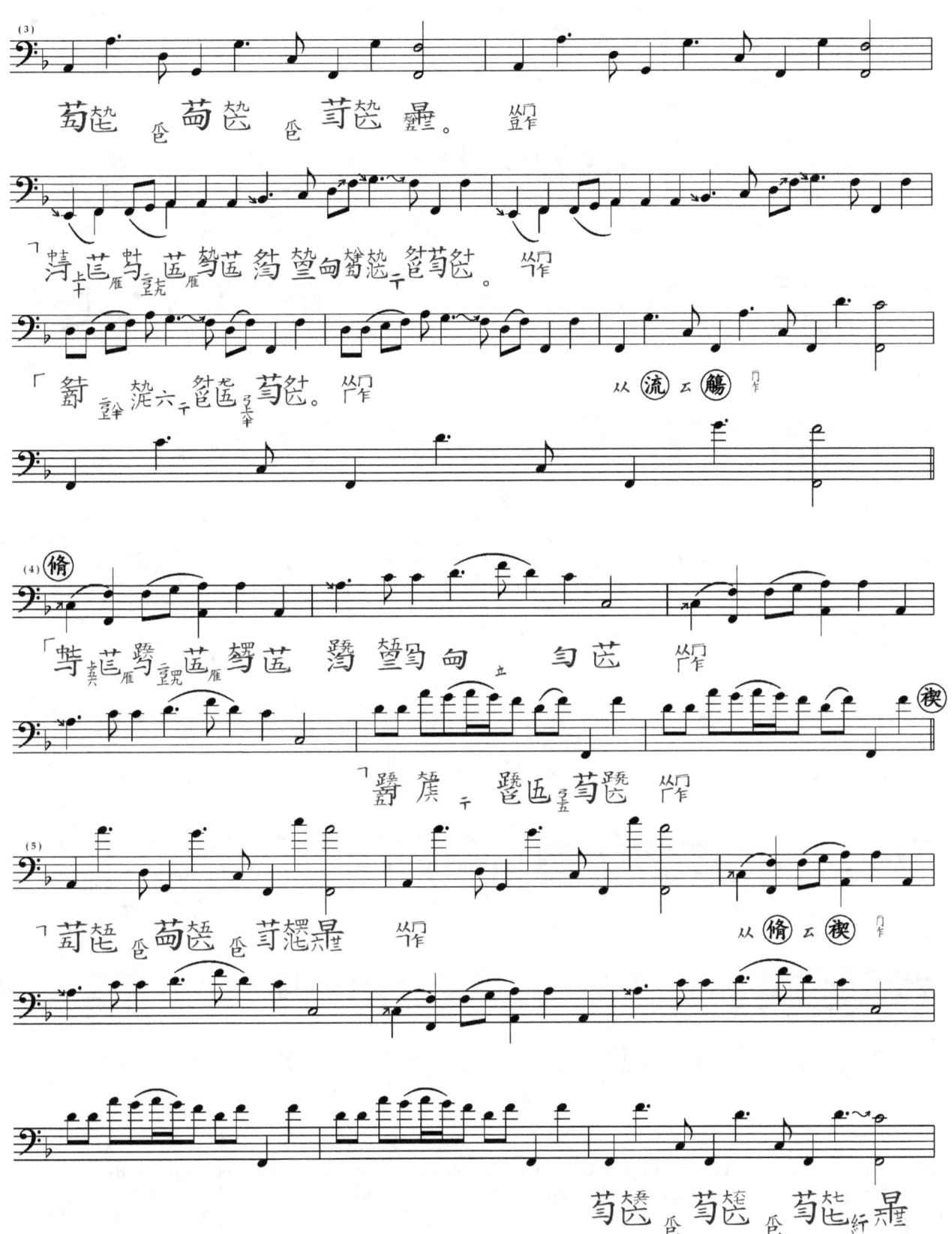

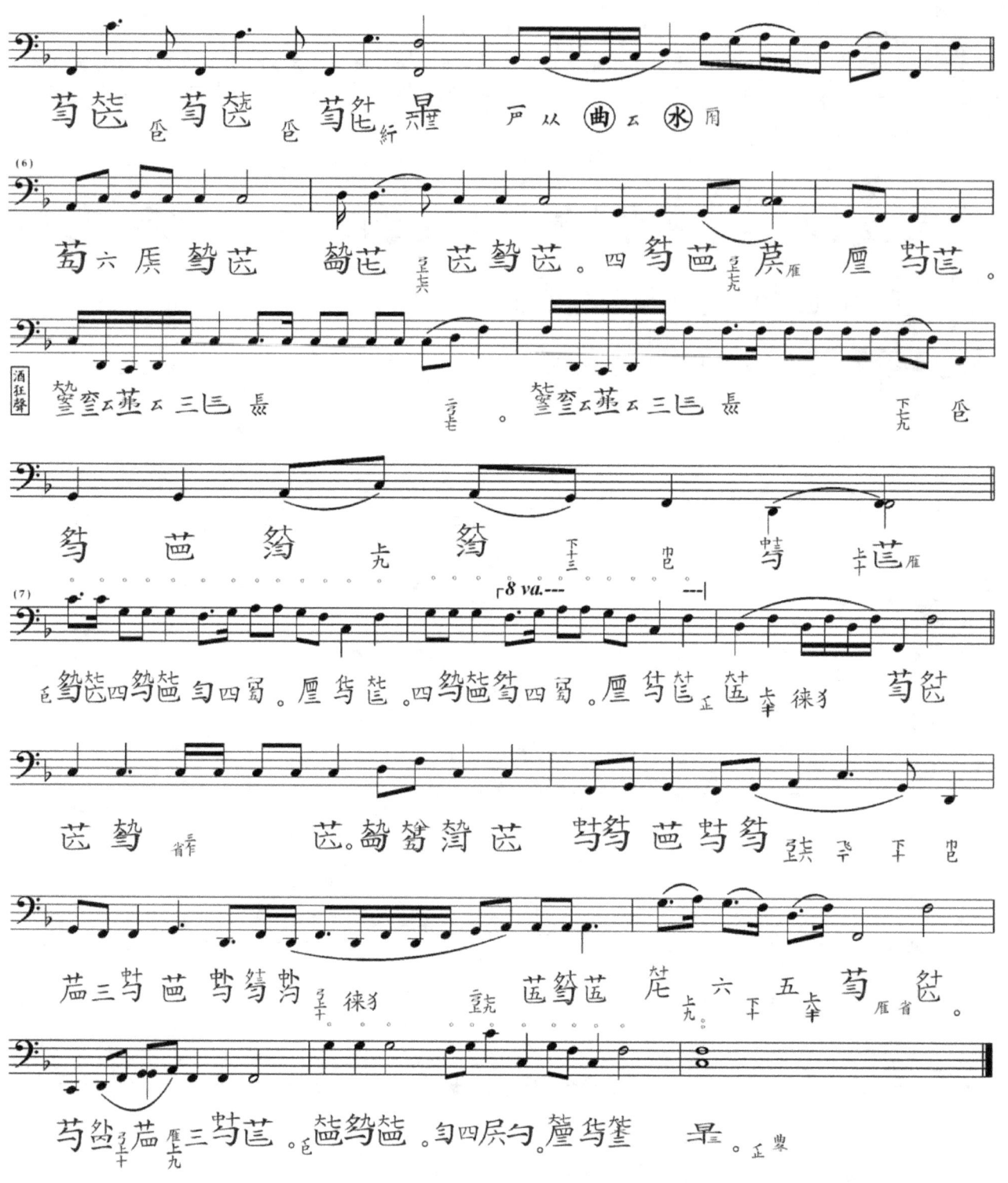

NOTE: On the 4th to last bar, left hand positions have been shifted to the right in order to better reflect the intention to match the open note counterparts, although it could have been intentional to have the left hand *precede* the right hand movements to enforce the drunken *rubato*. To compensate, one may also add an open string VI on the outstanding 8.5 pressed position.

英語琴統初階

## Lesson Pointers

- Can I handle the rhythm of this melody and maintain it throughout?
  - Is it unbiased from the more popular rhythm of *Jiu Kuang*?
- Can my left hand handle the technical requirements swiftly?
  - Avoid situational improvising (follow the score). Fingers may tangle up otherwise.
  - Utilize the left ring fingernail to press down on the kneeling movement (*guizhi* 跪指) for multiple strings. Remember that fingers push down themselves, and avoid straining the rest of your hand muscles in the process.
- Is the number of notes in longer 'chain' (*suo*) phrases right? (Follow the given rhythm to help keep count)
- Am I handling the new left hand movements according to their definitions, such as having rounded sounds for *yin* and sharp slides for *zhuang*, and firm slides?

流觴

# REPERTOIRE B

♫

# NON-STANDARD TUNING ETUDES

YANG GUAN SAN DIE
HUA XU YIN
QIU XIAO BU YUE

# Yangguan Sandie

*Three Variations on the Yang Pass Theme* is an adaptation of a famous Tang dynasty poem by Wang Wei 王維 titled "*Seeing Yuan Er off to Anxi* 《送元二使安西》", where Anxi is a part of the Tang frontier, between modern-day Gansu and Xinjiang.

Due to the reference of Wei city (where this poem is composed), this piece is also called *Weicheng Qu* 渭城曲 or "Wei City Song". Even today, this piece is popular among not just guqin players, but for all instruments as a signature piece of Han Chinese music.

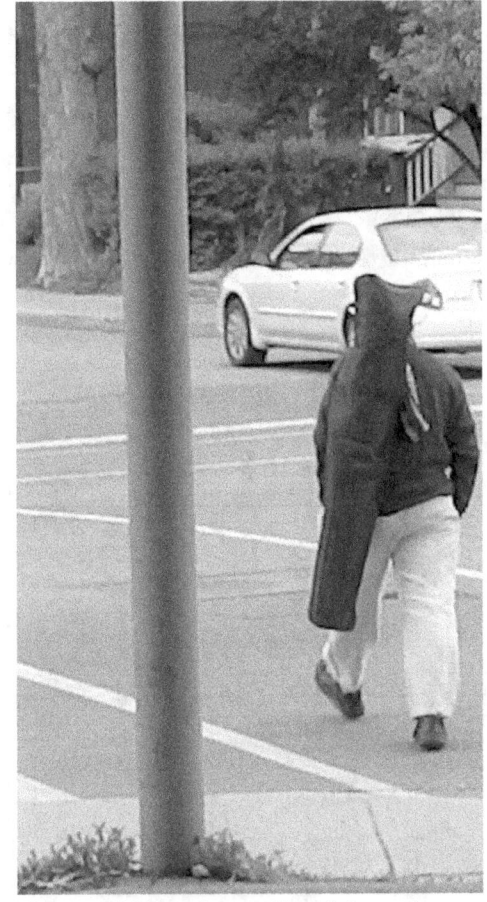

**Players bidding farewell and departing after a Toronto guqin gathering.**
**"The hostels are verdant and the willows are fresh…" – Wang Wei**
**Photo taken by the author, June 2007.**

陽關三疊

This popular tune was first recorded as a guqin piece in the *Zheyin Shizi Qinpu* 《浙音釋字琴譜》 of 1491, and has appeared in over 30 surviving texts in various lengths and versions, with additional lyrics from the original poem below:

> 渭城朝雨浥輕塵。客舍青青柳色新。
> 勸君更盡一杯酒。 西出陽關無故人。
>
> *The morning rain at Weicheng dampens the light dust,*
> *The inn is green with the color of new willows.*
> *I offer thee one more cup of wine.*
> *For west past Yangguan, there will be no old acquaintances.*

# 陽關三疊 Three Variations on the Yang Pass Theme

Modified from Guqin Quji (1962)
Score rearranged by Juni Yeung

Ruibin Tuning 蕤賓調 (+5)
Tuning: Match harmonics: String III @ 4th/10th *hui* with String V @ 5th/9th *hui*; tighten V.

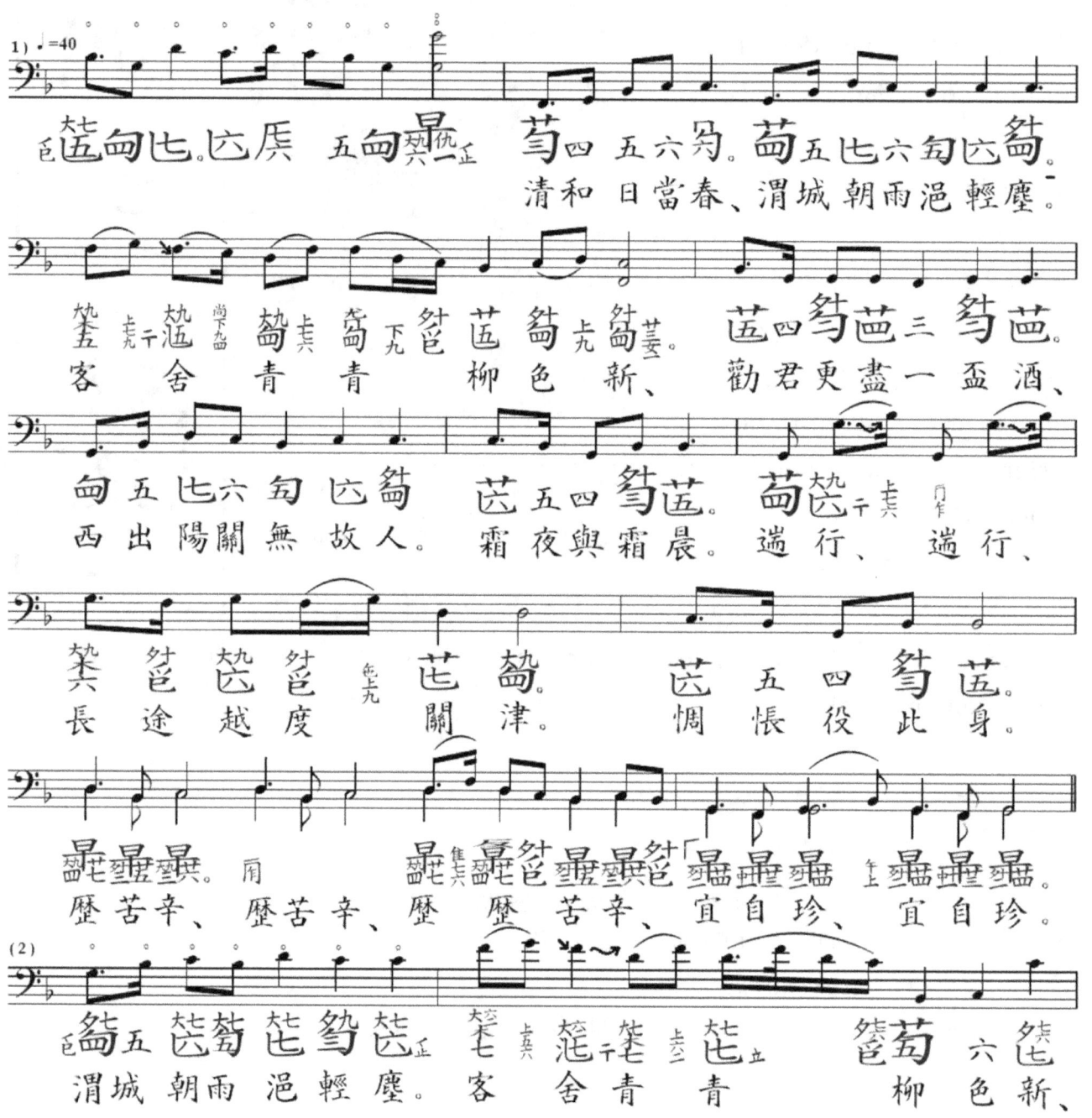

英語琴統初階

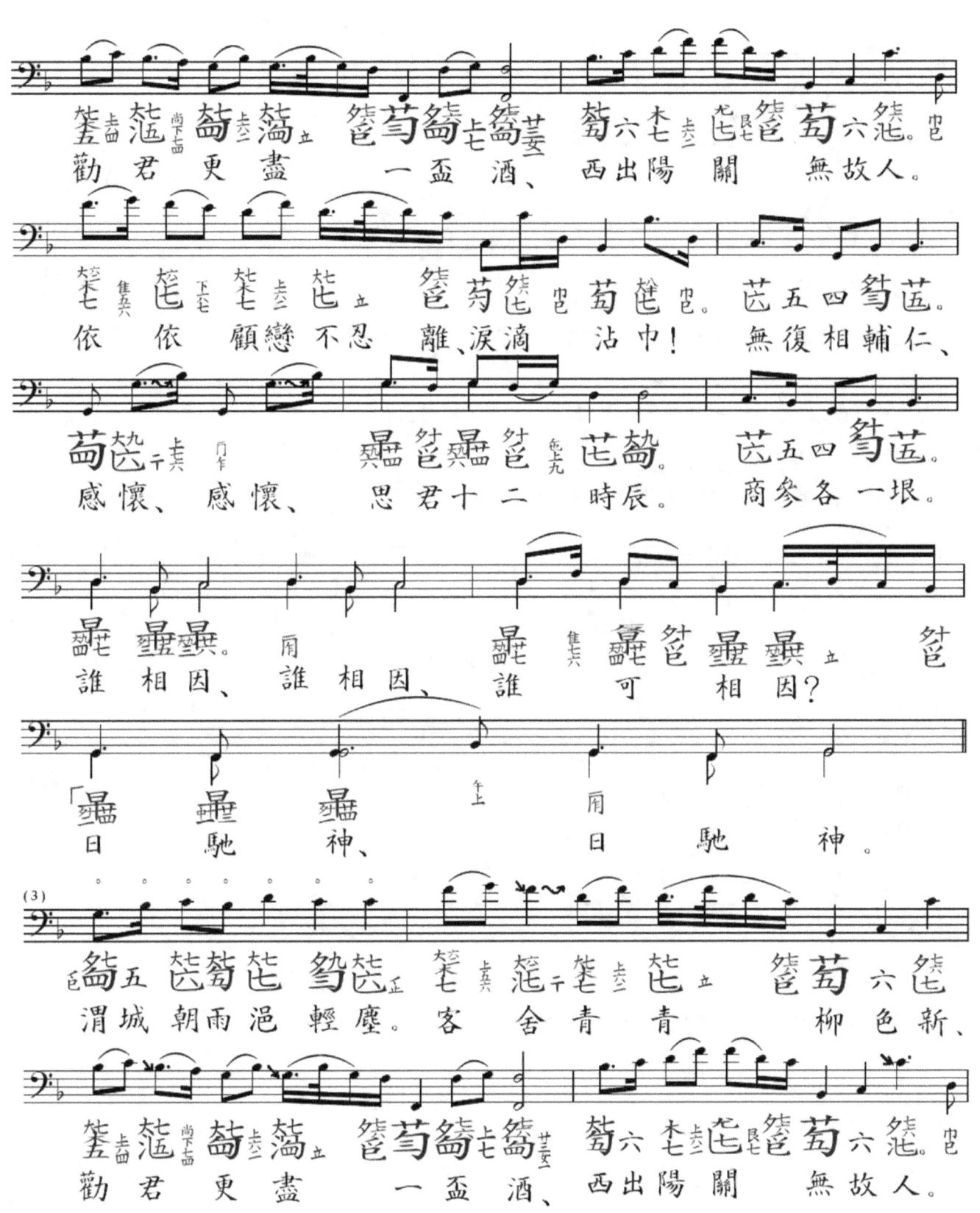

勸君更盡 一盃酒、 西出陽關 無故人。

依依 顧戀不忍 離、淚滴 沾巾! 無復相輔仁、

感懷、 感懷、 思君十二 時辰。 商參各一垠。

誰 相因、 誰 相因、 誰 可 相因?

日 馳 神、 日 馳 神。

渭城 朝雨 浥 輕塵。 客舍青青 柳色新、

勸君更盡 一盃酒、 西出陽關 無故人。

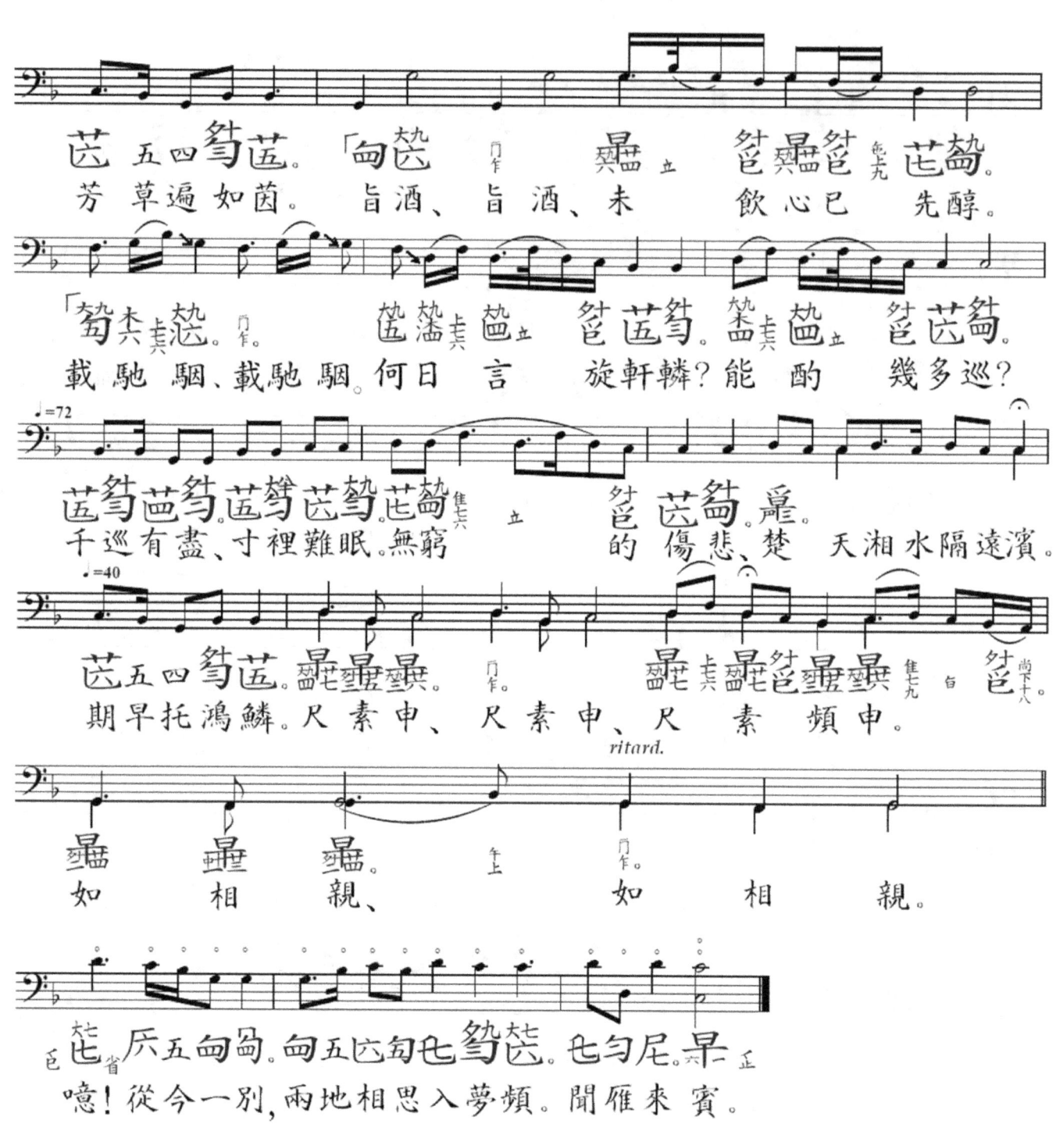

芳草遍如茵。旨酒、旨酒、未　飲心已　先醇。

載馳驅、載馳驅。何日言　旋軒轔？能酌　幾多巡？

千巡有盡、寸裡難眠。無窮　的傷悲、楚　天湘水隔遠濱。

期早托鴻鱗。尺素申、尺素申、尺　素　頻申。

如　相　親、　　如　相　親。

噫！從今一別，兩地相思入夢頻。聞雁來賓。

## Lesson Pointers

- Am I keeping the phrases separate and distinct, as if reciting the original poem?
- Can I memorize this piece without mistaking the sections from each other?
  - Remember the distinct features of each "variation" – there are unique phrases in each one, and if you remember the order of appearance for these phrases, you can cut down on redundant memorization.
- Am I controlling and adding my own treatment of the phrases to embellish the performance?
  - Try to grab a feel on your artist's credit – add little decorations here and there, and experiment where the limit is and how floral a piece may be, especially when it is accompanied by song or another instrument.
- Is my new tuning correct?
  - Double check using two ways:
    - Match open string V, with pressed 10th *hui* of string III,
    - Harmonics 9th *hui* of string V, with (harmonics) 10th *hui* of string III.
  - Make sure that other strings or pegs aren't loosened while adjusting to the new pitch.

## Notes

英語琴統初階

# Huaxu Yin

*Prelude to a Utopian Land* describes a tale from the book Liezi 《列子》, about the journey of Huang Di 黃帝, the Yellow Emperor, going into 3-month seclusion after feeling dissatisfied from his 15 years of rule over the newly united Chinese tribe. Huang Di dreamt of a land called Huaxu 華胥, where the inhabitants had no extraneous desire, and with a naïve nature they knew no malevolence. Achieving this understanding, Huang Di returned to his people and by the 28th year of his rule, the land was in harmonious rule.

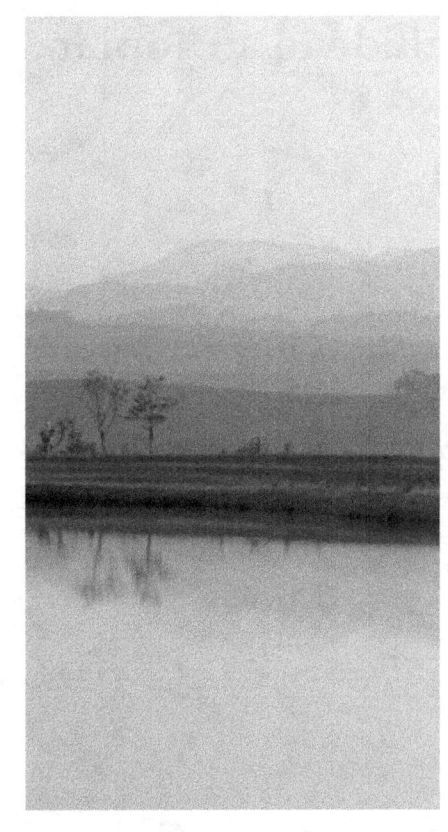
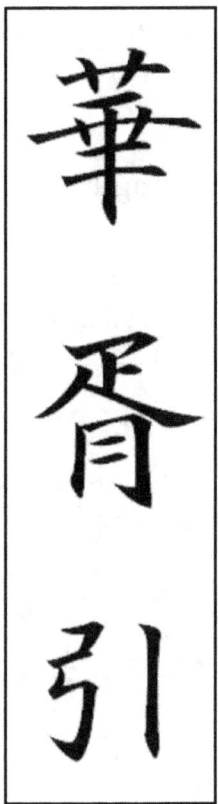

While originally undivided into sections, the piece can be largely split into three sections, with the first and last having largely parallel themes, but fine details are "completed" in the later section.

Two variations are suggested in processing the rhythm used in repeating phrases in this score, and the player may take some liberty in reinterpreting the musical themes in this profound "celestial air of antiquity", *Taigu Shenpin* 太古神品.

# 華胥引　Prelude to a Utopian Land

Adapted from Shenqi Mipu (1425)
Score by Wang Di, rearranged by Juni Yeung

Qiliang Tuning 淒涼調 (+2, 5)

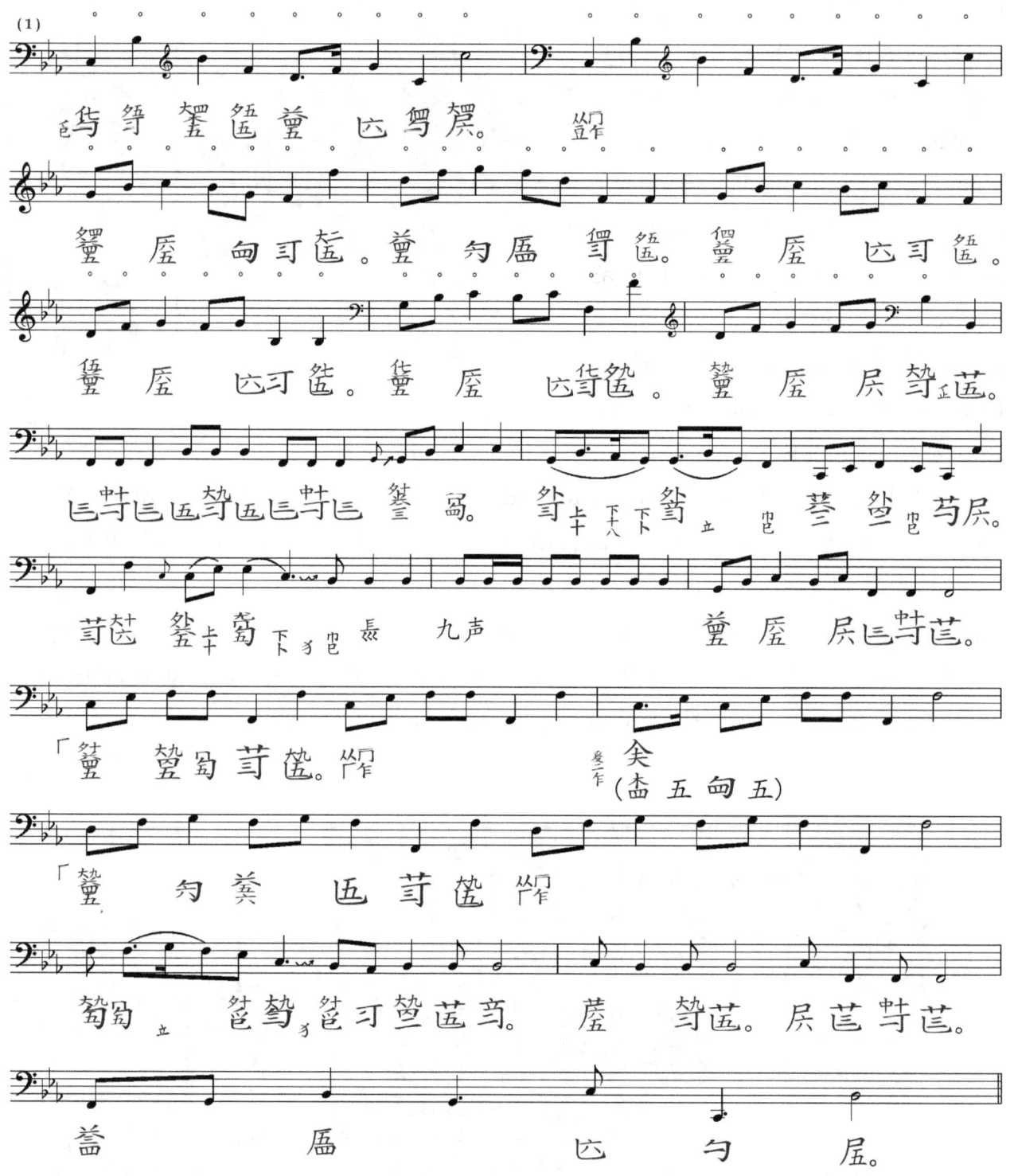

英語琴統初階

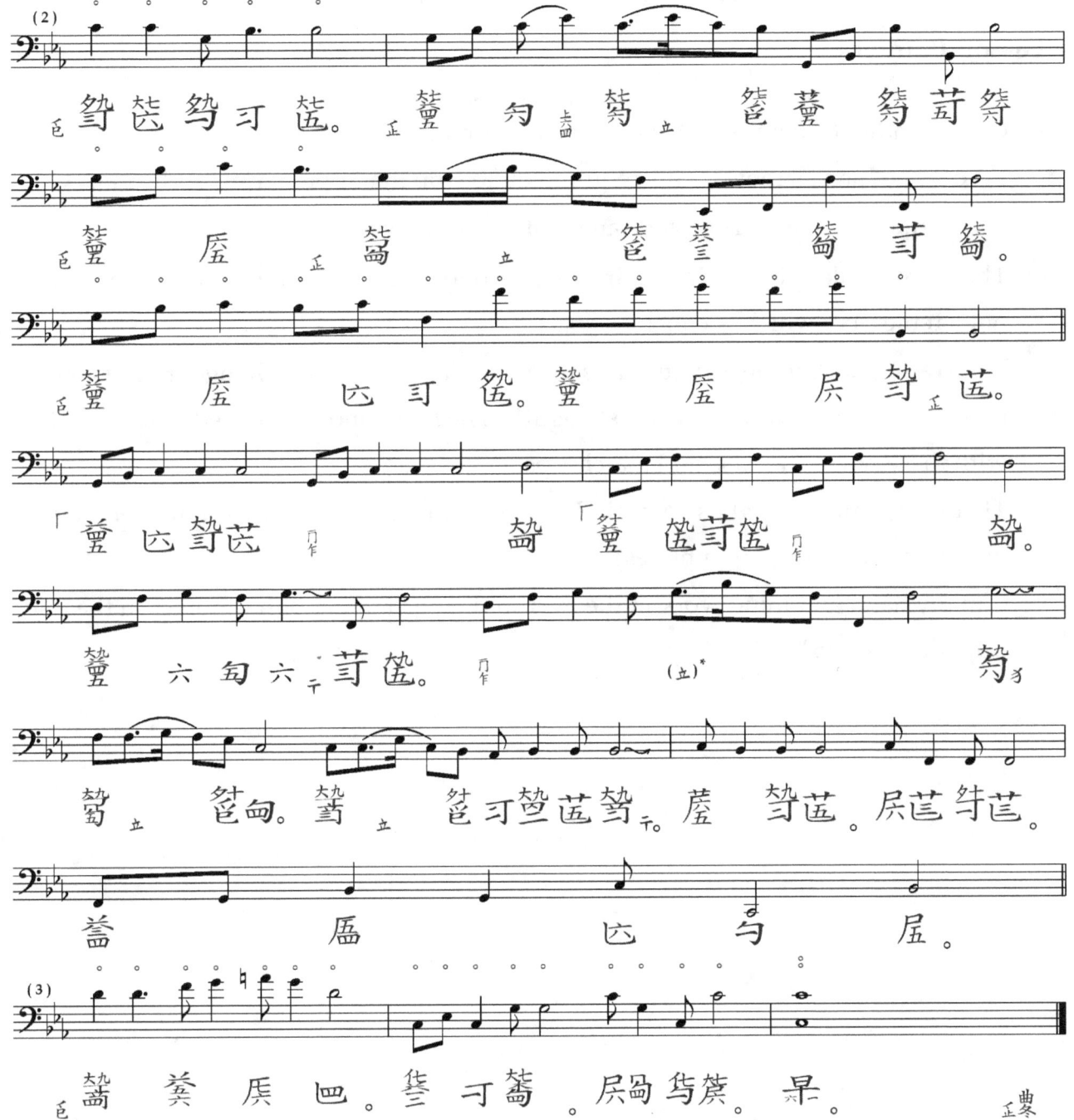

1: A Zhuang (collide, 撞) has been added here for balance, as referenced from Yao Bingyan's 姚炳炎 version recorded in Guqin Quji 古琴曲集.

NOTES: In the Guqin Quji, the various Diejuan 疊涓 movements are commonly but inconsistently interpreted as "using index and middle fingers to play consecutive strings quickly, producing 4 notes". According to Chen Zhuo 陳拙's fingering index (the definitions used in this book), all Diejuan involving multiple strings are defined as a quick stroke with index and/or middle finger on the strings, producing 2 notes, which makes the single instance of Quanfu 全扶 more emphasized.

The Diejuan/Quanfu confusion was an issue of many mid-20th Century interpretations, primarily because the more common single-string Diejuan has two sounds produced by the right middle and index stroking inwards quickly, and there was no clear consensus of how to do this movement prior to the rediscovery of Chen Zhuo's Tang dynasty text in the early 21st Century.

**Tuning Method:**

From *Ruibin* tuning, match harmonic @ 9th *hui* on string II with 7th *hui* on string V.

**Lesson Pointers**

- Can I handle the new right hand movements correctly?
    - The Juan 蠲 movements require you to stop the upper string of the pair with the next available finger, same with Quanfu 全扶.
- There are similar phrases in the first and second sections with the difference of one note: remember which is which.
- Like Yangguan Sandie, new tunings mean left hand positions change from usual habits (e.g. the use of 10th *hui* on string III). The hand and mind needs to be familiar with these new situations and match-ups.
- There is an emphasized use of right hand ring finger, both in and out movements (as with many Taigu Shenpin pieces).
- Can my hand and mind work in the mirrored environment of harmonics in the mid-upper register (5th *hui* and up)?

**Notes**

英語琴統初階

# Qiuxiao Buyue

*Strolling Under the Moon in the Autumn Evening* is a piece recorded only in the Xilutang Qintong of 1525 in pre-modern manuscripts. Being set in the extremely rare Biyu Diao 碧玉調 tuning, this piece is seldom played past and present. This piece was brought back into attention when Yao Gongbai 姚公白 made a recording of this piece and it became a part of the "Old 8" recordings.

The piece was composed by Liu Shilong 柳世隆 of Southern Qi,

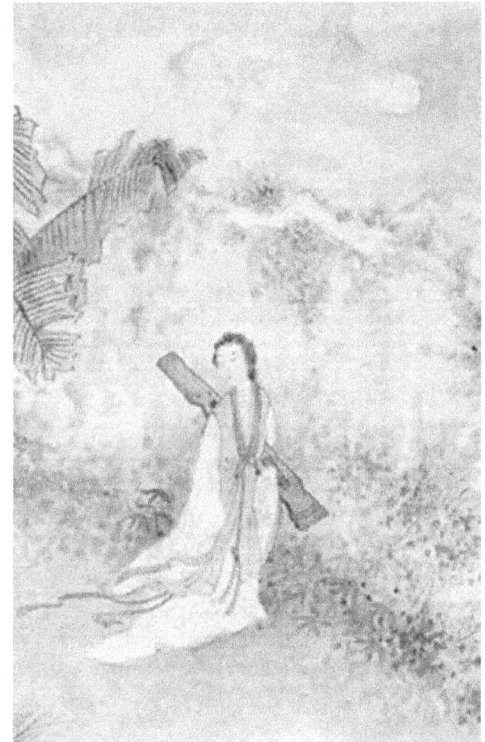

Su Liupeng (1798-1862),
*Carrying Qin in the Moonlit Night*
(Portion of horizontal scroll)

one of the Six periods during the first Age of Disunion in 5th Century China. The *Guangyue Ji* 《廣樂記》 writes: "…Liu Shilong was proficient with the qin, and is ranked first among the literati. His attitude of not being troubled by worldly matters brings him to play this piece on a moonlit night, as if taking a leisurely stroll in the garden. Its light-heartedness leads his followers to name this piece as such."

The primary challenge of this piece is in preparing the instrument in the right tuning prior to playing the piece itself. Unlike other tunings, Biyu Diao must be adjusted by using stopped notes on pressed strings, and requires the player to have great precision in its process (as the tuning process is irreversible and one has to restart from standard tuning if he or she fails in the middle). Otherwise, this is an excellent piece and relatively easy to play.

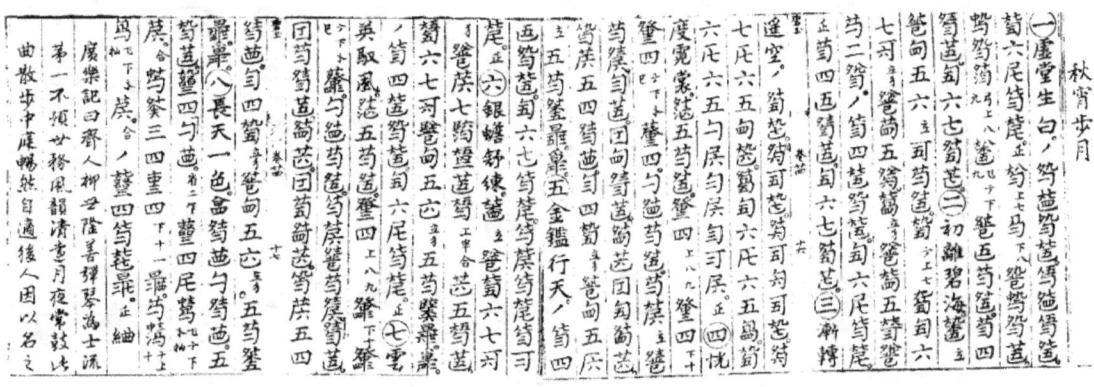

# 秋宵步月　Strolling Under the Evening Autumn Moon

From Xilutang Qintong (1525)
Score by Juni Yeung

Biyu Tuning 碧玉調 (-1, 4, 6; +3[½

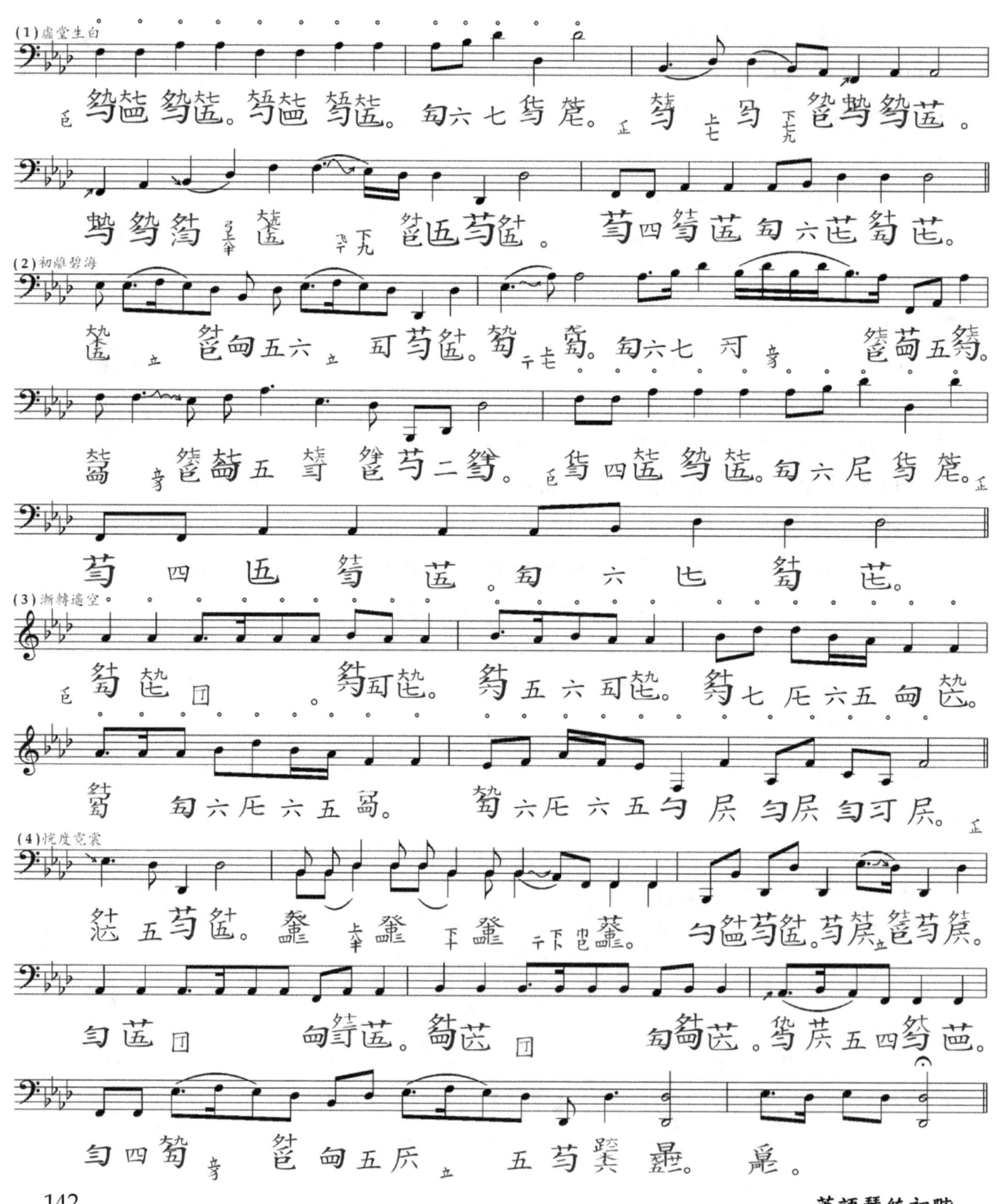

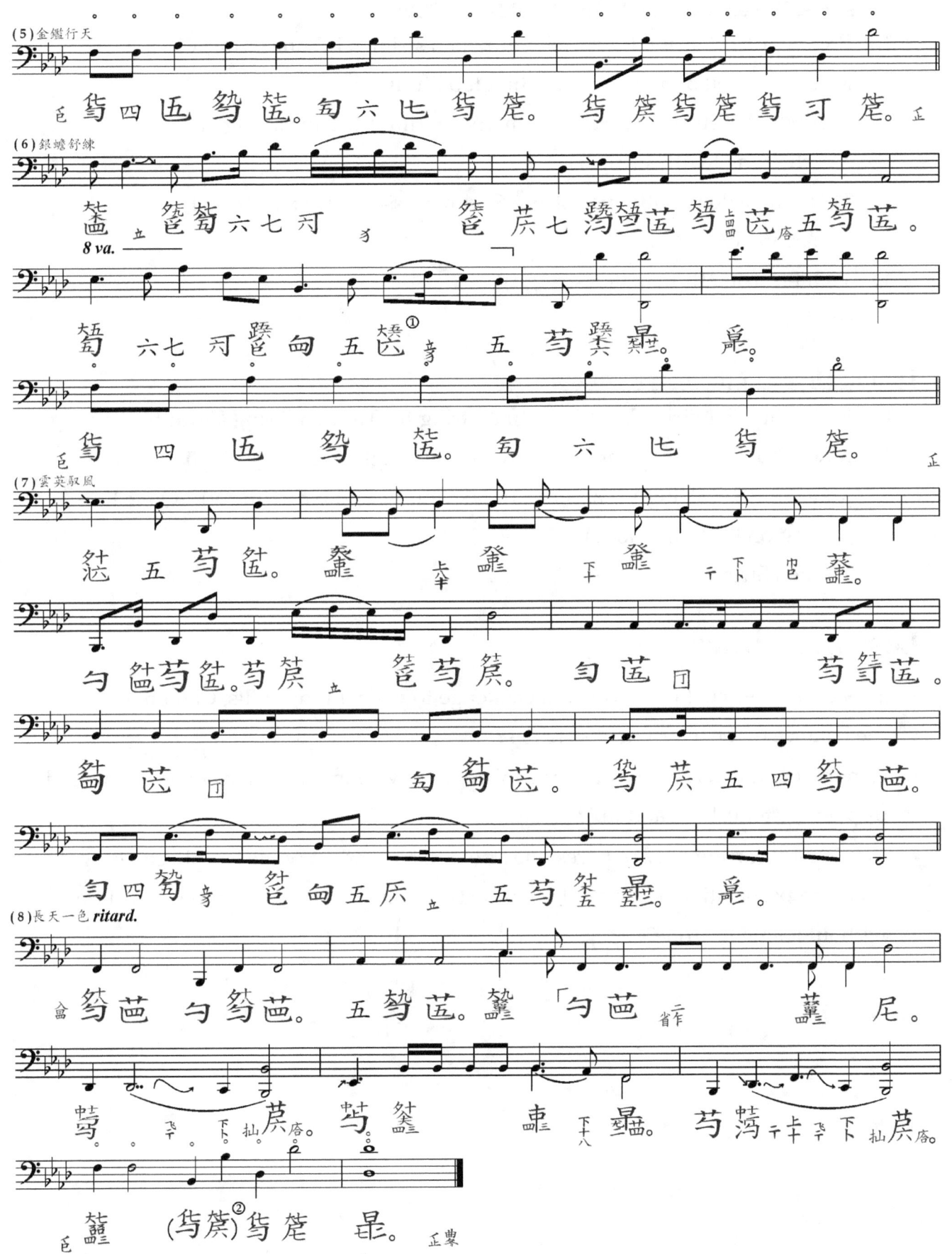

1: Changed to using left thumb 大指 for smooth playing.
2: Added in as per Yao Bingyan's rendition.

**<u>Tuning Method 1 (as recorded in Xilutang Qintong):</u>**

1.  Press @ 10.8 of string IV, match with open string VI. Tune string VI. Make sure you do this exactly! This step is critical.

2.  Press @ 10 of string IV, match with open string VI. Tune string IV.

3.  Match string I with string VI.

    This can be done with open string 6 with pressed 7th *hui* @ string I, or harmonic @ 10th *hui*.

4.  Tighten string III to match string IV.

**<u>Tuning Method 2 (harmonics only):</u>**

1.  Match hui 9 @ string V and hui 10 @ string III; Tighten String V (Ruibin Tuning)

2.  Match hui 7 @ string V and hui 9 @ string II; Tighten String II (Qiliang Tuning)

3.  Match hui 9 @ string VII and hui 10 @ string V; Tighten String VII (Qingshang Tuning on Jiazhong mode)

4.  Tighten String III to match IV.

# Lesson Pointers

*   This tune is selected primarily as a challenge to your tuning skills. Can I maintain the balance of the instrument's strings?

*   Can my hand and mind work in the mirrored environment of harmonics in the mid-upper register (5th *hui* and up)?

*   Previously, barring only requires one string to be pressed while simply covering the others in preparation. Now can I press on two strings at the same time, and slide without losing the tone?

英語琴統初階

# Notes

# Repertoire C

♫

# Performance Pieces

Gu Feng Cao
Yu Qiao Wen Da
Kong Zi Du Yi
Song Xia Guan Tao
Sanzang Jin Tianzhu

英語琴統初階

# Gufeng Cao

*Etude in the Style of Antiquity* first appeared in the Ming Dynasty manuscript *Shenqi Mipu* (1425) under the Celestial Airs of Antiquity *Taigu Shenpin* collection of pre-Song Dynasty pieces. According to *Qinshi Chubian* 《琴史初編》 by Xu Jian 許健, it is reminiscent of Wei-Jin era (4th Century C.E.) styles of composition.

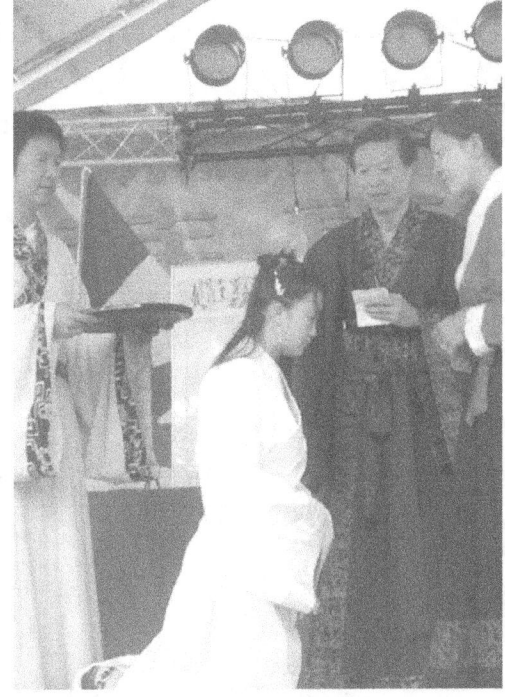

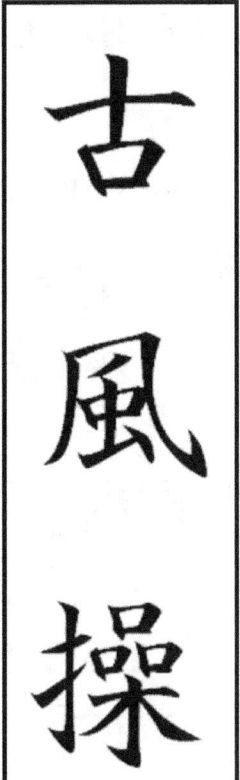

Coming-of-age ceremony organized by Toronto Association for the Revival of Hanfu, at CPAC Huaxia Festival, Toronto. Photo taken by the author, August 2008.

The piece is annotated as a tune of remembering the installation of ritual and order by King Wen of Zhou (11th c. B.C.E.), and remembering the ideal antiquity where "they could hear each other's chickens and dogs, and yet during their whole lives not visit each other. Not having likes or dislikes, and not having evil addictions". However, Xu Jian notes that the last section emphasizes on a then modern style of music and falling out of proper pentatonic progression, potentially implying a critique of present corruption, much like Xi Kang and the Seven Sages of the Bamboo Grove from this era.

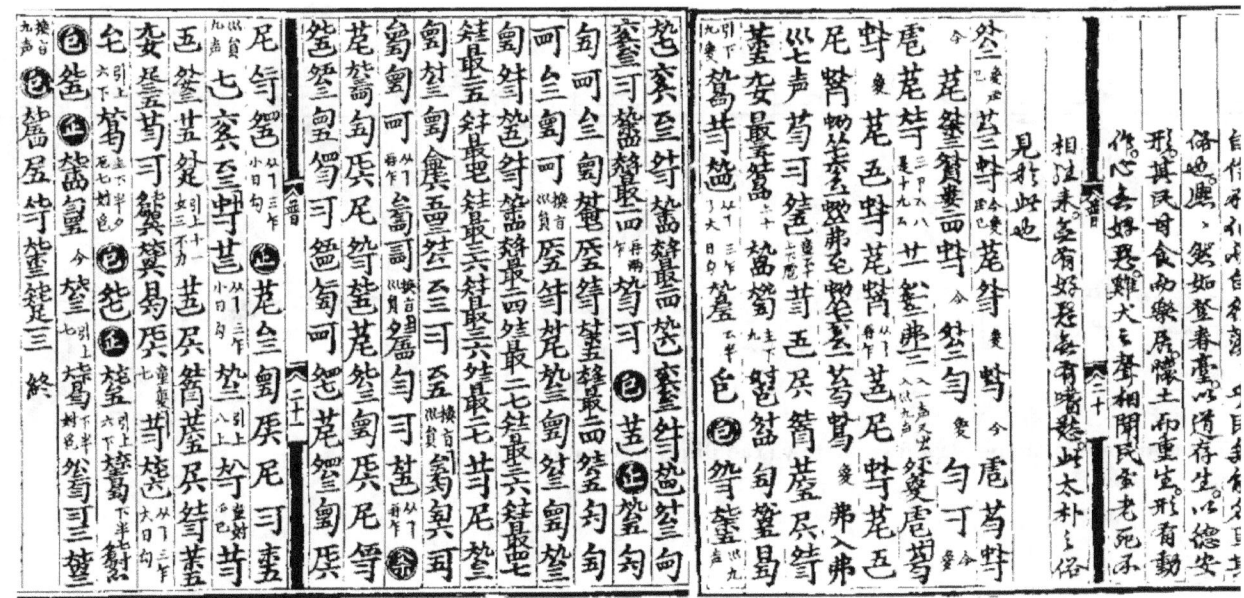

# 古風操　Etude in the Style of Antiquity

From Shenqi Mipu (1425)
Score by Juni Yeung

Standard Tuning 正調

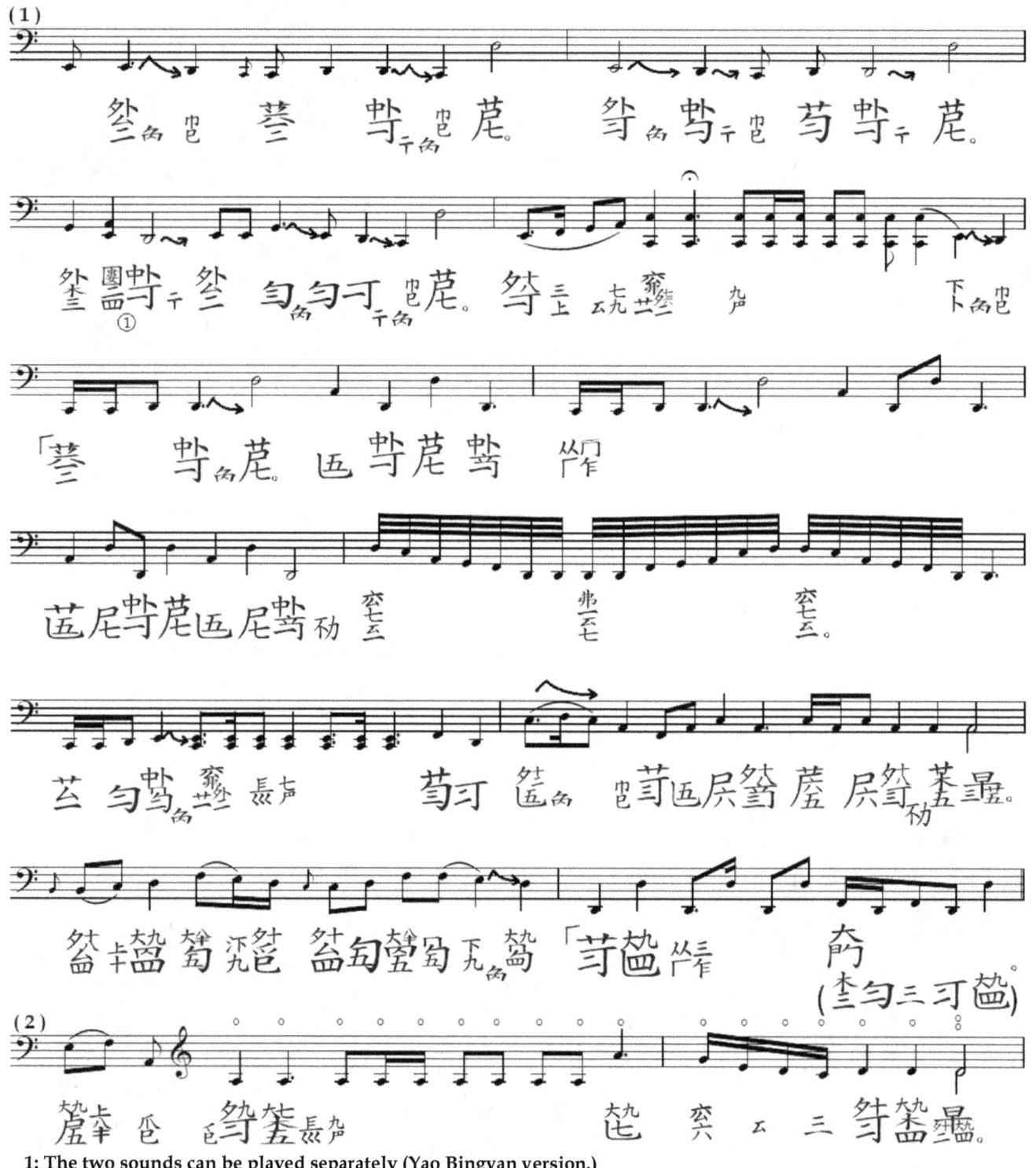

1: The two sounds can be played separately (Yao Bingyan version.)

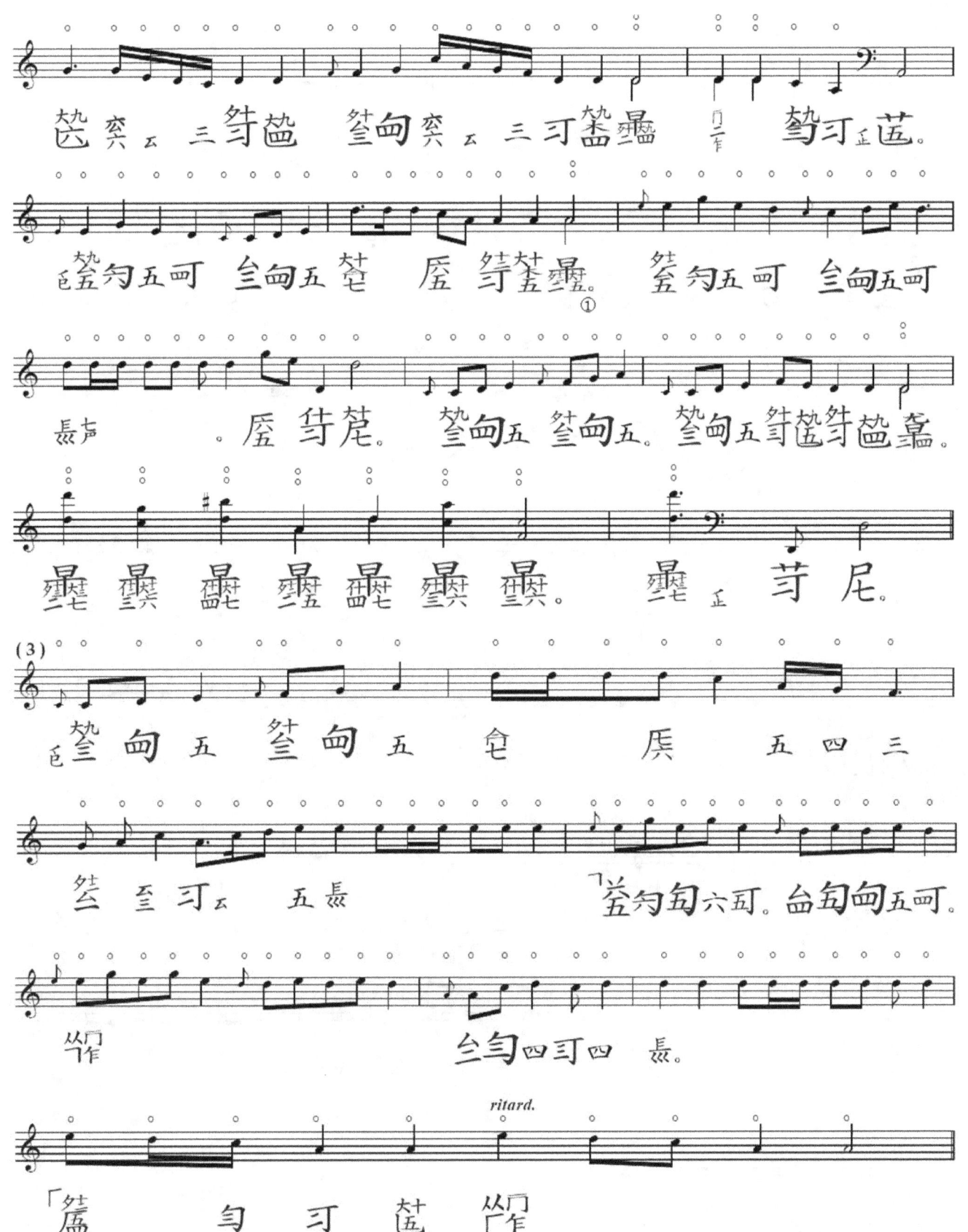

1: Originally marked as strings II and IV. Corrected now as II and V, as proven from the two previous notes.

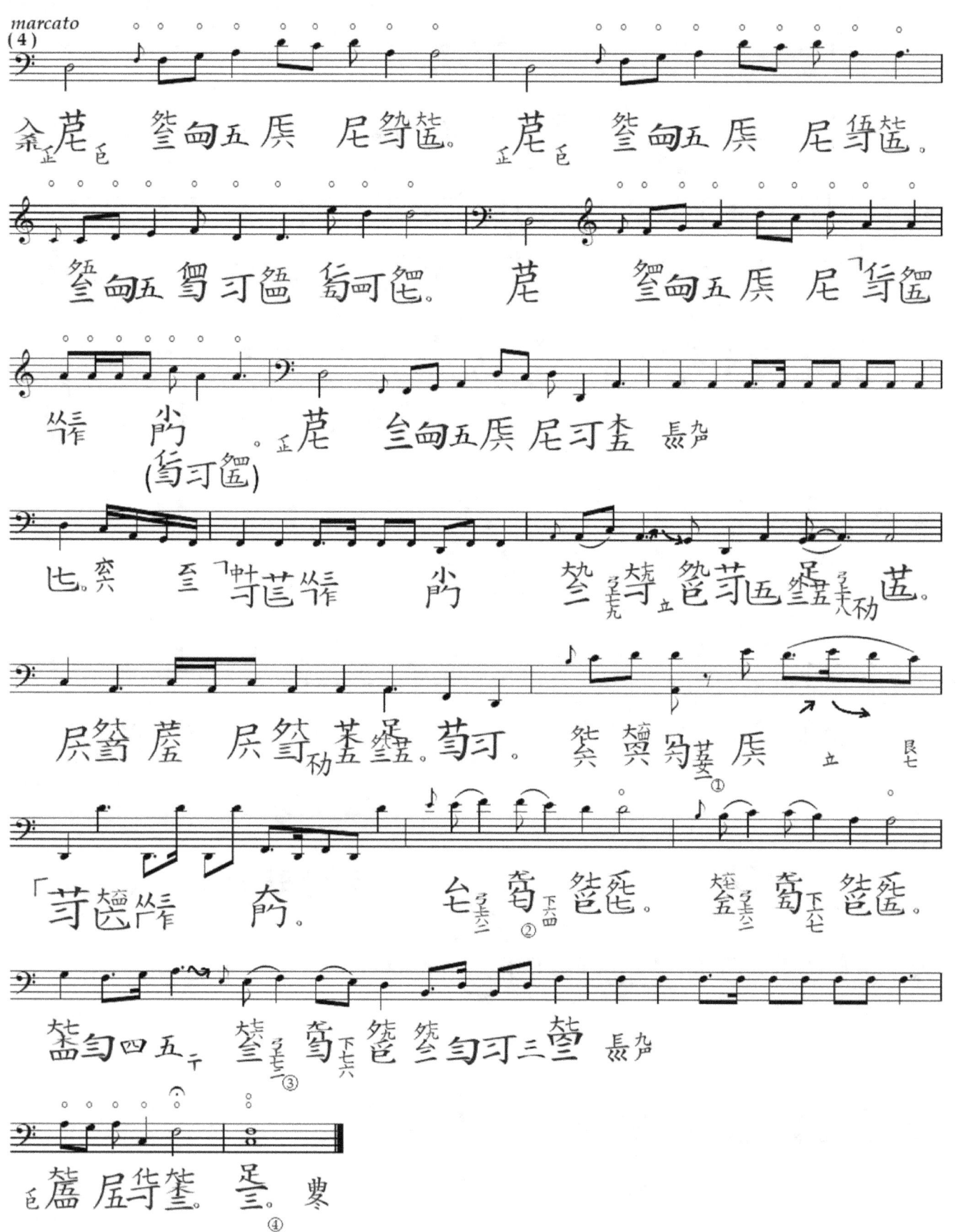

1: Added by the writer for performance effect, did not exist in original score.
2: Originally marked on 6th *hui*, now put as 6.2 to match previous position.
3: Originally marked on 7th *hui*.
4: Can be played separately (Yao Bingyan version.)

英語琴統初階

NOTE: In this manuscript, many musicians have attempted to tackle the problem of a strong dissonance repeated 9 times , played as open string I, and ring finger @ 7.9 on string II (Bar 4 in this book.) John Thompson moves the entire set down by one string to strings II an d III, while Gong Yi enforces the dissonance with the accompaniment of an orchestra.

The revision manuscript *Fengxuan Xuanpin* also by Zhu Quan repeats this by changing string II (only) to III. Here, I have opted for a simpler approach by moving the left hand to 7.6 on string II to maintain the original strings used, hence not needing to change the right hand movement.

Another explanation for justifying this can be: in the Ming *huiwei* system, 7.6 is written as 7-8, but as with many misprints of the 1425 score, the 7 of 7-8 was omitted as a mistake. Melodically, it would have been illogical to play a *bianzhi* (flat-sol) tone when this section emphasizes the use of *qingyu* (sharp-la).

## Lesson Pointers

- This piece includes many rare fingerings: Do I made a clear understanding of what they are from the fingering index?

    o This is especially true for the Dajiangou 大間勾 and Xiaojiangou 小間勾.

    o In an emergency, use your best guess based on other information provided and context.

- There is a broad variety of left hand vibratos used in this piece – have I made an effort in presenting them each as unique movements, while linking them up into one continuous performance (i.e. not choppy in connections)?

- There is a phrase in the middle of the piece that has pairs of harmonics played together in rapid succession. Be sure to read clearly beforehand, separating position 12 from 13, and aim your left hand fingers carefully and accurately to produce the light and crisp sounds.

- Above and beyond: The original score is provided with the interpretation. If you were to write this music score from reading only the source text, what would you have done differently? If you didn't know what the rhythm was, how would you handle it?

## Notes

英語琴統初階

# Yuqiao Wenda

*Dialogue Between the Fisherman and Woodcutter* is a piece made popular in modern times by Wu Jinglüe 吳景略 of the mid-20th Century. These two character archetypes in Chinese literature and popular lore portray a free-spirited character, living at his own pace in the rural village and in nature, taking casual chitchat with each other, interspersed with the sounds of their labour – the rowing of oars and the chop of the hatchet.

The earliest surviving manuscript with this piece is in

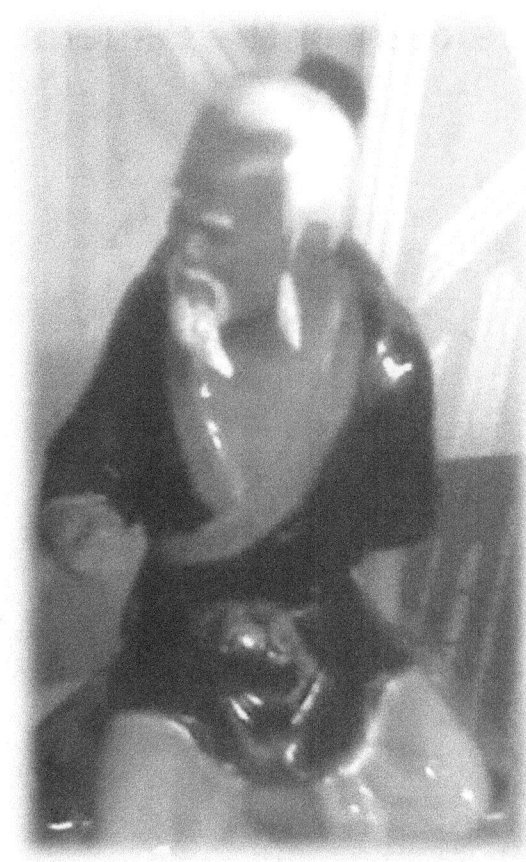

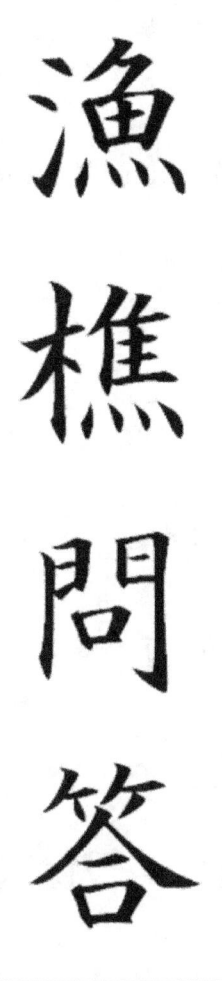

A ceramic figure of an old fisherman, found in Toronto's Chinatown. A fisherman is thought to be the disguise of a sagely character. Photo by the author, 2005.

the *Xingzhuang Taiyin Xüpu* 《杏庄太音續譜》, although some later manuscripts claim that this piece may have existed in *Zixiadong Qinpu* 《紫霞洞琴譜》, the Song Dynasty (12th Century) compendium of guqin scores, now lost. This proves that for over half a millennia, this piece has retained its popularity musically and ideologically, and the simplicity of its motif will continue to be appreciated by future generations.

# 漁樵問答　Dialogue of the Fisherman and Woodcutter

From Guqin Quji (1962)
Score by Juni Yeung

Standard Tuning 正調

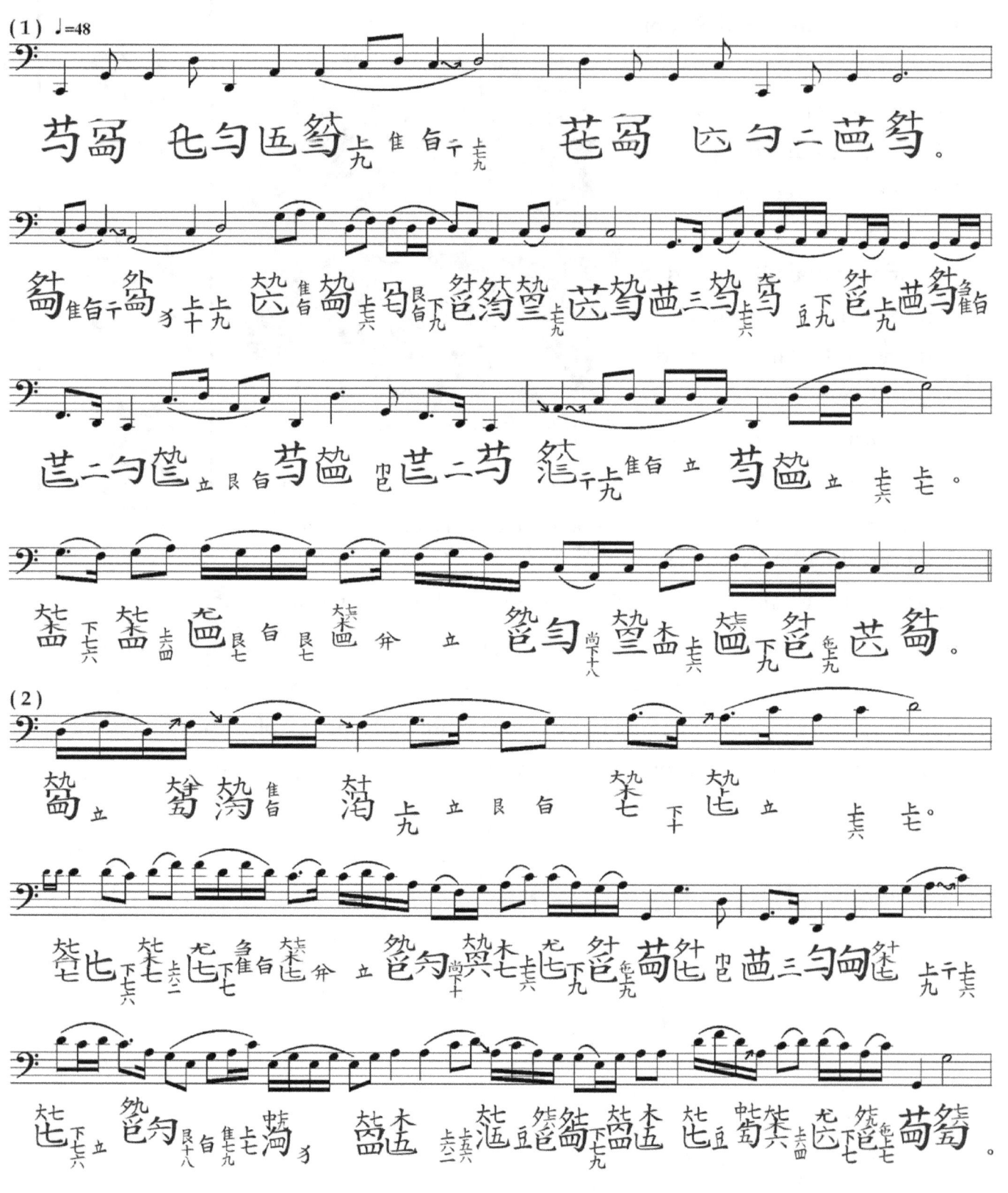

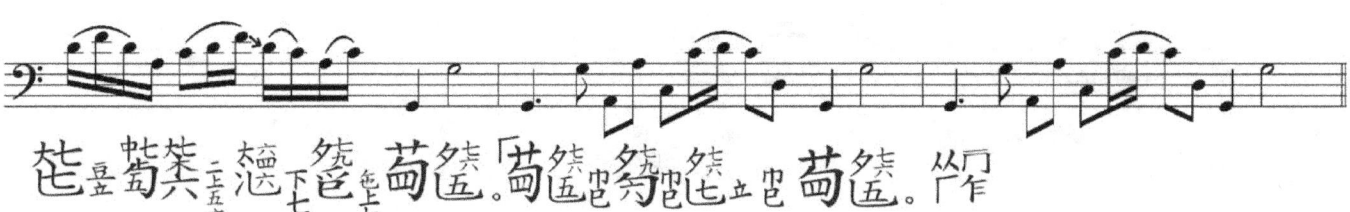

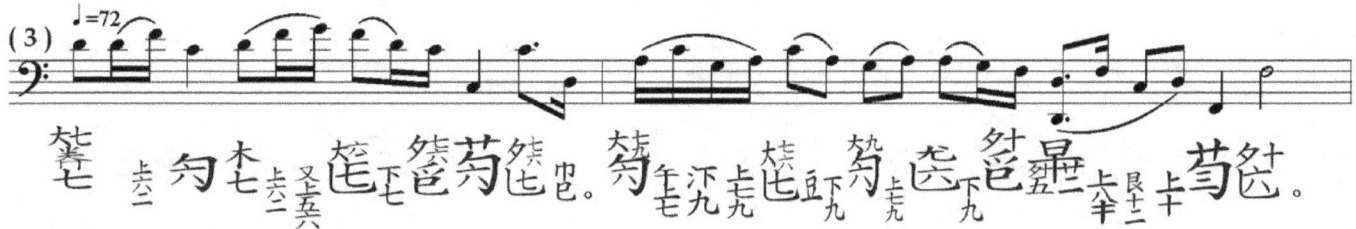

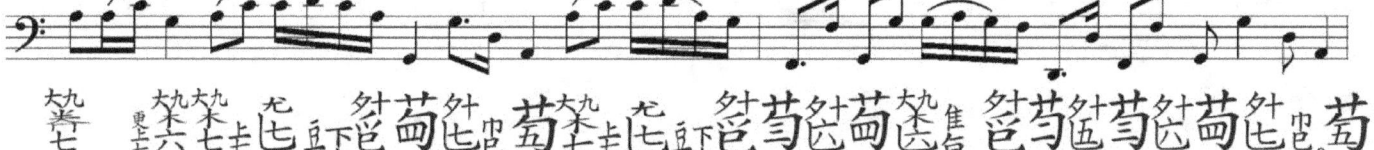

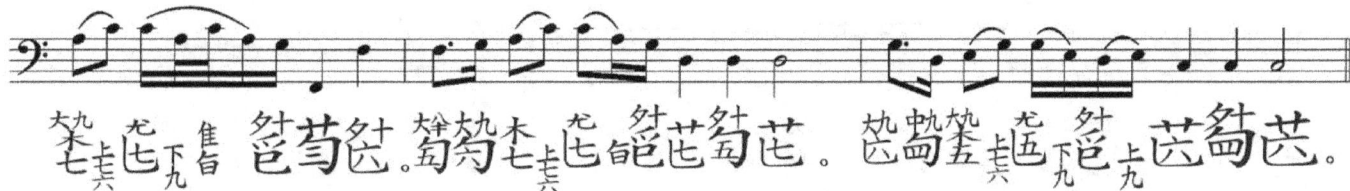

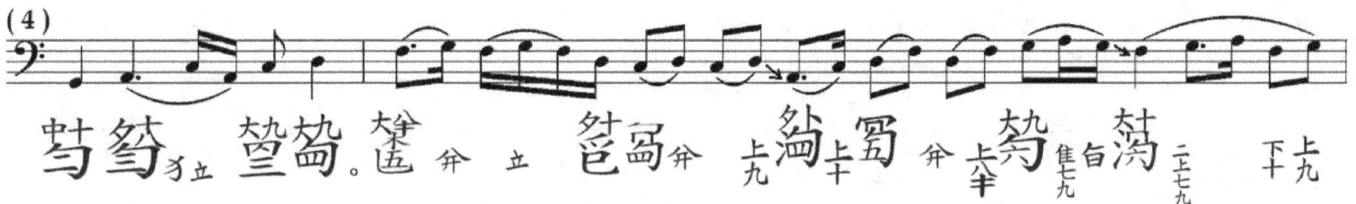

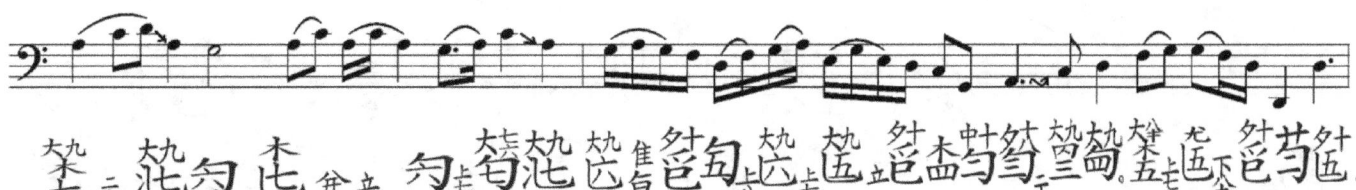

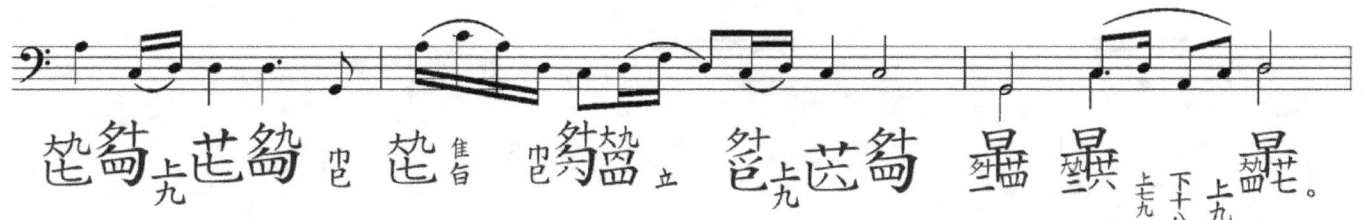

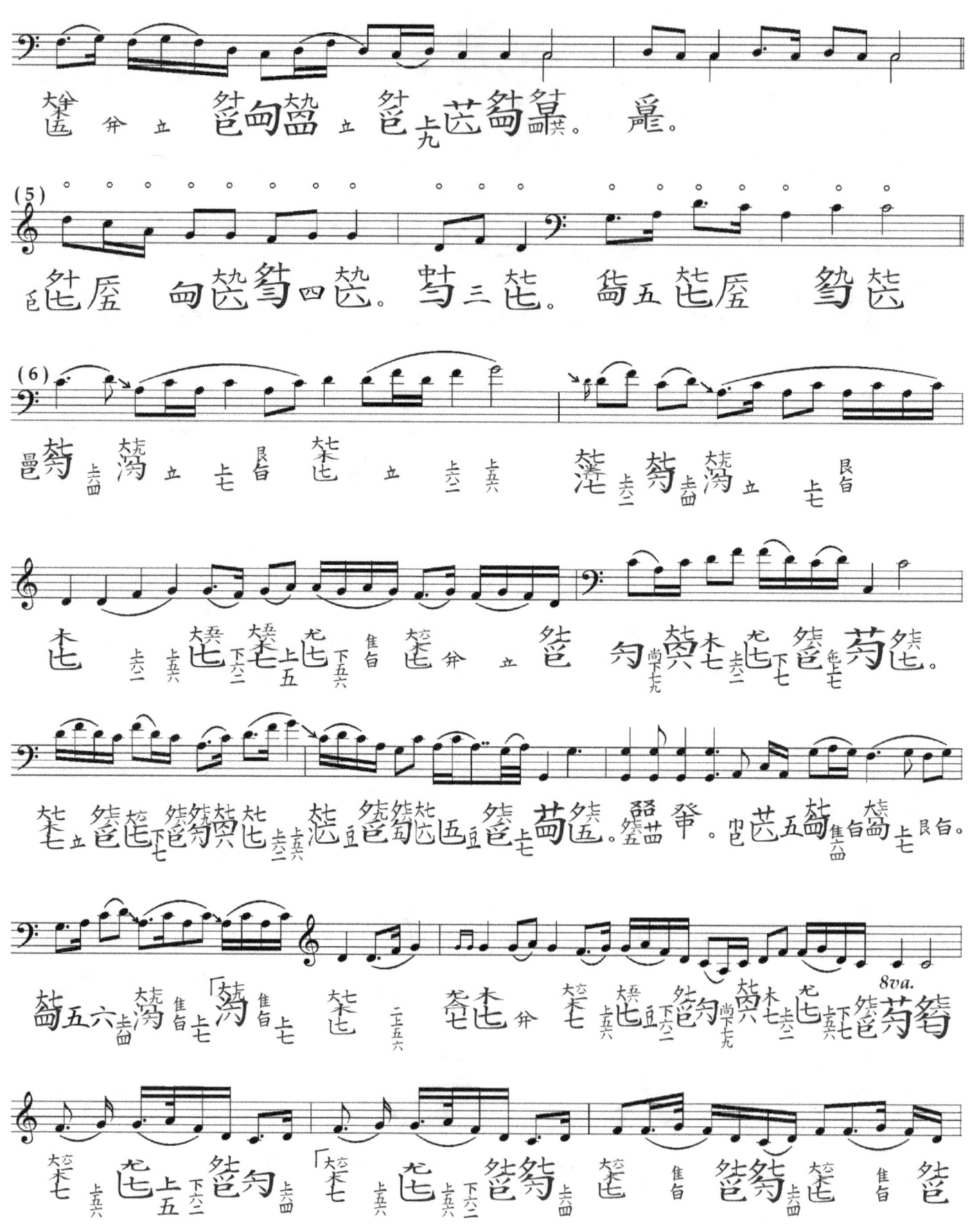

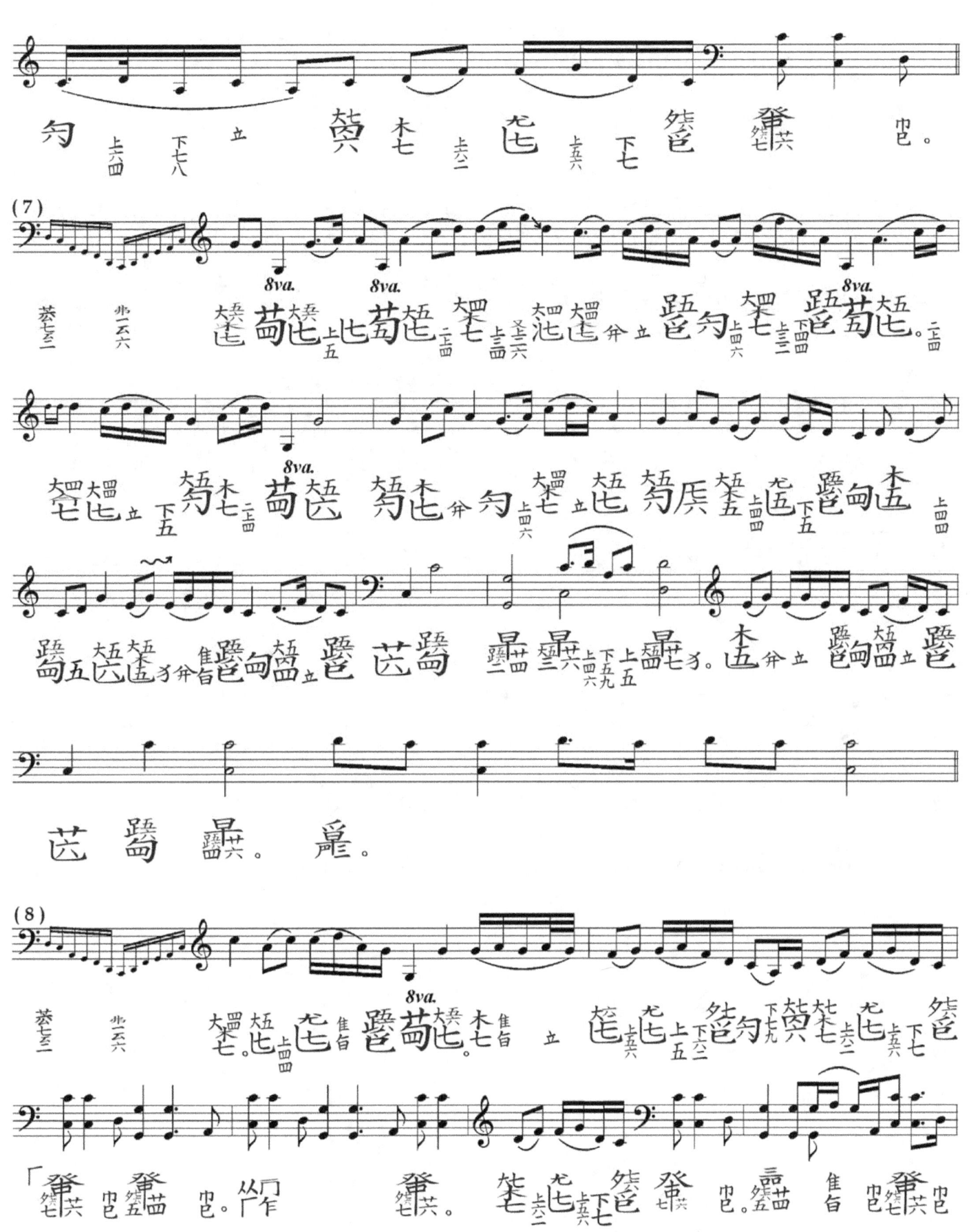

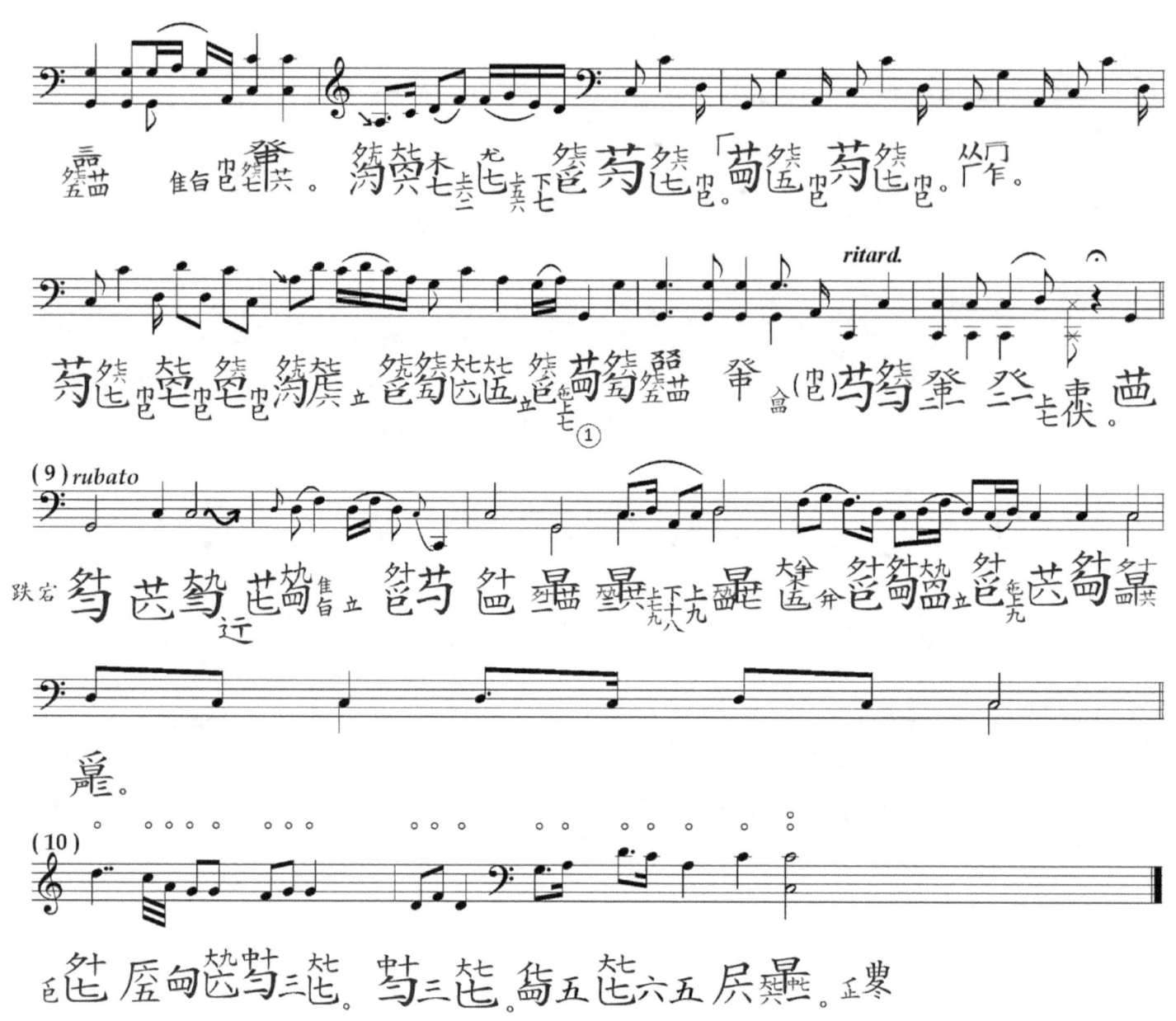

1. Originally uses string VI, changed to string V for ergonomic performance.

# Lesson Pointers

- This is the first long piece in the entire book, with over 5 minutes in performance time. Can you memorize it without memory lapses?
    - Practicing by section and remembering the order of them based on the opening phrases can be a way to memorize the piece.
- This is the first piece where "collide" and "provoke" (*Zhuang* and *Dou*, 撞/逗; 立/豆) are used synonymously. These two movements have very similar descriptions, but sound very different – make sure to understand and perform them according to their descriptions.
    - *Dou* can be easily recognized/represented by plucking while sliding up, followed by a feather-touch return.
- Are techniques from all previous lessons accumulating and put into practice across different sections of this piece?

## Notes

英語琴統初階

# Kongzi Duyi

*Confucius Reading the Book of Changes* is a popular topic in Chinese lore, depicting the perseverance of Confucius studying despite his stature and increasing age. He reaffirmed King Wen of Zhou's objective to use the *Yijing, The Book of Changes* as an ontological doctrine, legitimizing it as proper knowledge rather than the craft of shamans and fortune-tellers. The most well-told portion of this story is about how the cowhide binding of the bamboo scroll disintegrated with wear and tear, that he had to have it replaced three times – a sign of how frequent and how thorough he was in analyzing the classic text.

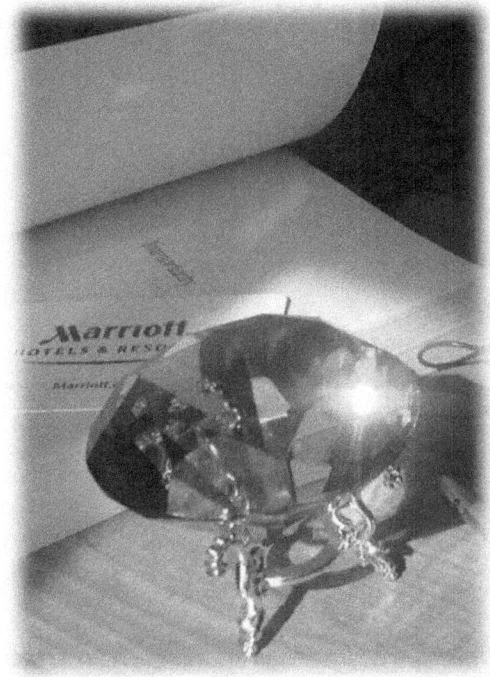

**On a classic theme of reading and recluse:**

*Two scrolls of the Daoist Canon and a three-foot sword;*
*A nine-section bamboo cane and a seven-stringed qin.*
    **(From *The Collected Poems of Ancestral Master Lü* 《呂祖詩集》)**

Photo by the author, 2005.

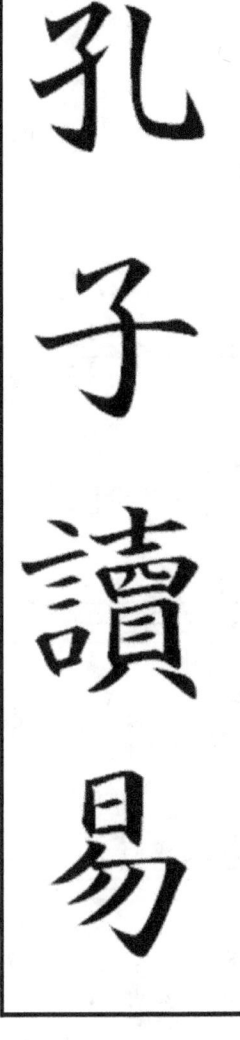

孔子讀易

The piece today is a signature of the Sichuan guqin school, and is loved by students of all guqin traditions old and new for its bold use of double-*zhuang* to imitate the sound of a person reciting a book out loud (perhaps with a hint of dozing off). This modern score also is significantly modified from the original version, as the original version requires the player to switch back and forth on string tunings in every new section for the large half of the piece. The frequent change of modality in this piece is also significant to the theme of the *Book of Changes* itself, and how the 64 trigrams are arranged and presented, evolving from great separation towards perfect harmony, and back again.

# 孔子讀易 Confucius Reading The Book of Changes

From Qinxue Beiyao (2004),
Score by Juni Yeung

Standard Tuning 正調

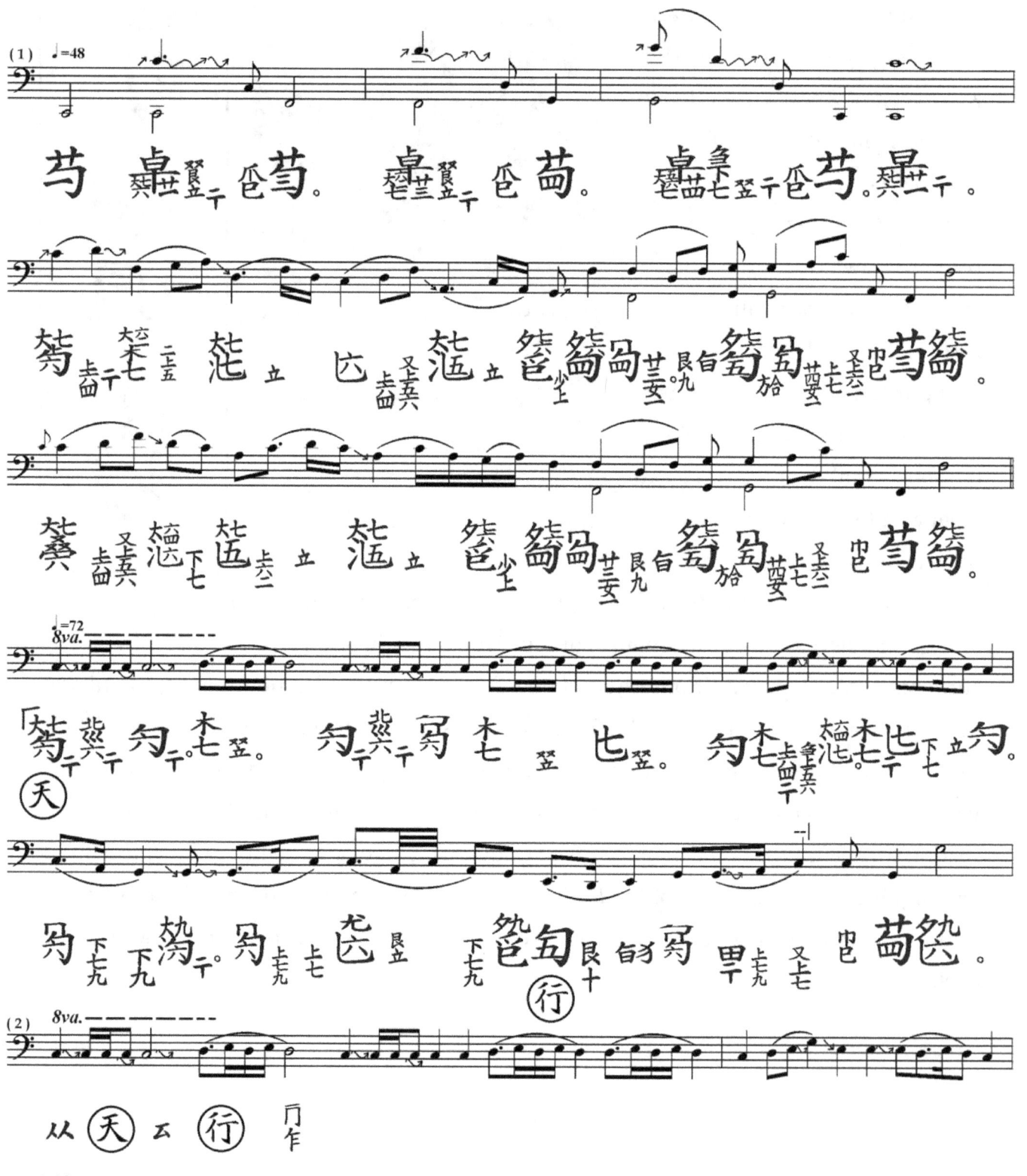

英語琴統初階

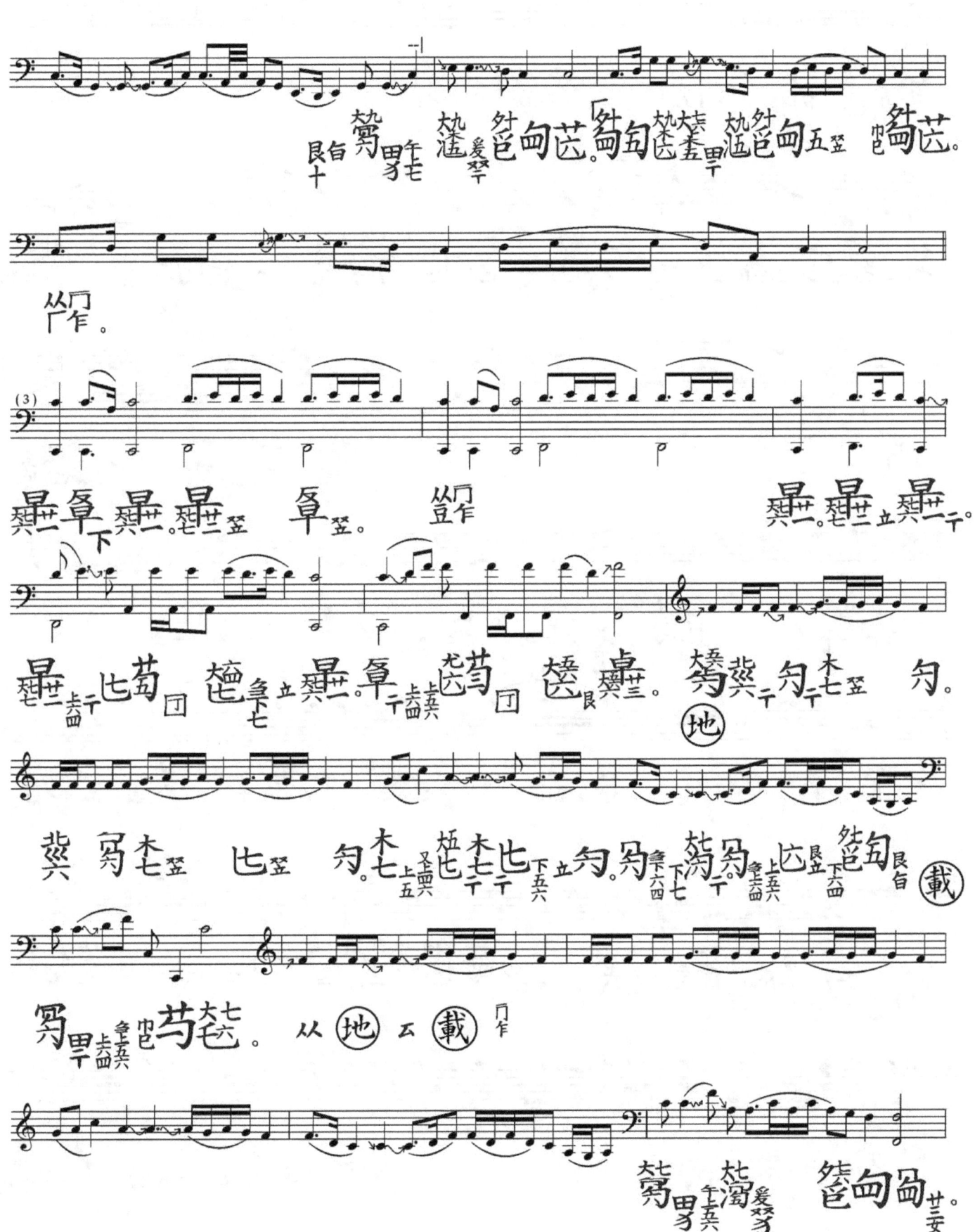

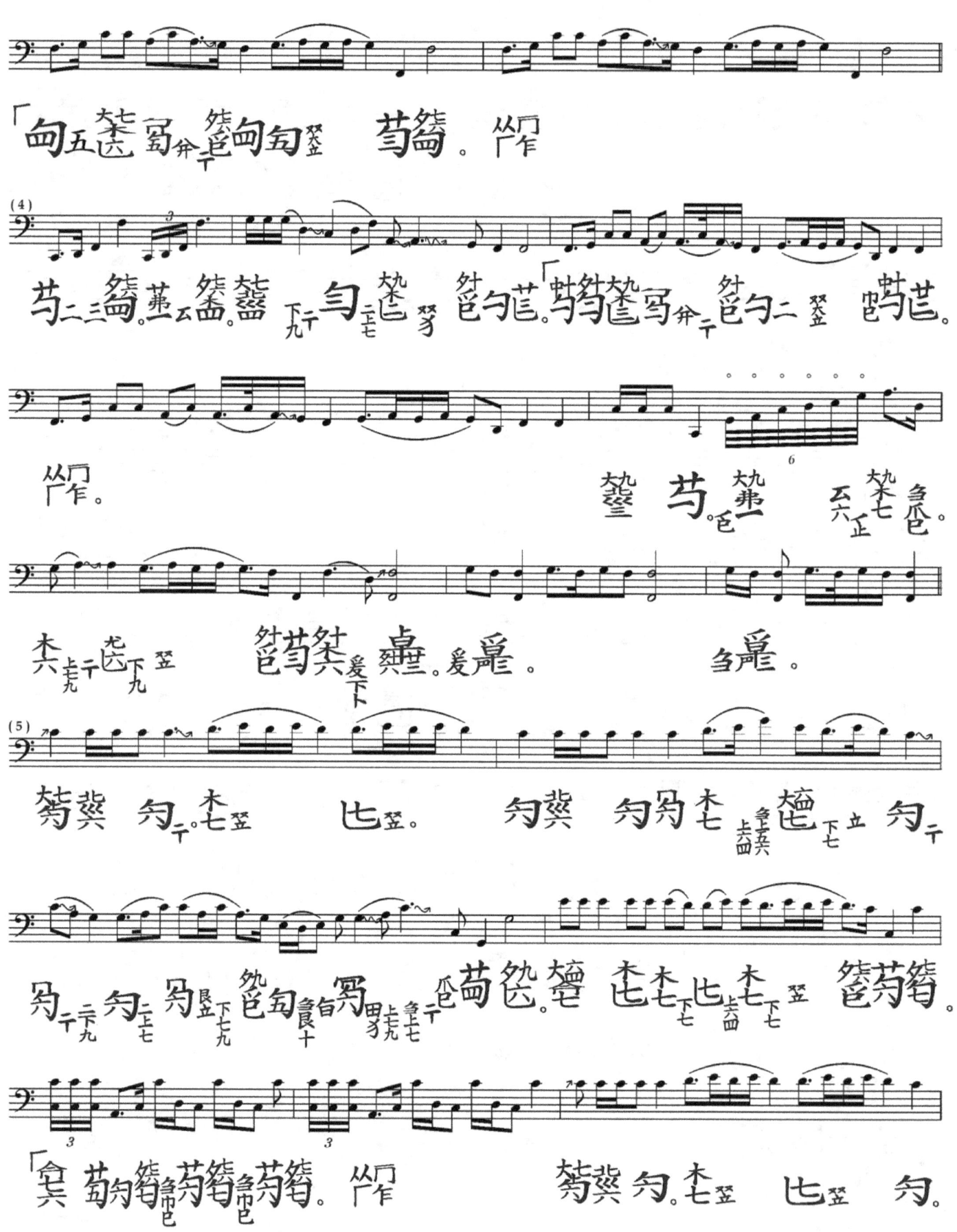

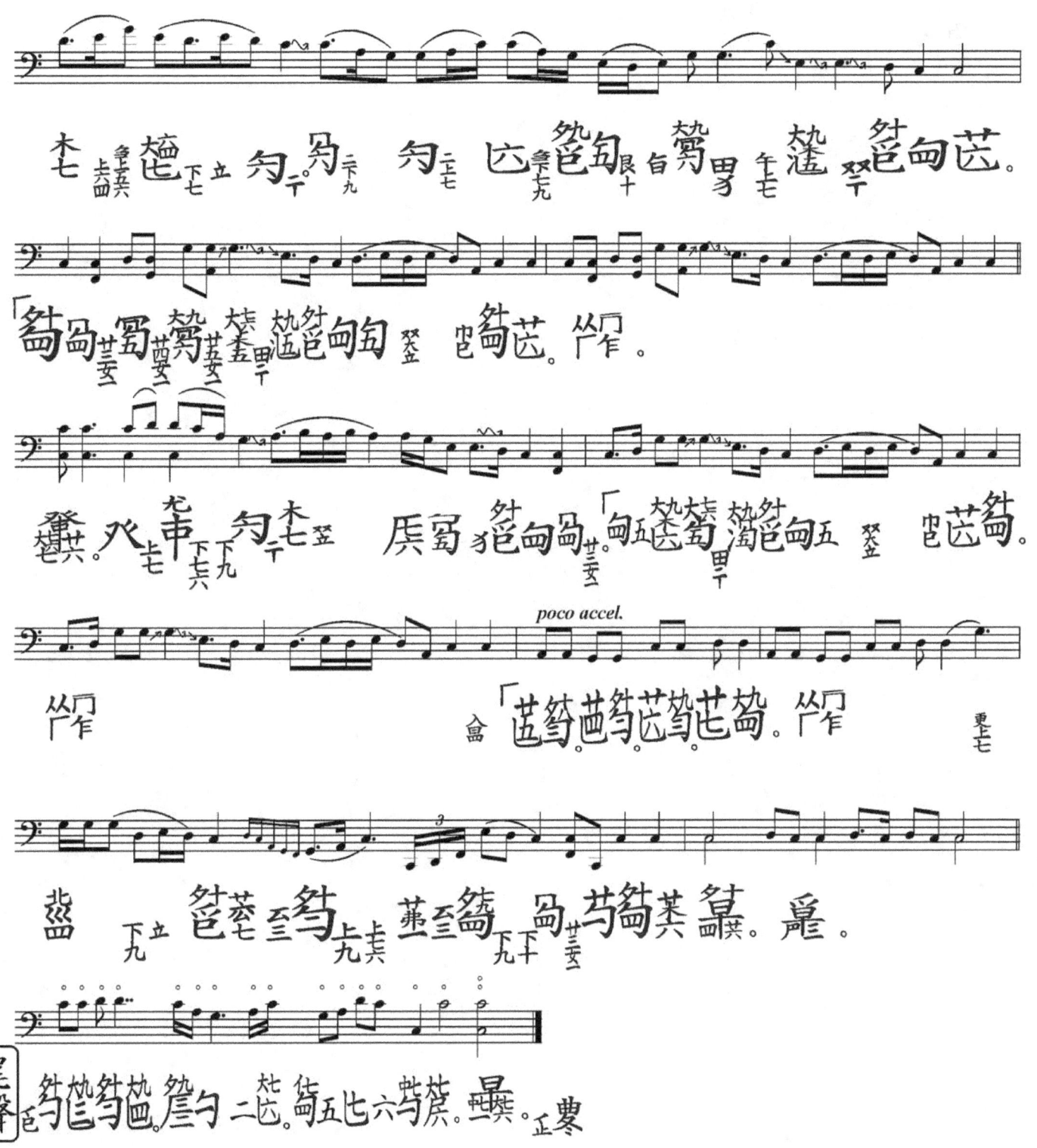

## Lesson Pointers

- This piece features the use of "double collide" (Shuang-zhuang 雙撞/双立). Be sure to emphasize the way it is delayed before the double waves.

# Songxia Guantao

From Yanlulou Qinpu (1766)

*Watching Waves from Under the Pines* is a typical example of a technically demanding piece composed in the later eras that emphasized the division between musician and literati qin music. While the origins of this piece are not recorded in detail, the *Kumuchan Qinpu*《枯木禪琴譜》 (1893) attributes it to Shi Zhihe 釋智和, a Southern Song dynasty (early 13th Century) qin-playing Buddhist monk. While the structure of this piece corresponds with the technical flamboyance of composition in the period, Xu Jian comments on the

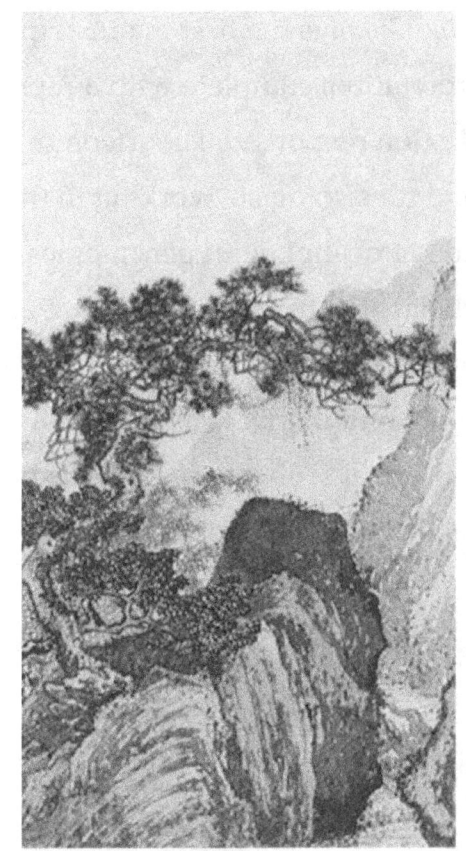

Tang Yin (1470-1523),
"Dreaming of Immortality in a Thatched Cottage" (section), Freer Art Collection.

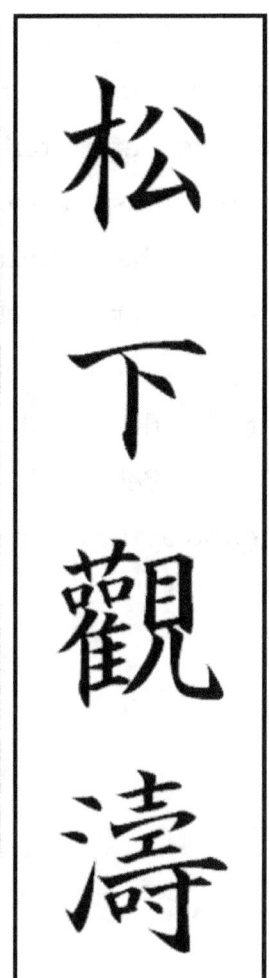

Daoist (rather than Buddhist) flair of the piece's philosophical theme.

There are several surviving manuscripts that carry this title, with the first being *Qinyuan Xinchuan* 《琴苑心傳》 (1670), and the only version to carry an appending commentary. Unfortunately, this commentary only records the author's process of listening to a performance of the piece and attaining a copy of the score from a player named Yang Wuxiu 楊五修 of Jinlingzhen (a town near Yantai, Shandong Prov.), as well as praise for its technical finesse and refinement.

The author has chosen this piece for interpretative dapu upon request by Christopher Evans of England in July 2008, and its interpretation was first performed in public in Kingston University, at the Asian Music Circuit Summer School, on August 1, 2009.

*Standards of the Guqin* is the first manuscript in the world to carry this tune with a modern dapu interpretation, complete with a report detailing on methodology, theme analysis, and a reflection on potential shortcomings on the process. It is my hope that future musicians and musicologists working in this field would follow suit, in hopes of ending the confusion of dealing with genealogies of different versions on the same piece that many scholars confront, by providing equal (or better) accountability of their analytical and re-interpretative process, setting an example that allows the possibility of tracing the evolution of guqin pieces as a continually innovating tradition in detail.

(Below: The original 1766 manuscript, sections 1 to 5. The remainder can be found at the last page of the interpreted score.)

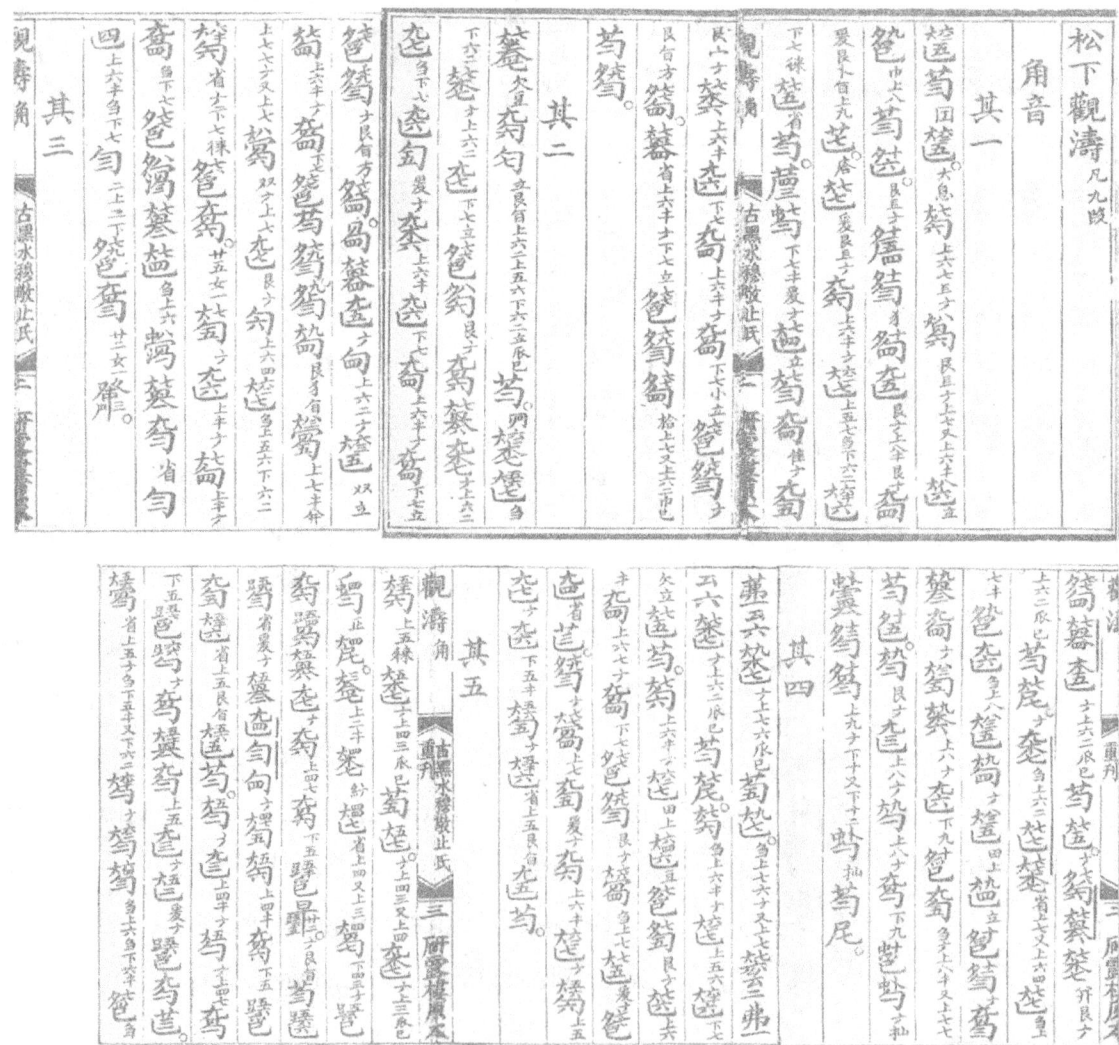

英語琴統初階

# 松下觀濤 Watching Waves from Under the Pines

From Yanlulou Qinpu (1766)
Score by Juni Yeung

**Standard Tuning 正調**

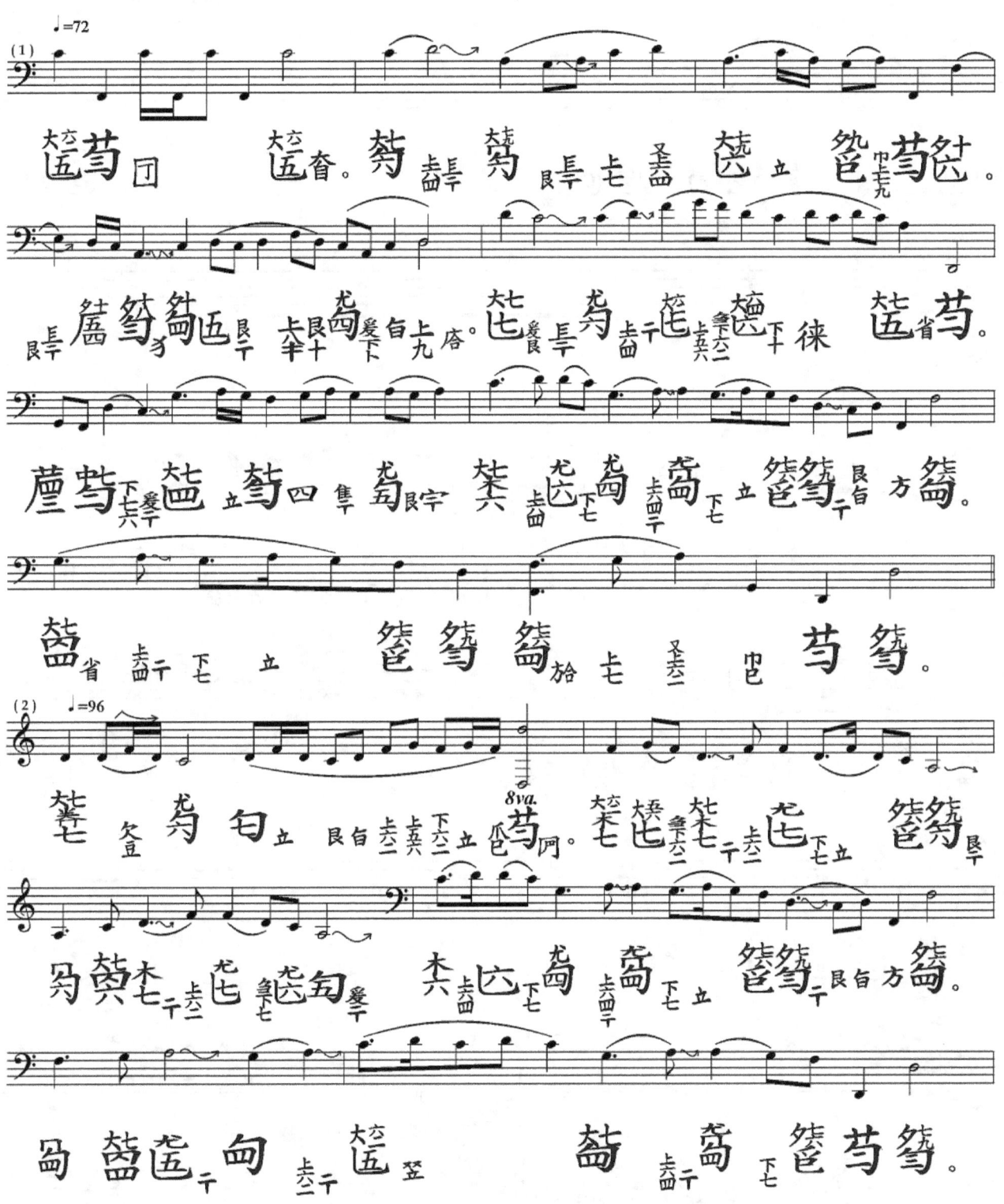

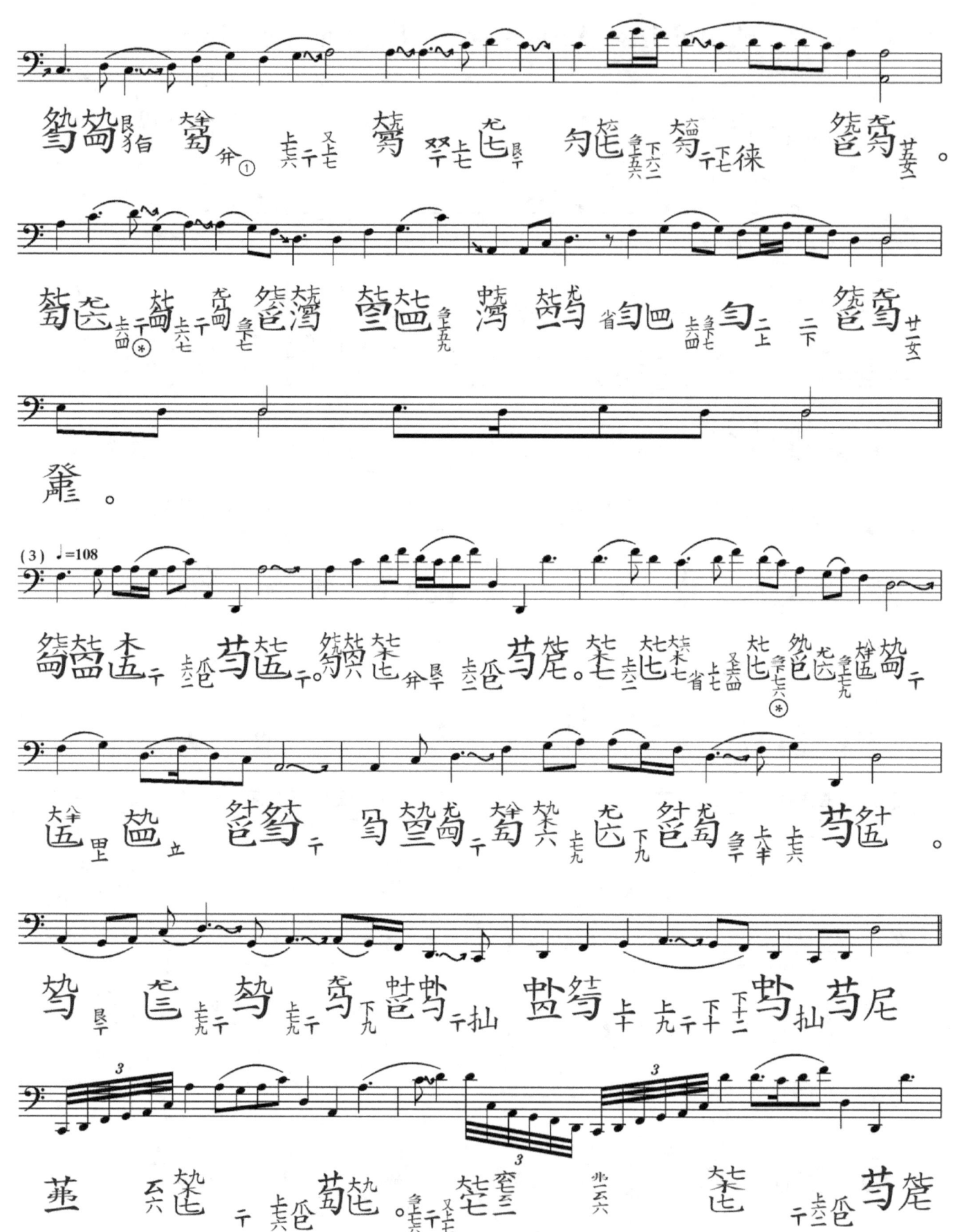

1: Originally "8.3 Gou-ti V, up 7.5 fenkai, up 7.7, yin, again up 7."
*: Minor positional adjustment here due to inconsistencies with positional systems.

英語琴統初階

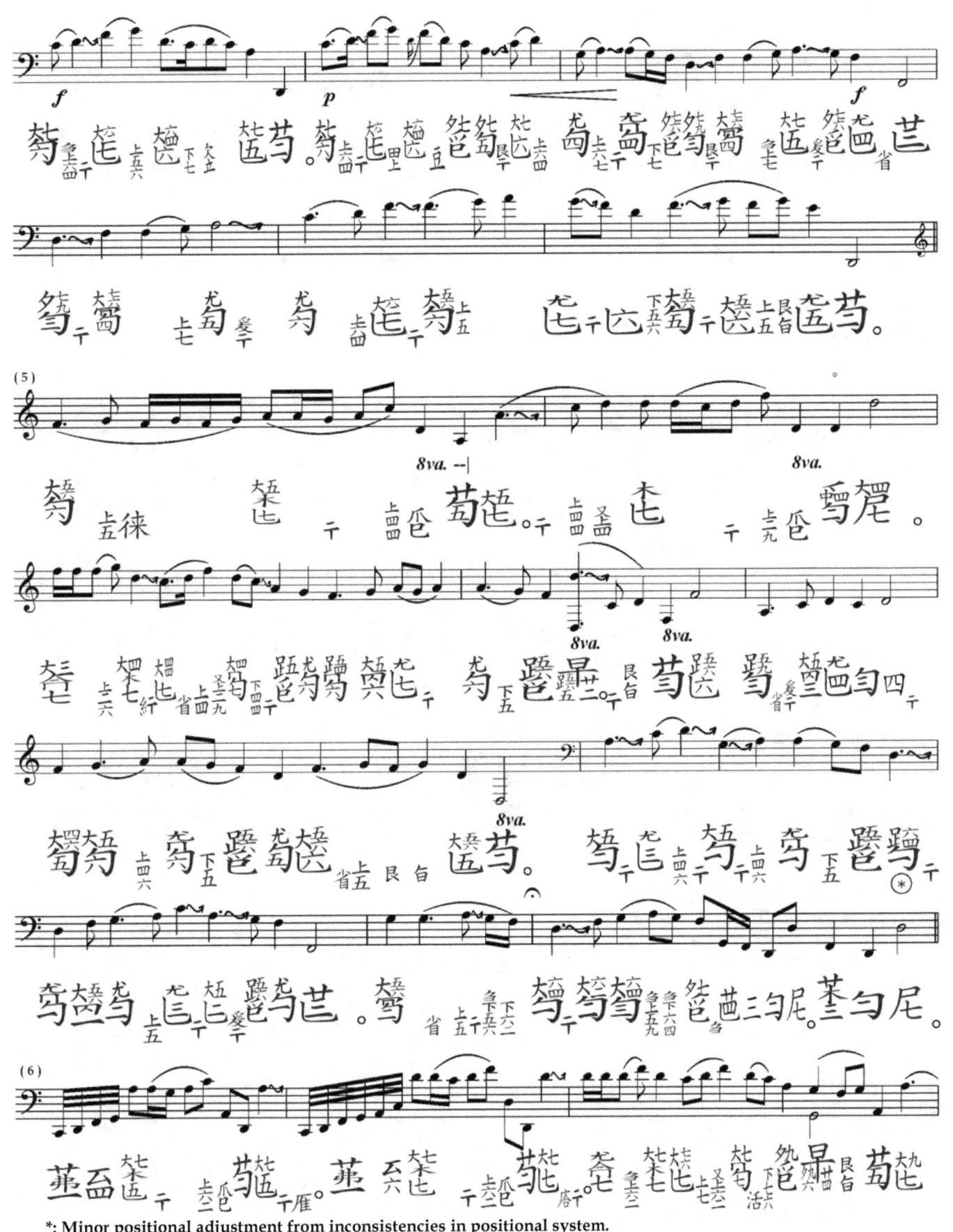

*: Minor positional adjustment from inconsistencies in positional system.

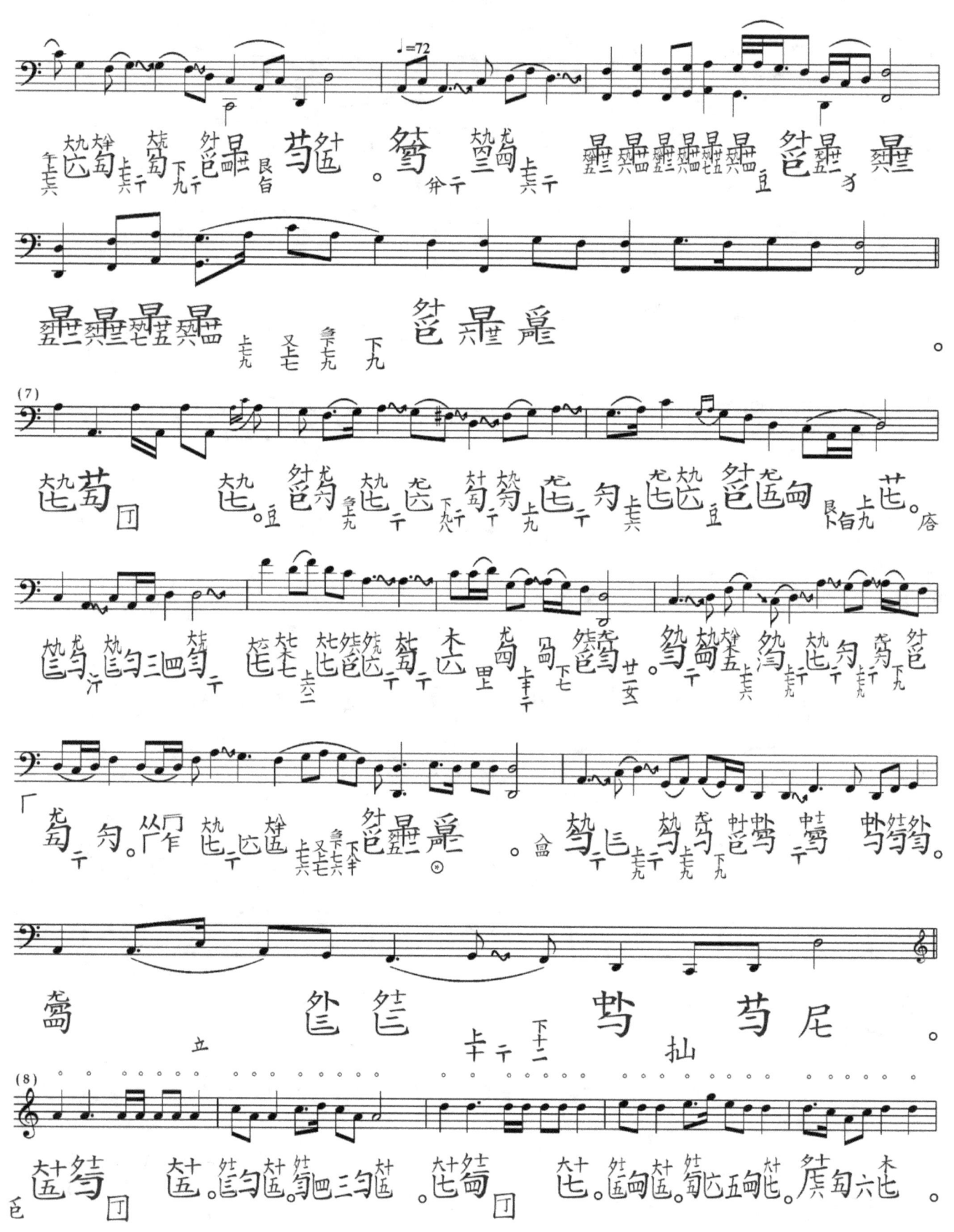

英語琴統初階

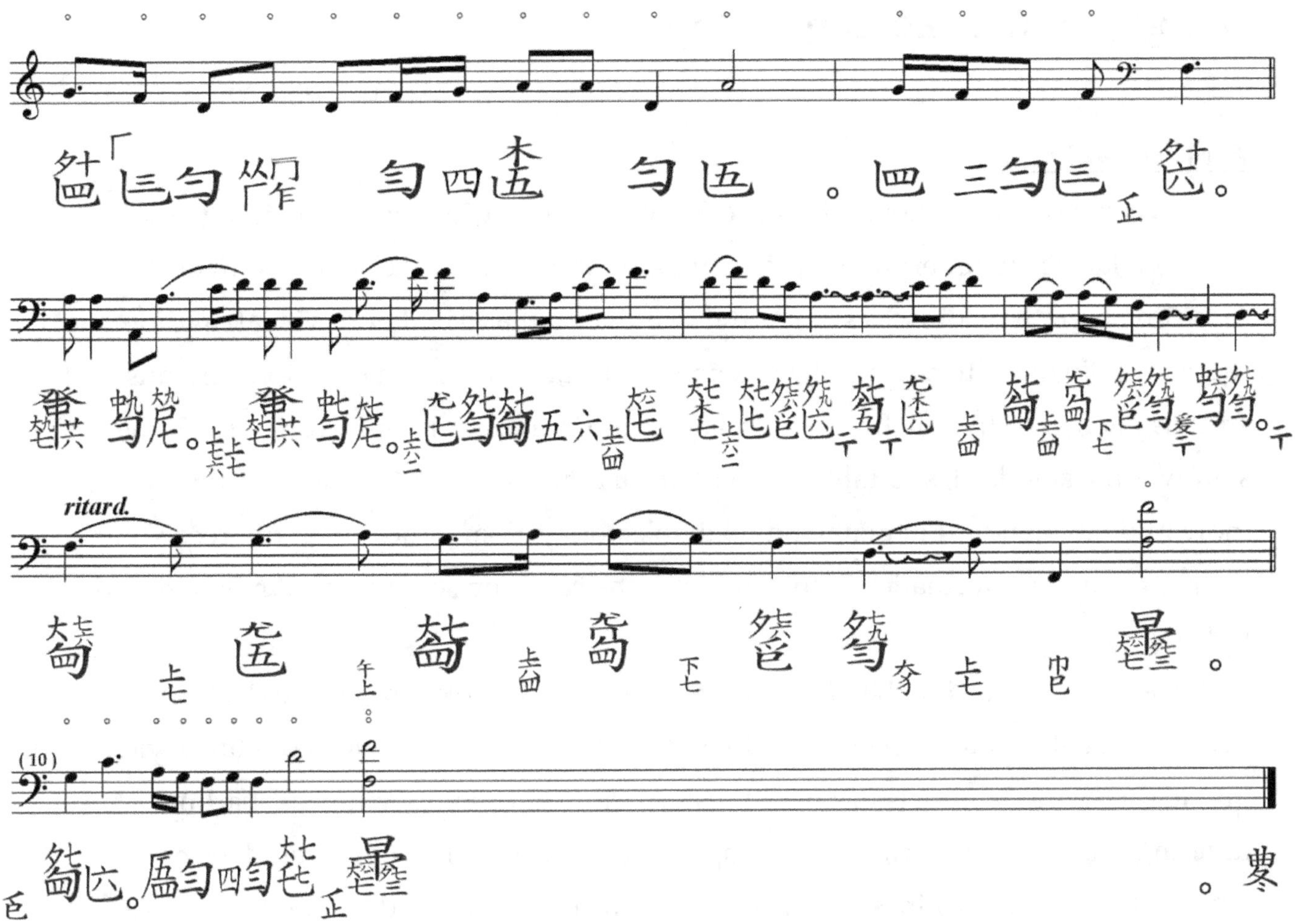

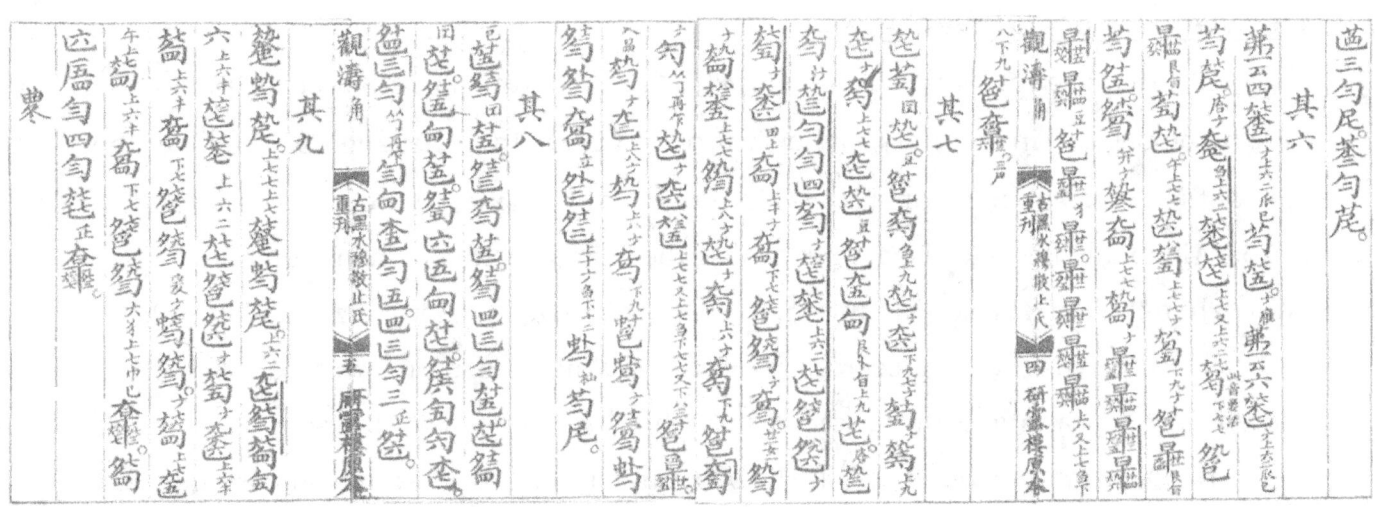

# Songxia Guantao Dapu Report

Juni Lefeuille Yeung, FXKQS

## A blurb on Dapu

*Dapu* is a long, if not tedious process of taking guqin scores containing only finger tablature and interpreting them into a playable melody. Usually, it involves recording them with devices such as the five-line staff and cipher or visual/audio recordings, in order to capture the missing information from the traditional manuscript, such as pitch and rhythm. In the latter half of the 20th century, tablature with 5-line staff was the standard, and tablature with *jianpu* (Numbered Musical Notation) the more popular standard in mainland textbooks today. Sometimes, an audio recording supplements the information, and completes the common set of tutorial media found today.

And since starting the *Standards of the Guqin* textbook project in 2005, I have decided that all written *dapu* work I do will continue with my preferred 5-line style, giving due credit to my history with Western musical training, with half-barlines dividing phrasing rather than dissecting meter precisely. This, however, does not suggest the idea that Chinese music has no regard for meter and an objective sense of rhythm – quite contrary, there is a strong sense of *rubato* (or the Chinese term *die-dang* 跌宕) that dictates the rise and fall of musical phrases and notions. Hence, *dapu* is a work of deduction and postulation in recreating (or even re-inventing) these elements that is otherwise lacking in the written tablature.

## The Manuscript and the Piece

The manuscript *Yanlulou Qinpu* 《研露樓琴譜》 was named after the personal style name of Cui Yingjie 崔應階, The Viceroy of Fujian and Zhejiang (閩浙總督) at the time of the book's publication. He was famed for composition in poetry, music, and various fictional tales. He also helped revise the local gazette of Chenzhou and Yuntaishan (Cloud-Terrace Mountain, formerly classified under Haizhou County).

Based on Zha Fuxi's research on existent guqin titles, there are at least five known existing variations of this piece, with the chronology as follows:

1. Qinyuan Xinchuan 琴苑心傳 1670, same title, with description. cf. QQJC 2e. Vol.11 p.364)

2. Songfeng Ge Qinpu 松風閣琴譜 1677, under name *Songfeng Yin* with lyrics and commentary. cf. QQJC 2e. Vol.12 p.422)

**3. Yanlulou Qinpu 研露樓琴譜 1766, no description. cf. QQJC 2e. Vol.16 p.459)**

4. Yilulou Qinpu 浥露樓琴譜 (1802+?)

5. Tianwenge Qinpu 天聞閣琴譜 (1876)

6. Minghsheng Ge Qinpu 鳴盛閣琴譜 (1899)

Hence, judging from the chronology, the work is not an original of Cui, but simply a part of his collected repertoire. Songfeng Ge Qinpu furthers this account by attributing the lyrics and score to a Cheng Yin'an (程隱庵 文譜, possibly a misprint of the author Cheng Xiong's title "Ying'an 穎庵"?). However, comparisons with older scores indicate that he did process the score into modern notation, especially concerning the transitioning of Ming-style *huiwei* system into the "metric" *hui-fen* system. Typical of scholarship at the time, there are mistakes, which must be taken into account in the reading and interpretation process.

Since the Yanlulou copy has no descriptions for pieces, the earliest traced account goes to the *Qinyuan Xinchuan*. According to this:

*"The piece can be traced to even earlier origins ("It is an ancient piece 古曲也"). The theme is a Daoist practitioner sitting under the stout pines and watching the unending waves. Looking upwards to the progression of the Way (daohua 道化) and downwards upon the feeling*

*of things (觸物情). There is a heavy feeling of sorrow - someone lamenting on the passing of things by a riverside. Hence, this piece is clear, transcendent, and conveys the mood of a poetic recital of emotion."*

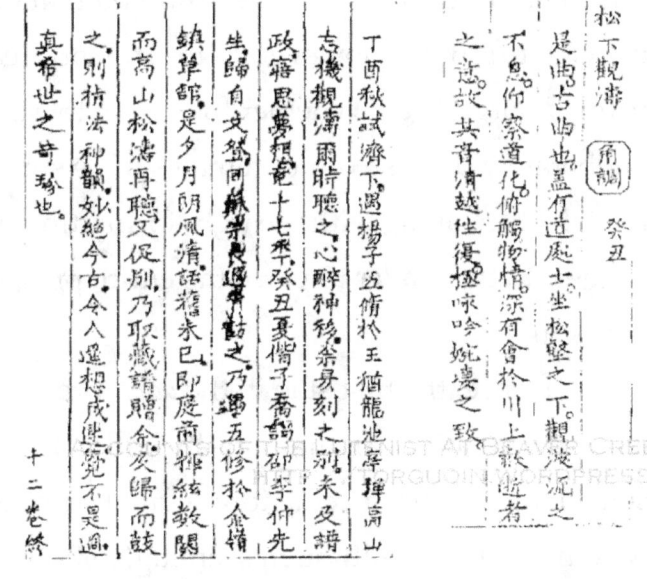

The piece is recorded as a piece in *Jue* mode. According to prestigious texts from the Ming Dynasty, explanations such as the *Shen Qi Mi Pu*, characterized the third string (the "*Jue*" string) as the *gong* sound, or the primary tonal centre upon a standard tuning of the instrument, resulting in the setting **5 6 1 2 3 5 6** (1=gong). It is also characterized by the strong use of its relations with its *Jue* sound (3, open 5th string) and its *Yu* sound (6, open 2nd/7th string). From the sectional analysis shown below, this piece can be justified as a *Jue* mode under these classification requirements.

From the first look on the first page of the original score, one may notice that Cui is indeed well-versed in musical theory for the guqin. Obvious if not somewhat unsettling to the modern reader, the left hand positioning suggests at first sight rather uncommon examples, such as "8 (八)" and "7-½ (七キ)" along with familiar and obviously modern-looking decimal positions, such as "6.2 (六二)" and "5.6 (五六)". The former system is known as the *hui-wei* system, popularly used in pre-1683 scores to denote positions relative to one or two *hui*, such as "7-8" denoting "between 7 and 8th *hui*", whereas the latter *hui-fen* system divides the space between two *hui* (despite the

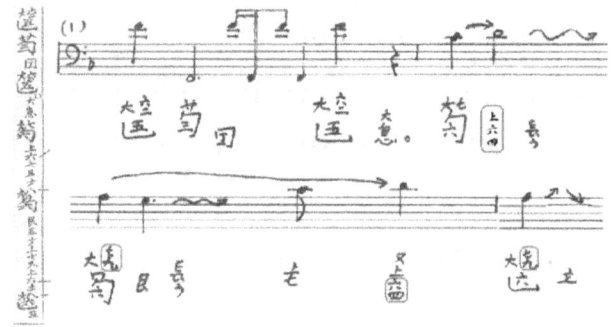

**The first line of the score. Changes are marked.**

varying distances) into ten equal parts and noting all positions between them as a decimal of the distance in between. In the earlier years of implementing this system, some manuscripts spend great detail explaining the innovation and ideas which failed in practice. For example, recording the second decimal (such as 7.76 or 12.23) for the space simply did not allow such amount of information to be possibly printed clearly and picked up by the eye. The mixed use of these two systems proved that Cui knew of both systems, and accepts its use concurrently – however, to the modern reader it is a sign of confusion and a sign of being disorganized. Whether the use of these two systems in the same piece was deliberately done so or not remains to be studied. On a side note, the vertical layout of the tablature along with the tight formatting of the left hand subtext also tends to suggest to the reader to parse the entire progression in one go, which is somewhat stressful.

Hence, the first step in the *dapu* process is to rewrite the entire score so that the left hand positions are universally in the decimal system. In the draft copy, consideration into spacing for the final copy and dividing general phrasing and sections was the first task. Although seemingly straightforward with 'just copying' the score horizontally under five-line staffs, questions occur on the use and changes of the original score, be it position rewrites, or discovering incorrect notes or misprints and correcting them (such as having a pressed note on one string before, but an empty slap

英語琴統初階

with the left thumb on an adjacent string right after). Any changes will have to be footnoted, and justified on a case-by-case basis.

Next, using a table with all the relative pitches for pressed and harmonic notes, the pitches are drafted onto the five-line staff with whole notes. As one creates rhythm by interpretation in practice (as in repeatedly sight-reading and analyzing the melody), and records it in pencil. This is a tedious task that can be processed much quicker if there was the existence of a computer software that can automatically interpret pitches onto the alternate staff based on tuning and position, which can be easily processed by spreadsheet. However, it is most regretful that nobody in my knowledge has created such a digital calculator or assistant that is openly available yet. After finalizing the above, one then proceeds to rewrite the entire score in ink, carefully marking in fine print and lines, and equally spaced out to ensure that the bars (phrases) fit onto a single line as best as possible. The product is scanned, and then published. When possible, an audio or video recording to accompany the results as aid is recommended.

## Section-by-Section Analysis

### Section 1 of 9

The piece begins in broad *lento* but with powerful cycling of octave-spanning chords. The use of *chang-yin* ("long murmurs") give hint to the slower tempo. Every phrase almost ensures the feeling of great power (as in the roaring waves of the rocky Fujian coast) as every finale was backed with a lingering lower pitch, with the second 'attempt' being a highlight, as one could see the left hand dragging up from the far end of the instrument up to meet the crisp Yu sound of an open 7th string. (Theme O-1)

A technical note: As shown in the picture above, the opening line contains originally a "6-7" and a "6.4" at the same time. It is up to the discretion of the player to determine whether the 6-7 should be interpreted as a 6.7 instead, given the possibility of just-intonation position recalculation done by the author to achieve a novel temperament to imitate local Fujian music patterns.

Beginning with the *Wang-lai* and *li* of the 4th line, speed up slightly and limit the degree of left hand movement from here on until the *release* at the end of the section for dramatic effect.

The first hint of the two-line primary theme (A) in this piece is suggested after the chord at *tongsheng* (just before the first footstop.) This theme of simple slides from 7th *hui* of each string to one or two sounds upward is varied once here (A-2) and resolved with a declining action back on *Jue* sound (page 2, open 5th string *as one* with pressed 6th string, 1st footstop). To resolve the theme as a full section, the author repeats theme (A) one more time in its simplest denomination on *zhi* and concludes with a lamenting *bo-la sansheng*.

### Section 3 of 9

The new two-line theme (B-1) is strongly indicative of a rising action, picking up the pace. The first "line" (two footstop sections, depicted here as first line of section 3) is a parallel image, suggesting that the player play in a swinging manner, with the use of in-out right hand movements and two-step *glissandos* (a *yin* counts as a step if the slide only goes up one tone, to account for parallel rhythm). A melodic line sings majestically and high-strung on the *yu* sound to denote the climax of the section before returning to the lower ranges, but refuses to extinguish itself, with consistent use of *push-out* movements and resolves with the bang of a loud *yu* (open 7th).

### Section 4 of 9

A climax of the entire piece, with lavish use of *gun-fu* rolling sounds to decorate the previous theme (B-1*). This section changes the modality by a fifth to *zhi* (so) sound, traditionally understood as a tone for outcries of expressive emotion, and is further expressed by the increasingly higher positions demanded on the left hand. However, it is important to observe the slight cooling off at the end of this section with the use of non-pentatonic *he* (si, E) sound before closing off with the open *zhi* sound at the end. A minor correction has been made to a note here, where the original reads "thumb 5th *hui* slap [*yan*] 2nd string", but should be 3rd string since the previous note was there. Should it be played on 2nd string, the author would have used empty-press/slap [*xu-yan*] instead.

### Section 5 of 9

This section may be the most technically demanding for the left hand, as it involves various techniques of moving, *gui-zhi* (kneeling-finger), and pressing on the upper register (which is difficult on any instrument, but especially poorly-made ones). Instead of *gun-fu* rolls, it is replaced with subtle left hand movements in *wanglai* 往來

英語琴統初階

back-and-forths, and this subtlety is confirmed even more so with the use of a single harmonic at the end of the theme line. While the middle of this section is similar in treatment to the previous sections, it was somewhat difficult to link up the concluding open string notes as it suggests a slowdown, but the overall theme goes otherwise.

**Addendum:** After much experimentation, I have still failed to rationalize the last phrase of this section to my satisfaction, and I am continuing to look into connecting this interlude with the rest of the piece without sounding obviously disjointed from the style of the rest of the piece.

### Section 6 of 9

This section begins the cool down variation, as the theme (C-2) from last section (C-1) is taken down an octave and recreated with the *gun-fu* but to a lesser degree. The climax of this section is the extensive use of chords in *cuo* movements (which must not slow down), followed by a conclusive *taocuo sansheng* movement. This is the final variation of the main themes used since section 3, hence concluding the body of the piece.

### Section 7 of 9

The conclusion begins with a declaration on returning to the original *Jue* sound and varies on the opening theme (O-2). While the notes may seem to have similar layout, length and progression with section 1, it is also important to consider the context of the previous and next sections - hence not copying the tempo and rhythm of the beginning. This theme finishes off in a formulaic *taocuo sansheng* and enters the second half with the reintroduction of the two-line theme (A-2) in *ruman*, or "entering slow-beat".

### Section 8 of 9

This section is played almost entirely by harmonics – an often obligatory feature of larger guqin pieces. The melody does not deviate far from the base mode of *Jue* but stands unique in its content.

The last section maintains securely on a *Jue*-mode based melody line, emphasizing its tonality by sweeping motions (*bo, la*). Notice the non-perfect chord produced in the middle of the first line (*zhi* and *yu* sound together from open 6th and pressed 7th strings) – probably due to maintaining parallelism in the technique and visual aspect of performance, but it also emphasizes the open *zhi* sound to express a sense of sadness (the traditional understanding of the tone) and imperfection. Remnants of the first theme (A) echo for one last time before entering the ending sequence which repeats the *gong* sound twice as a faint pressed-harmonic chord.

### Process Notes

The writing of this report itself took over a month, as I had to learn the analysis of melodies and modality as I wrote along. At least three major revisions were made on the historical information, as I lacked the proper previous research on the number of re-occurrences in other manuscripts of the exact same piece. Thanks to Christopher Evans for keeping me updated on this. Also a big thank you to Dr. Tse Chun-Yan for his work on Ming-Qing dynasty tablature differences, Mr. Jim Binkley and Mr. John Thompson for email crash-courses on modality, and the members of the Facebook International Qin Society for all their enthusiasm, support, and feedback!

(Source: http://torguqin.wordpress.com/2009/06/19/dapu-songxia-guantao/, with additional comments and modifications for this textbook, various times during 2010.)

英語琴統初階

# Sanzang Jin Tianzhu

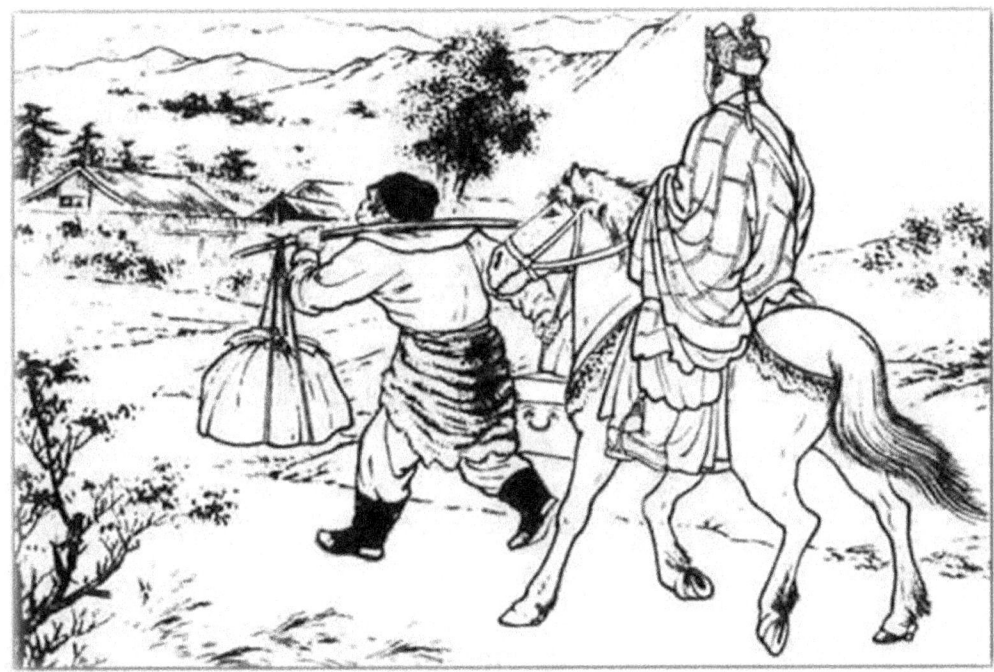

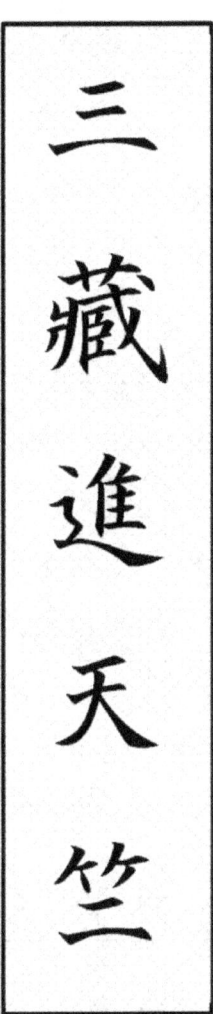

This 2020 new composition depicts the moment in the book Xi You Ji 西遊記 (Journey to the West) when the monk Tang Sanzang (or Tripitaka) and his entourage, including the Monkey King Sun Wukong, enter India for the first time. The composer Brian Blugerman omits the Jue (mi) sound by lowering 2nd and 7th strings by a semitone and raising the 5th string by a semitone, making the scale Gong, Bian-shang, Qing-jue, Zhi, Qing-yu, Gong (1/♭2/4/5/♭7/1). This gamut is not native to the Chinese modal system but rather to that of an Indian *raag*, and reflects the exotic airs of the foreign setting.

## 調絃法 Tuning Method

緊五一山，慢二七各一山 Tighten V by 1 lü. Loosen Str. II/VII by 1 lü

First method: 𢀖 → 𢀖 / 𢀖 → 𢀖 / 𢀖 → 𢀖

1. 三絃四徽對五絃五徽、調五絃。Tighten Str. V by matching Hui 4 @ Str. III with Hui 5 @ Str. V
2a. 三絃四徽對二絃三徽、調二絃。Loosen Str. II by matching Hui 4 @ Str. III with Hui 3 @ Str. II.
3a. 以二絃四徽對七絃七徽、調七絃。Loosen Str. VII by matching Hui 4 @ Str. II with Hui 7 @ Str. VII.

Alternatively: 𢀖 → 𢀖 / 𢀖 → 𢀖 / 𢀖 → 𢀖

2b. 五絃二徽對七絃三徽、調七絃。Loosen Str. VII by matching Hui 2 @ Str. V with Hui 3 @ Str. VII.
3b. 以七絃七徽對二絃四徽、調二絃。Loosen Str. II by matching Hui 7 @ Str. VII with Hui 4 @ Str. II.

* 凡"下外"按位均為十三徽六分，而非十三徽二分徽外之位。

"Lower Outside" indicates pos. 13.6 rather than 13.2 𢀖 = 𢀖

# 三藏進天竺 Tripitaka Enters India

原作/Original Composition by Brian Blugerman
減字譜、原譜/Jianzipu and Score by Brian Blugerman
譜面電子化/Score Digitization by Juni L Yeung

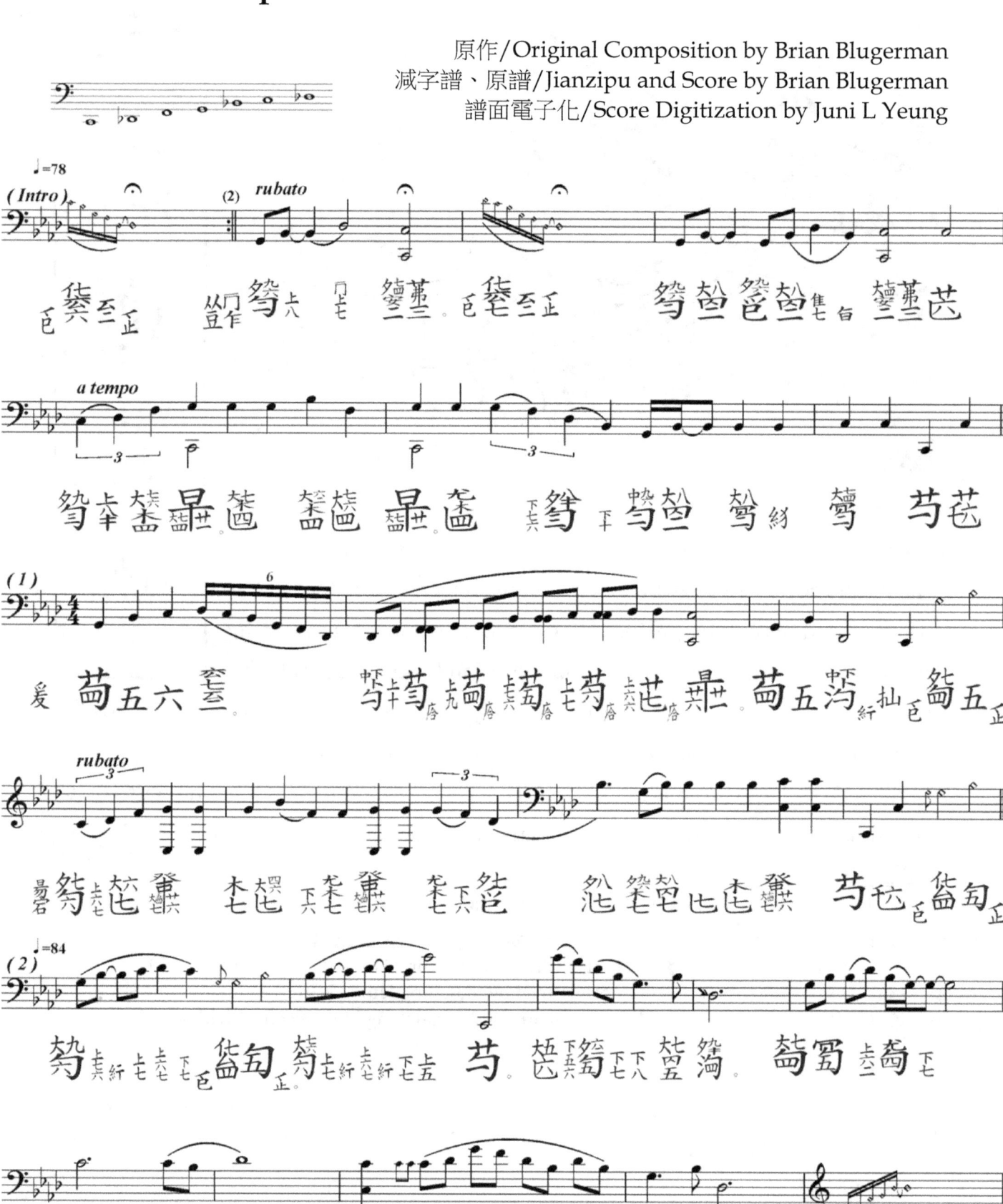

英語琴統初階

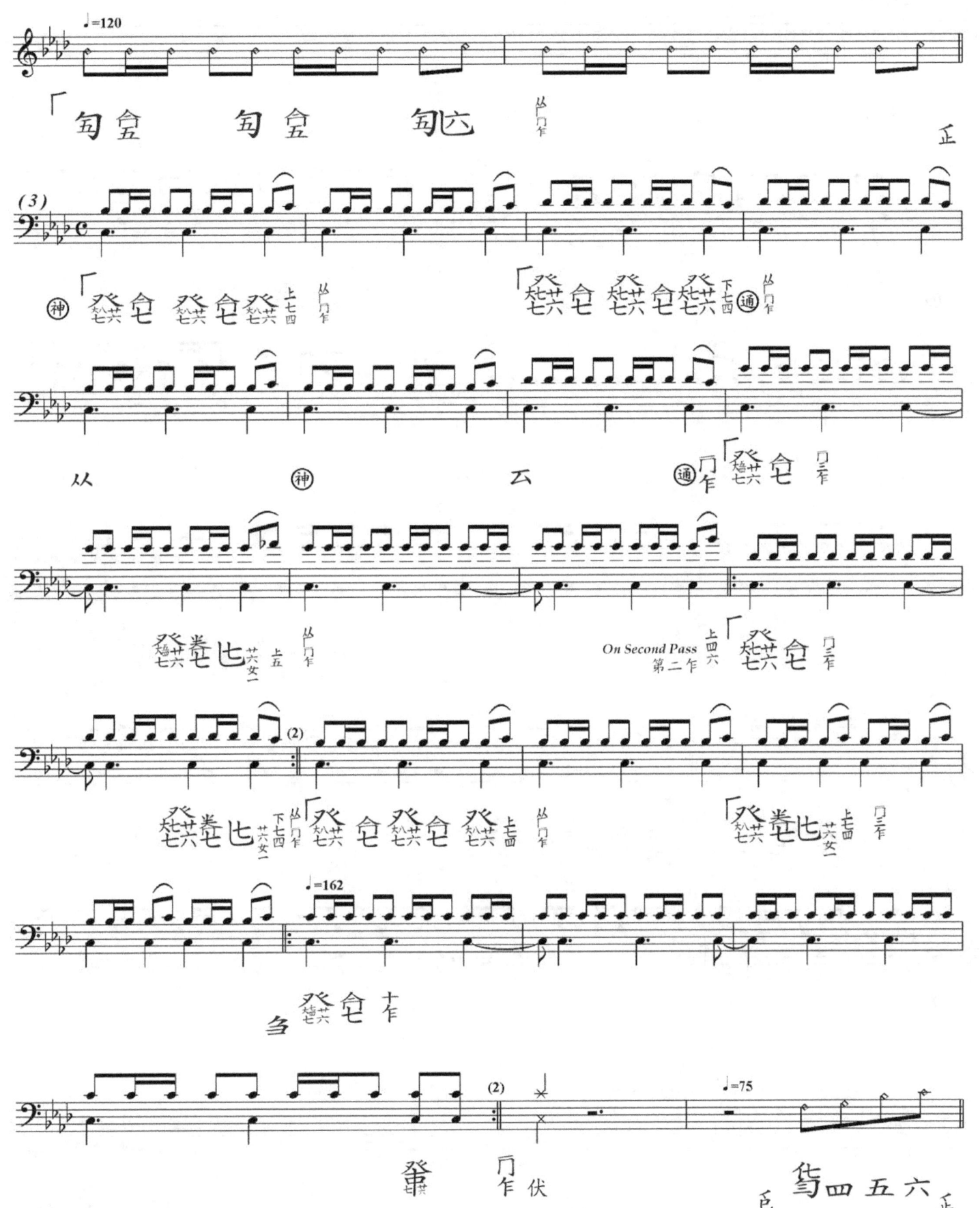

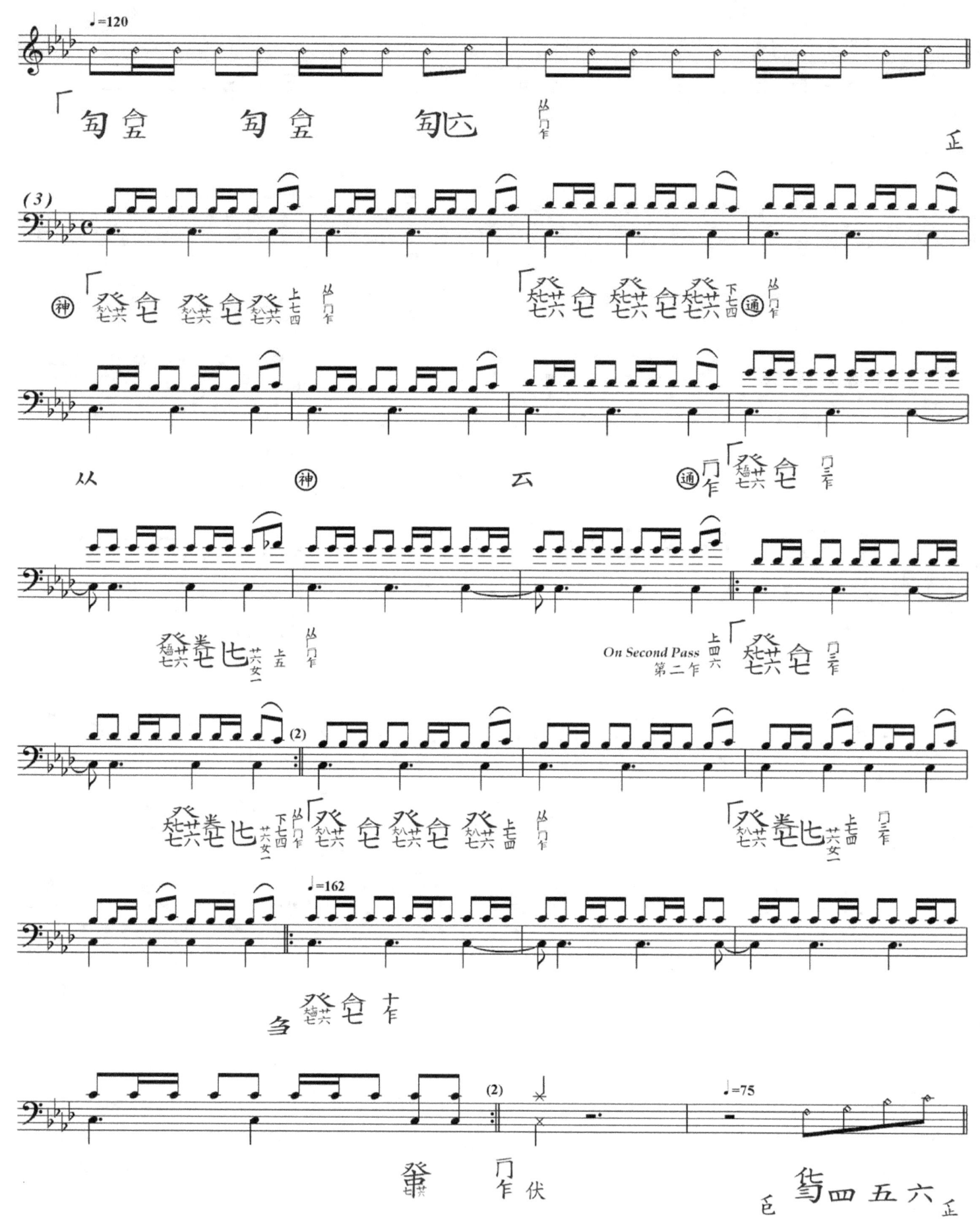

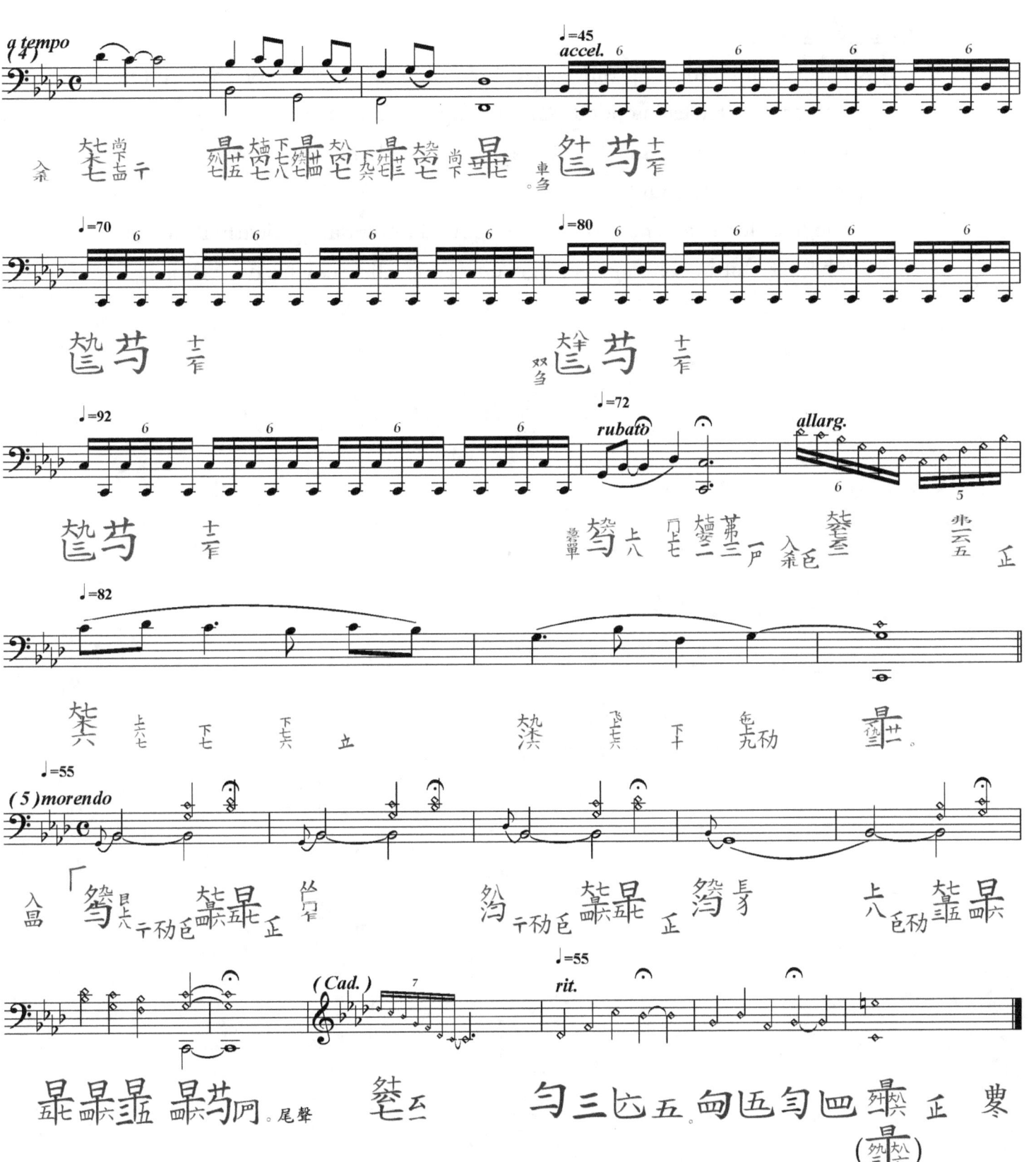

## Learning Pointers:

- This is a modern composition. The time values and tempo on the five-line staff are written as intended. Am I noting the changes?

- There are sections with 10 or 12 repeats. How do I group them in a way so that it's easier to count?

- The middle section *lun* movements: Am I differentiating clearly the ones where it's hitting only one string, versus ones that may hit two strings?

## Notes

英語琴統初階

# REPERTOIRE D

♫

# SCORE INTERPRETATION EXERCISES

# (BASIC SKILLS) SHANG YI: TAI GU
# (INTRA-TEXTUALITY) YIN DE
# (INTER-TEXTUALITY) SHANG YI

*This is where you will have to write your own score!*
*The wise musician always drafts in pencil.*

# Foreword to Repertoire D

It is expected that by reaching this chapter, the student has attained a solid foundation in technique and history of the music as a reference point – mastering the performance of all pieces in Repertoires A, B, and C would be a minimum point of reference before proceeding.

*Dapu* is the recursive interpretation of an existing guqin tablature score into a playable piece. According to the *Zhongguo Yinyue Cidian* (Chinese Musical Dictionary), *dapu* is "a jargon referring to the process of playing out a qin melody from a qin manuscript. Since qin manuscripts do not directly record musical notes but only string positions and fingerings, as well having a considerable flexibility in rhythm interpretation, *dapu*'ers must be familiar with conventions in and performance technique to deduct the melodies' progression, and then to recreate it. Its aim is to reproduce the state in which it was originally performed – since most surviving pieces are lost in practice, one must undergo the *dapu* process to restore the music." (p.64; cf. Cheng Gongliang p.3)

As primarily an oral tradition, students studying under a master would not have to encounter the *dapu* process as melodies would have been passed from performance imitation, without drawing from a written medium. The function of the manuscript acted as a fingering archive in case of forgetfulness. However, this assumes the student has a mental impression of the melody and rhythm, which will supplement the tablature. As the majority of surviving written scores are no longer passed down in performance, however, we do not have the luxury of doing so, and will have to recursively discover what has been lost.

英語琴統初階

# Shang Yi: Tai Gu

This is the first piece of Folio 8 from Xilutang Qintong of 1525, a 125-piece compendium of qin melodies large and small, coupled with four folios on music theory and guidelines for qin players' decorum with the instrument. Unfortunately, the surviving copy does not include Folio 5 containing the fingering tablature explanations. Because of this, one will have to look to other manuscripts of the era for explanations on uncommon fingerings – the index of the *Taiyin Daquan Ji* (a Song dynasty manuscript) reprinted in the Zhengde Era (1506-1522) is a common substitute.

According to Zha Fuxi and John Thompson's research, there are over ten manuscripts carrying versions of this modal prelude, the earliest being *Taiyin Daquan Ji* sometime during the Southern Song dynasty (11th c. C.E.). The title and listed order suggests that this motif is a model for subsequent pieces in the section, depicting the notes of the scale and its positions on the qin, common variations of melodic progression.

## The Basic Process of Written Dapu

The dapu process will require, if done by hand, two to three rewrites. The first draft is a rough rewrite of the score, converting original tablature into another system that records pitch and time value, as well re-express parts or entire symbols into more recognized tablature systems today. The second draft refines and finalizes the corrections made throughout the interpretation processes of the first, while the third and final copy is a space-adjusted, proportionately and carefully scribed copy in ink or pen. With computer-assisted score writing programs, the spacing issue on the second draft can be solved with professional ease.

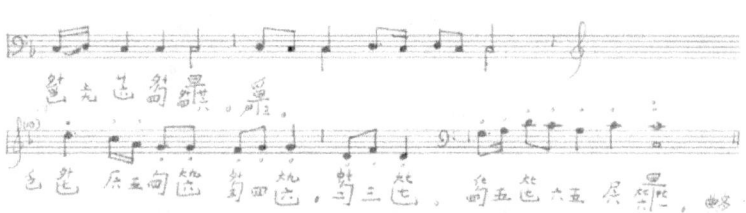

Start writing your first draft after looking through or roughly playing through the music, making sure that when you copy the tablature, you don't have to start on a new line or page during an intensive moment of the music. On a separate sheet of paper, prepare a reference chart with the common pressed and harmonic positions and

> First write out the tablature, then write the pitches on the five line staff as whole notes that can be altered by adding stems or filling in later. Leave more space for movements that involve multiple notes, and be consistent with the level of detail of score rendition, such as markings for slides, harmonics, and use of bar-lines.
> Things may change as you polish your work, so remember to draft in pencil!

their pitches in their relative tunings. Converting from tablature to pitch-based scores (whether number or on the five-line staff) is a straightforward task but requires meticulous care and concentration, as it is easy to miscalculate or miswrite by one or two tones.

## Before putting pencil to paper

Although for the purpose of simplicity in this book, the subsequent exercises are all in standard tuning – it may not hurt to first look at the title and subtitle labels for hints whether a given piece may be in a non-standard tuning. This may either come as a label indicating the piece to be in a certain mode (or explicitly a tuning), or may come as a post-script, perhaps along with instructions on how to tune it.

英語琴統初階

# The First Look-through

Let's start by breaking down this piece into recognizable phrases. Beginning with the first bit (right), we see two notes, a "pause-do-thrice (2 more times)", followed by the identical note as the first before going onto something foreign. This series of movements is identical to a Da-yuan, so this is one phrase on its own.

The remainder of the line (left), we see a bunch of notes that we do not know when it ends as a phrase. Furthermore, there is a left hand – qi (lifting) symbol with a top portion never encountered before (and not included in the fingering index in this book). Let's solve this mystery at a later time.

Here, we see "two drag ups (to) 8-above", giving evidence that this score uses the non-decimal *hui-wei* system. We know that the closest equivalent on string V is 7.9. Make note of that and go on.

Playing the first half of the second line, we hear a somewhat 'odd' phrase – many possibilities exist here – does the phrase start from the "Thumb 9 *tiao* VI" (left) until the same symbol on the next line? Or is it somewhere else, possibly from the "*Zhu* Thumb 10 *gou* V" (right)? Should we group them by tone and quickly play it through, or give ample time to each to dilute its octave jumps which may sound odd?

It is safe to say that the third line can be divided into a new phrase from the "*Zhu* middle 11 *gou* I", as there is little agency with the previous note, in addition to the repetition in the following notes.

The series of subscript left-hand movements presents a new challenge: "Up-9, *wang-lai* (back-and-forth), *dai*". While we know *daiqi* (ring finger lift-up) is a common movement, could *dai* (without the *qi* 'up') mean something else, such as *dai-shang* 帶上, which is a slide upward?

On the fourth line (right), we see the *dai* again, followed by a similar –*qi* movement from the first line, but potentially different, as this is written with a mouth (□) under it, becoming *heqi* 合起 or *shiqi* 拾起, or "to match/pick up". Adding this to our list of mystery characters, we shall leave this until we find internal and external proof whether both variants exist, or if it is a misprint.

The latter half of the fourth line (left) may be a longer string of tablature, but based on practical expertise and the "Xianweng" principle of dividing phrases by two pitches using two different methods, it becomes evident that three notes form a short phrase. It is important not to overlook the intricacies of longer strands of left hand slides, such as the one at the end of this line – the resulting performance should give some sort of rhythmic symmetry to the previous phrases of the line, and the retreating *yin* should have a distinct space-time from the slide down to 11 (position 10.8).

We see the *heqi* (?) again in the middle of the fifth line (right above), making the mystery –*qi* characters go up to three counts, with two having a "mouth" and one without. With this many examples, one can start playing both possibilities and ponder on the validity of the hypotheses. Say, if this –*qi* movement is a slide up, assuming that it goes up by one whole pentatonic tone, does it "match up" as its name mentions? Or, if it is a lift up, does the sound make a perfect unison, fourth, or fifth interval with the previous or next note?

Finishing up the fifth line (left), make sure to connect it to the next line as the *la* movement on string II (the number 2 being spliced by the *la* middle stroke) is connected to the "open string I as one" description next page. Be wary of compound characters and don't miss a note because of it.

The last lines show a long series of slides and a unique use of the *feiyin* or "flying *yin*" which implies a large amplitude jump, again pay attention to its timing. There is a large space after the left hand string that we can assume to be a misprint for the lack of a *fanqi* (begin harmonics) symbol, as we can see the stop symbol at the end of the piece. The "stop piece" symbol used here also gives an indication to the composition type of this song as a *yi* (意), or motif, and may have greater meaning when analyzing the structure of entire pieces later.

英語琴統初階

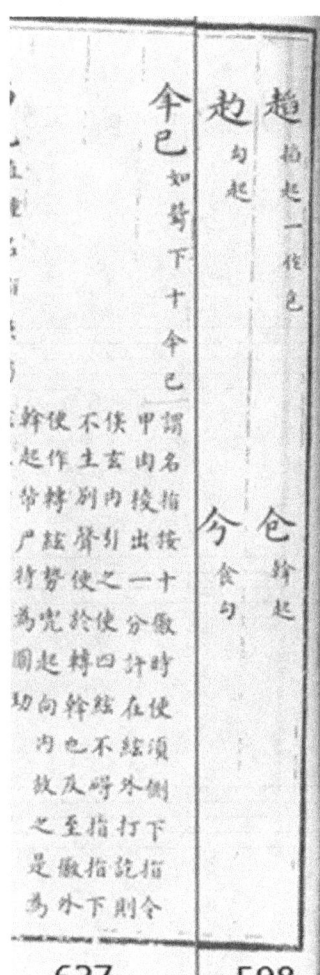

627 | 598

Since the Xilutang Qintong does not have its own fingering index, the next best alternative is to find other external sources from the same period. In page 598 and 627 of the Yongle Qinshu Jicheng (1403~1425?, reprinted 1983) or its simulacra Qinshu Jicheng (1590), we can find a very similar symbol with the name *woqi*, or "scoop up." The description is as follows on p.627:

*"Woqi: For example when ring finger presses on 10th hui [of string V], lie the finger on its side// using half flesh and nail, with 1/10 of the finger strutting out past the string. Perform the* da *(ring finger inwards), then // stay on the string and drag/pull it [towards yourself], so that string IV does not block your fingers // and create other noises. Twist it [the pressing finger] in a scooping [inward] motion towards hui-wai (outside position) // and scoop inwards as if switching to another string. Hence, it is called //* woqi *[scoop up]. The back-lift-up sound (written in jianzipu) is especially rounded in strength.*

Whether all 3 instances of the mystery symbol can be defined with this movement, is up to the rationalizing of the interpreter.

Another method of confirming or attempting to solve such mysteries is done by investigating other similar records from other sources. This will be done in the third part of this repertoire.

# 商意-太古 Shang Motif: Upper Antiquity

From Xilutang Qintong (1525)
Score by

Standard Tuning

英語琴統初階

# Shenpin Gu-Shang Yi
# (Shenqi Mipu)

Recorded in the earlier compendium *Shenqi Mipu* of 1425, it is one of two pieces that shares the name "Shang motif", this one being differentiated with the term "gu (ancient)". Comparing the contents one can clearly see that this is a predecessor or source text for the 1525 version seen in the previous lesson.

Some thoughts to consider are: What changed over the course of one century? What are things you find odd-sounding in this version, and what has been changed in the version a century later? Why do you think they happened? Since the two manuscripts are written in two styles of *jianzipu* and have different penchants for organizing their text, does that reflect onto performance style as well? Are some of the previous "mystery characters" solved because of alternative accounts with different jianzipu writing systems?

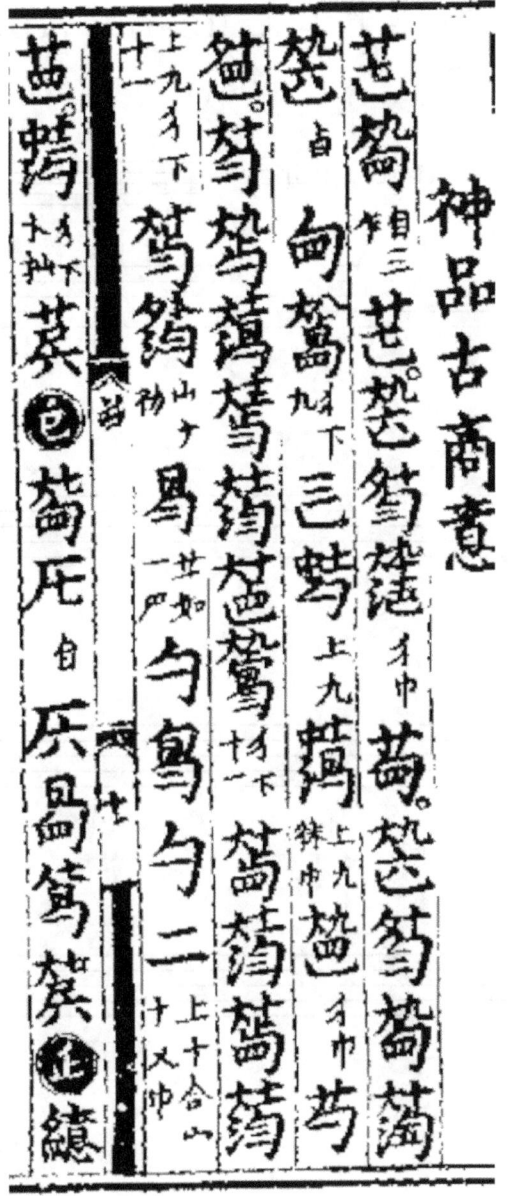

# 神品古商意 Celestial Air: Ancient Shang Motif

From Shenqi Mipu (1425)
Score by

Standard Tuning

英語琴統初階

# Yin De

Also from the Shang mode repertoire in *Xilutang Qintong* Folio 8, the title *Hidden Virtues* can also be found in five different manuscripts from the Ming to the early Qing period, where then a similar variation was found in Songxianguan Qinpu of 1614 under the title *Qiujiang Yebo,* or *Autumn River Night Anchorage.* Since then, 27 manuscripts carried variants and facsimiles of the piece under the latter name.

There is no attached commentary in this manuscript, although Shenqi Mipu annotated the following by the author:

> *As for this piece, in the ancient time (when the Dao was followed),*
> *resolute gentlemen and benevolent men had uncommon talents, and were born*
> *with pure and lofty goals. Whether in seclusion amongst the cliffs and gullies, or*
> *living in the market place, they wore rough clothing and maintained their values,*
> *so as to nurture their heroic spirit; they were not known to (common) people. So*
> *it is said, the gentleman has great virtue while looking like an ordinary coarse*
> *fellow; and so this piece was written in order to communicate with the deities,*
> *and speak of their own objectives.  (tr. John Thompson, silkqin.com)*

# 隱德 **Hidden Virtues**

From Xilutang Qintong (1525)
Score by

Standard Tuning

英語琴統初階

# Standard Tuning Positions Chart

## Open & Pressed Tones

| Str | Open | Out | 13 | 12.3 | 12 | 11 | 10.8 | 10 | 9.5 | 9 | 8.5 | 8 | 7.9 | 7.6 | 7.3 | 7 | 6.7 | 6.5 | 6.2 | 6 |
|---|---|---|---|---|---|---|---|---|---|---|---|---|---|---|---|---|---|---|---|---|
| I | --C | --D | | | | | --E | --F | | --G | | | --A | | --B | -C | | -D | | -E |
| II | --D | --E | | --F | | | | --G | | --A | | | --B | -C | | -D | | -E | -F | |
| III | --F | --G | | | | | --A | | --B | -C | | | -D | | | -F | | -G | | -A |
| IV | --G | --A | | | --B | | --B | -C | | -D | | | -E | | | -G | | -A | | -B |
| V | --A | --B | | | -C | | | -D | | -E | -F | | | -G | | -A | | -B | C | |
| VI | -C | -D | | | | -E | | -F | | -G | | | -A | | | C | | D | | -E |
| VII | -D | -E | | -F | | | | -G | | -A | | | -B | C | | D | | E | | |

| Str | Open | 5.6 | 5.2 | 5 | 4.8 | 4.6 | 4.4 | 4.2 | 4 | 3.8 | 3.5 | 3.3 | 3 | 2.7 | 2 | 1.5 | 1.2 | 1 |
|---|---|---|---|---|---|---|---|---|---|---|---|---|---|---|---|---|---|---|
| I | --C | -F | | -G | | -A | | -B | C | | D | | E | | G | A | | | +C |
| II | --D | -G | | -A | -B | C | | D | | E | F | | G | A | | | +C | +D |
| III | --F | | -B | C | D | | E | F | G | | A | | +C | | | | | +F |
| IV | --G | C | | D | E | F | | G | A | | +C | +D | | | | | | +G |
| V | --A | D | | E | F | | | A | B | +C | | +D | +E | | +G | | +A |
| VI | -C | F | | G | A | | B | +C | +D | | +E | | +G | +A | | | ++C |
| VII | -D | G | | A | B | +C | | +D | | +E | +F | | | +A | | ++C | ++D |

## Harmonic Positions

| Str | Open | Out | 13 | 12 | 11 | 10 | 9 | 8 | 7 | 6 | 5 | 4 | 3 | 2 | 1 |
|---|---|---|---|---|---|---|---|---|---|---|---|---|---|---|---|
| I | --C | +E | +C | G | E | C | -G | E | -C | E | -G | C | E | G | +C |
| II | --D | +F♯ | +D | A | F♯ | D | -A | F♯ | -D | F♯ | -A | D | F♯ | A | +D |
| III | --F | +A | +F | +C | A | F | C | A | -F | A | C | F | A | +C | +F |
| IV | --G | +B | +G | +D | B | G | D | B | -G | B | D | G | B | +D | +G |
| V | --A | ++C♯ | +A | +E | +C♯ | A | E | +C♯ | -A | +C♯ | E | A | +C♯ | +E | +A |
| VI | -C | ++E | ++C | +G | +E | C | G | +E | C | +E | G | C | +E | +G | ++C |
| VII | -D | ++F♯ | ++D | +A | +F♯ | D | A | +F♯ | D | +F♯ | A | D | +F♯ | +A | ++D |

Each + or – denotes one octave higher or lower from the middle octave.

# Reading List

Guqin players are often trained under the guidance of teachers and a textbook of the said tradition, but since the advent of communications technologies and institutionalized curricula, players have sought for learning from different schools and styles, as well share ideas on music and musicological findings. Thanks to research efforts in China, Hong Kong, Taiwan and the United States, much modern scholarship provide detailed aspects for further research into musicology, aesthetics, and more.

## Essential Scorebooks:

中國藝術研究院音樂研究所 Zhongguo Yishu Yanjiuyuan Yinyue Yanjiusuo & 北京古琴研究會 Beijing Guqin Yanjiuhui. 古琴曲集 Guqin Quji, Vol.1&2. People's Music Publishing House. Bejing, 1983, 5th reprint 2003. ISBN 7-103-0117-0 & 7-103-0117-1.

李祥霆 Li Xiangting. 古琴曲集 Guqin Quji, Vol.1-3. People's Music Publishing House. Beijing, 2009. ISBN 7-103-03465-6.

龔一 Gong Yi. 古琴新譜 Guqin Xinpu. Shanghai Music Publishing House. Shanghai, 2011. ISBN 7-807-51844-0.

## Manuscripts, Handbooks, Compendia, and Scholarly Research on them:

畢克禮 Binkley, James (transl.). Abiding Antiquity: Translations from the Yu-ku-chai-ch'in-pu 與古齋琴譜. Lulu.com, 2006. ISBN 978-1-4303-0346-6

卞趙如蘭 Pian, Rulan Chao. Sonq Dynasty Musical Sources and Their Interpretations. Harvard University Press. Cambridge, 1967.

呂卡 Pisano, Luca (translated and annotated by). The Qinshi (History of the Qin) by Zhu Changwen (1041-1098). Bilingual Edition. Bibliothek der Tang und Song 6. Ostasien Verlag, Gossenberg, 2023. ISBN 978-3-9-940527-27-1.

唐建垣 Tong Kin-woon (Tang Jianyuan). 琴府 Qin Fu, Vol.1 & 2. Lianguan Chubanshe, Taipei.

查阜西 Zha Fuxi. 琴曲集成 Qinqu Jicheng, Vols. 1-30. Third edition. Cloth Hardcover. Zhonghua Book Company. Beijing, 2010. ISBN 7-101-07383-6.

查阜西 Zha, Fuxi. 存見古琴曲譜輯覽 Cunjian Guqin Qupu Jilan. People's Music Publishing House. Beijing. 1958. ISBN 7-103-02379-4.

Lieberman, Frederic (transl.). Chinese Zither Tutor - Mei-an Ch'in-p'u. Hong Kong University Press. Hong Kong, 1991. ISBN 978-962-209-042-2.

英語琴統初階

## On Dapu (Interpretation) and Aesthetics:

林西莉 Lindqvist, Cecilia. Qin. (Swedish, hardcover) Albert Bonniers Förlag. 2006. ISBN 978-910010-5808.

高羅佩 van Gulik, Hans R.H.. The Lore of the Chinese Lute: An essay in Ch'in ideology. Hardcover, Tuttle Pub. 1969. ISBN 978-0804808699.

謝俊仁 Tse, Chun Yan Victor. From Chromaticism to Pentatonism: A Convergence of Ideology and Practice in Qin Music of the Ming and Qing Dynasties. (PhD thesis), Music Department, Chinese University of Hong Kong, Hong Kong, submitted August 2009.

榮鴻曾 Yung, Bell. Celestial Airs of Antiquity, Music of the Seven-String Zither of China, Madison, A-R Editions. 1996.

榮鴻曾 Yung, Bell. "Da Pu: The Recreative Process for the Music of the Seven-string Zither" in *Music and Context: Essays in Honor of John Ward* ed. Anne Dhu Shapiro, Music Department, Harvard University, pp. 370-384.

榮鴻曾 Yung, Bell. The Last of China's Literati: The Life and Music of Mme. Tsar Teh-Yun. Hong Kong University Press. 2009.

## Sources in Chinese:

葉明媚 Yip Mingmei. 古琴音樂藝術 Guqin Yinyue Yishu. Commercial Press, Hong Kong. 1991. ISBN 9620741447

顧梅羹 Gu Meigeng. 琴學備要 Qinxue Beiyao. Shanghai Music Press, 2003. ISBN 7-80667-453-5

成公亮 Cheng Gongliang. 是曲不知所從起-成公亮打譜集 Shiqu Buzhi Suocong Qi – Cheng Gongliang Dapu Ji. Shuzhizhai Publications, Hong Kong, 2005. ISBN 988-987392-3.

-----. 秋籟居琴話 Qiulaiju Qinhua. SDX Joint Publishing, Beijing, 2009. ISBN 7-108-03255-3.

姚丙炎 Yao Bingyan. 琴曲鉤沉 Qinqu Gouchen. Shuzhizhai Publications, Hong Kong, 2007. ISBN 978-9-88987-393-6.

王耀珠 Wang Yaozhu. 《谿山琴況》探賾 Xishan Qinkuang Tanze. Shanghai Music Press, Shanghai, 2008. ISBN 978-7-80751-213-4.

章華英 Zhang Huaying. 古琴 Gu Qin. Zhejiang People's Publishing House. Hangzhou, 2005. ISBN 7-213-02955-X.

## Websites:

- Wikipedia. <u>List of Guqin Societies.</u>
  http://en.wikipedia.org/wiki/List_of_guqin_societies
- John Thompson's Website. http://www.silkqin.com
- James Binkley's *Yuguzhai Qinpu* Project. http://www.lulu.com/content/402391

  - Facebook. <u>Guqin - 古琴</u> (Facebook Group).
    http://www.facebook.com/group.php?gid=2212903582

英語琴統初階

# Beijing Central Conservatory of Music Guqin Examination Repertoire List

With the release of the third revision of Guqin Quji《古琴曲集》in 2010, the latest revision to the officially-recognized examination repertoire is as follows.

The asterisk (*) denotes multiple entries or multiple versions in the Guqin Quji.

| Level | Title (ZH) | Title (English) | Comments |
|---|---|---|---|
| 1 | 古琴吟 | *Guqin Yin* / Song of the Guqin | |
| | 鳳求凰 | *Feng Qiu Huang* / Phoenix seeks his mate | |
| | 慨古吟 | *Kai Gu Yin* / Song of the Sigh of Antiquity | |
| | 蘭花花 | *Lan Hua Hua* / Small Orchid Flower | Modern composition. |
| | 小白菜 | *Xiao Baicai* / Little Cabbage | Modern composition. |
| | 秋風詞 | *Qiu Feng Ci* / Ode to the Autumn Wind | Listed in this book. |
| 2 | 極樂吟 | *Jile Yin* / Song of Paradise | |
| | 良宵引 | *Liangxiao Yin* / Prelude to a Fair Evening | Listed in this book. |
| | 清夜吟 | *Qingye Yin* / Song to a Clear Night | |
| | 湘妃怨 | *Xiangfei Yuan* / Mourn of the Xiang Maiden | |
| | 雙鶴聽泉 | *Shuanghe Tingchuan* / Twin Cranes Listening to the Spring | |
| | 拉縴歌 | *Laqian Ge* / Boat Tracking Song | Modern composition. |
| | 滿江紅 | *Man Jiang Hong* / All the River is Red | Poem by Yue Fei. |
| | 泣顏回 | *Qi Yan Hui* / Lament Yan Hui | |
| 3 | 春曉吟 | *Chunxiao Yin* / Song to a Spring Dawn | |
| | 風雷引 | *Fenglei Yin* / Prelude to Wind and Thunder | |
| | 精忠詞 | *Jingzhong Ci* / Poem to Patriotic Loyalty | Poem by Yue Fei. |
| | 秋江夜泊 | *Qiujiang Yebo* / Autumn River Night Anchorage | |
| | 玉樓春曉 | *Yulou Chunxiao* / Spring Dawn at the Jade Tower | |
| | 映山紅 | *Yingshan Hong* / Mountain Covered in Red | Adapted from Revolutionary-era composition. |
| | 小草 | *Xiao Cao* / Little Grass | Modern composition. |
| 4 | 石上流泉 | *Shishang Liuchuan* / Flowing Stream on the Rocks | |
| | 神人暢 | *Shen Ren Chang* / Prose of the Immortal | |
| | 酒狂 | *Jiu Kuang* / Drunken Madness | Alternate form in book. |
| | 韋編三絕 | *Weibian Sanjue* / Thrice Worn-out book with Cowhide Binding | |
| | 孔子讀易 | *Kongzi Duyi* / Confucius Reading the *Yijing* | Listed in this book. |
| | 陽關三疊 | *Yangguan Sandie* / Three Variations to the Yang Pass Theme | Listed in this book. |

| | | | |
|---|---|---|---|
| | 歸去來辭 | *Guiqu Laice* / Returning Home | |
| | 秋夜長 | *Qiuye Chang* / Long Autumn Evening | |
| | 渴望 | *Hewang* / Desire | Modern composition. |
| | 信天遊 | *Xintian You* / Wandering Albatross | Adapted from modern song. |
| 5 | 鷗鷺忘機 | *Oulu Wangji* / Forgetting Intentions | |
| | 楚歌 | *Chu Ge* / Song of Chu | |
| | 關山月 | *Guanshan Yue* / Moon Over the Mountain Pass | Listed in this book. |
| | 高山 | *Gao Shan* / Lofty Mountains | |
| | 洞庭秋思 | *Dongting Qiusi* / Autumn Thoughts by Lake Dongting | |
| | 碧澗流泉 | *Bijian Liuchuan* / Azure Rivulet and Flowing Spring | |
| | 岳陽三醉 | *Yueyang Sanzui* / Three Drunks by Yueyang Tower | |
| | 採茶調 | *Cai Cha Diao* / Tea-Picking Tune | Modern composition. |
| | 茉莉花 | *Moli Hua* / Jasmine Flower | Modern composition. |
| 6 | 梧葉舞秋風 | *Wuye Wu Qiufeng* / Paulownia Leaves Dancing in the Autumn Wind | |
| | 長清 | *Chang Qing* / Long Clarity | |
| | 平沙落雁* | *Pingsha Luoyan* / Geese Landing on Flat Sands | |
| | 獲麟操 | *Huolin Cao* / Etude to Hunting a Qilin | |
| | 山居吟 | *Shanju Yin* / Song to a Mountain Residence | |
| | 醉漁唱晚 | *Zuiyu Changwan* / Drunken Fisherman Singing in the Evening | |
| | 雙乙反調 | *Shuang Yifan Diao* / Composition in Yifan Mode | Modern composition by Victor Tse Chun-Yan. |
| | 滄海龍吟 | *Canghai Longyin* / Song of the Dragon in the Sea | |
| | 普庵咒 | *Pu'an Zhou* / Incantation of the Pu'an Monestary | |
| | 憶故人 | *Yi Guren* / Remembering an Old Friend | |
| 7 | 長門怨 | *Changmen Yuan* / Lament at Long Gate Palace | |
| | 龍朔操 | *Longsuo Cao* / Etude of Longsuo Province | |
| | 佩蘭 | *Pei Lan* / Wearing Orchid | |
| | 天風環佩 | *Tianfeng Huanpei* / Jade Ornaments Clanging in the Heavenly Wind | |
| | 風雲際會 | *Fengyun Jihui* / Meeting of the Wind and Clouds | |
| | 春江花月夜 | *Chunjiang Huayueye* / Evening with the Flowery Moon by the Spring River | Adaptation from guzheng piece. |
| | 山水情 | *Shanshui Qing* / Feelings of the Mountains and Waters | Modern composition by Gong Yi for animation. |

英語琴統初階

| 8 | 高山流水 | *Gaoshan Liushui* / Lofty Mountains and Flowing Water | Adapataion from guzheng piece. |
|---|---|---|---|
| | 漁樵問答* | *Yuqiao Wenda* / Dialogue of the Fisherman and Woodcutter | Listed in this book. |
| | 梅花三弄* | *Meihua Sannong* / Three Variations of the Plum Blossoms | |
| | 欸乃(節本) | *Ao Ai* / Creaking Oars (Abridged) | |
| | 雉朝飛 | *Zhi Zhao Fei* / Pheasants Take Flight in the Morning | |
| | 漁歌* | *Yu Ge* / Fisherman Song | |
| | 孤館遇神 | *Guguan Yushen* / Meeting Spirits in the Lone Hostel | |
| 9 | 離騷(節本) | *Li Sao* / Grievance to Departure (Abridged) | |
| | 搗衣* | *Dao Yi* / Beating Clothes | |
| | 龍翔操 | *Longxiang Cao* / Etude to the Soaring Dragon | |
| | 烏夜啼 | *Wuye Ti* / Crows Cawing in the Night | |
| | 秋塞吟 | *Qiu Sai Yin* / Song of the Autumn Frontier | |
| | 墨子悲絲 | *Mozi Beisi* / Mozi Feeling Sadness from Silk | |
| | 陽春 | *Yang Chun* / Sunny Spring | |
| | 大胡笳* | *Da Hujia* / Large Barbarian Reed Tune | |
| | 樓蘭散 | *Loulan San* / Loulan Verse | Modern composition by Gong Yi. |
| 10 | 瀟湘水雲 | *Xiao Xiang Shuiyun* / Mists over the Rivers Xiao and Xiang | |
| | 樵歌 | *Qiao Ge* / Woodcutter Song | |
| | 廣陵散 | *Guangling San* / Guangling Verse | |
| | 胡笳十八拍 | *Hujia Shiba Pai* / Eighteen Beats of the Barbarian Reed | |
| | 幽蘭 | *Youlan* / Solitary Orchid | |
| | 梅園吟 | *Meiyuan Yin* / Song of the Plum Garden | Modern composition by Gong Yi. |
| | 三峽船歌 | *Sanxia Chuange* / Boat Song of the Three Gorges | Modern composition by Li Xiangting. |
| | 風雪築路 | *Fengxue Zhulu* / Building Road in the Blizzard | Modern composition by Li Xiangting. |
| | 春風 | *Chun Feng* / Spring Wind | Modern composition by Gong Yi. |

# REPERTOIRE E
♫
# MISCALLANI PIECES

# DAMING YITONG
# SANMIN ZHUYI
# O CANADA

英語琴統初階

# Daming Yitong

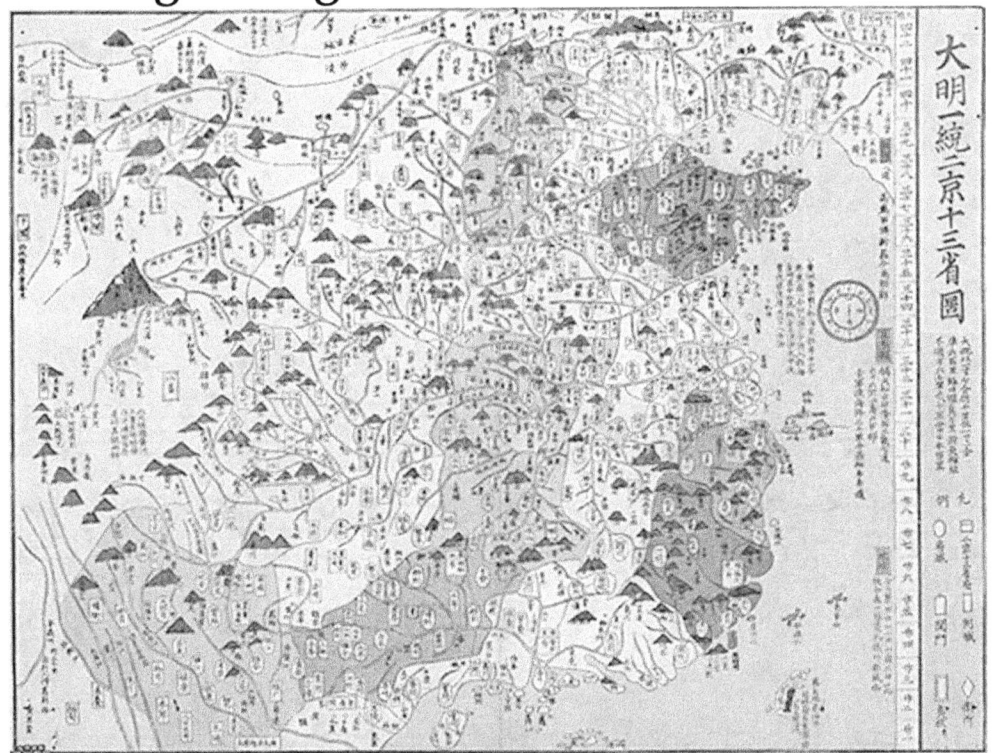
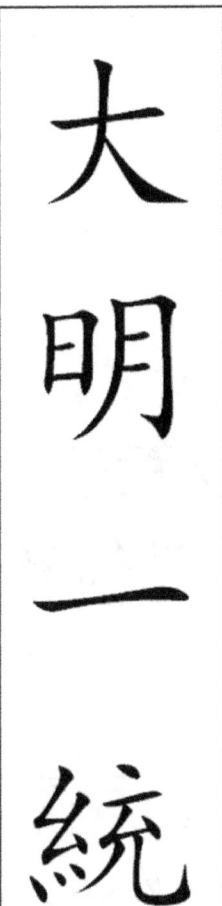

Found in the Fengxuan Xuanpin (1539) and Yuwu Qinpu (1589) to distinctly different music accompaniment, both sources depict a musical rendition to a two-part lyric attributed to Liu Ji, the key advisor to Zhu Yuanzhang, the founder of the Ming Dynasty. The song exemplifies the ideal Confucian relationship between the Lord and his Subject, with the former providing magnamity and leadership, and reciprocated with honesty and loyal sincerity.

This rendition here is from the 1539 manuscript, which claims that the music was composed in style of solemn court sacrificial ritual music – which is fitting, as the lyrics are written in two pre-Qin Classical Chinese styles: the first section of 14 lines is written in four-character *Pianwen* couplet, followed by the second section with 9 lines written in *Saoti*, or *Li Sao* style from the *Lyrics of Chu*. The 1589 version lacks the final line and harmonic coda in comparison to this version.

This rendition converts the original *huiwei* notation into the contemporary *huifen* system, in addition to several adjustments made as corrections to logical pitches and positions.

The English translation of the lyrics is provided after the score.

# 大明一統 Unity of the Great Ming

From Fengxuan Xuanpin (1539)
Score by Juni Yeung

Standard Tuning 正調

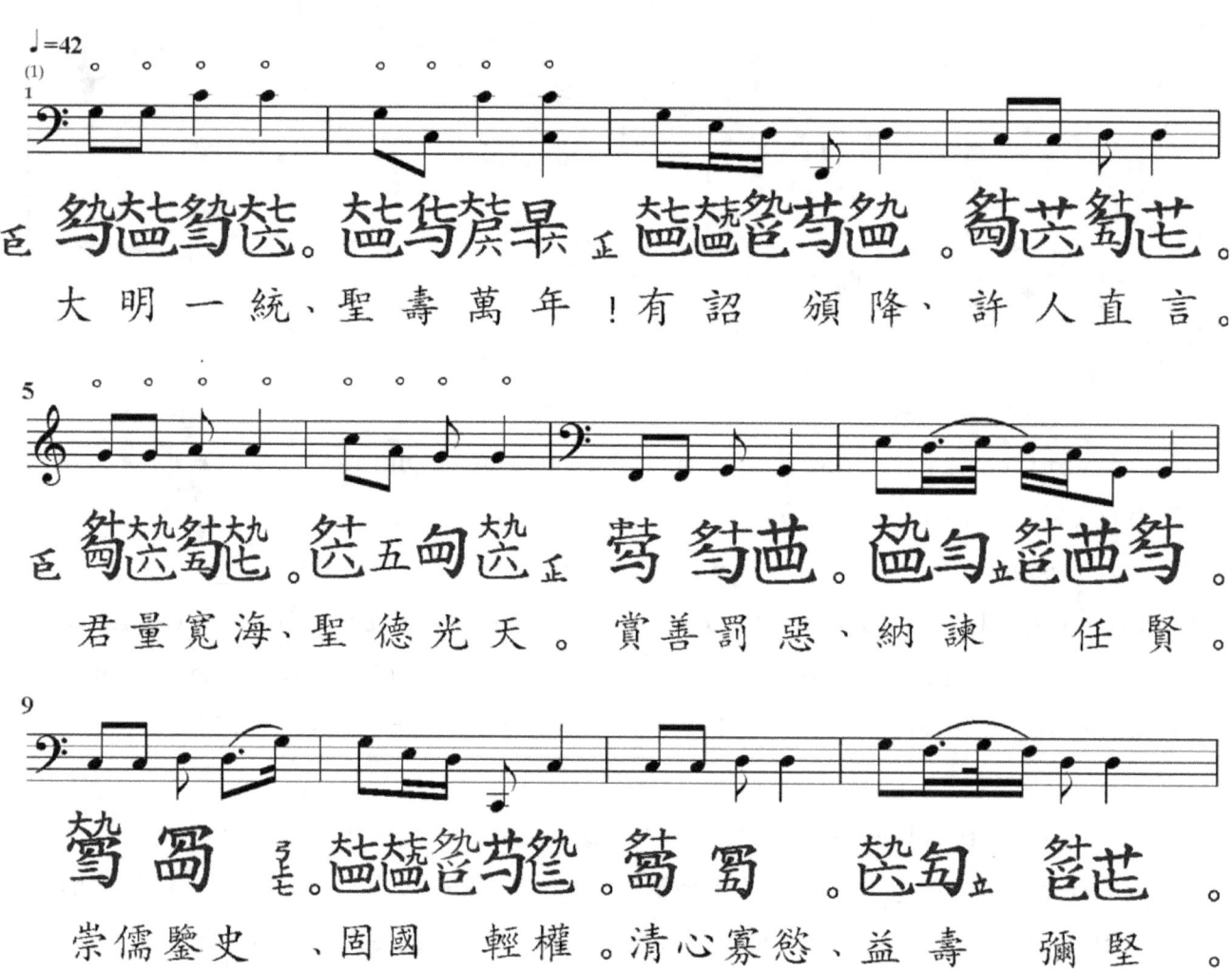

英語琴統初階

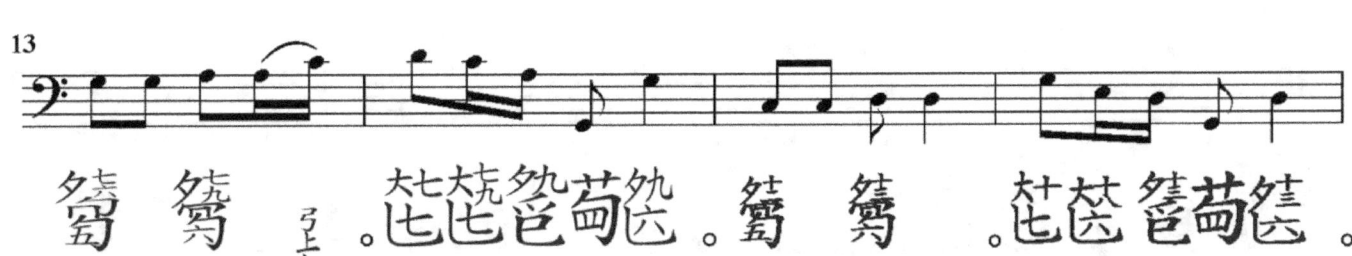

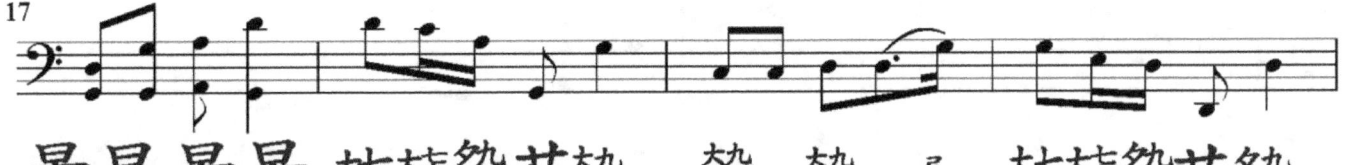

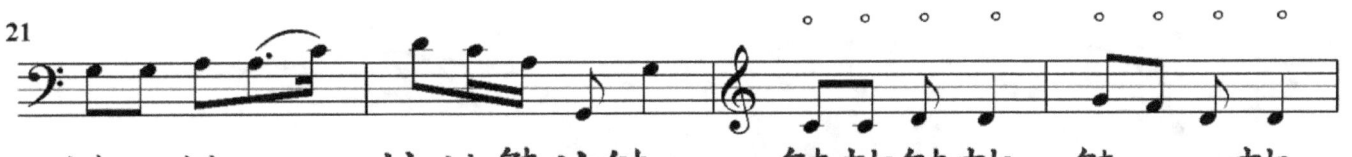

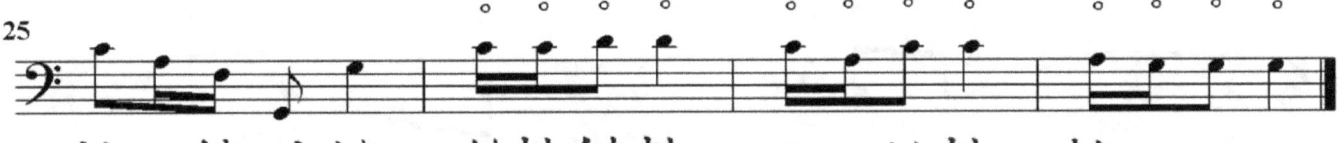

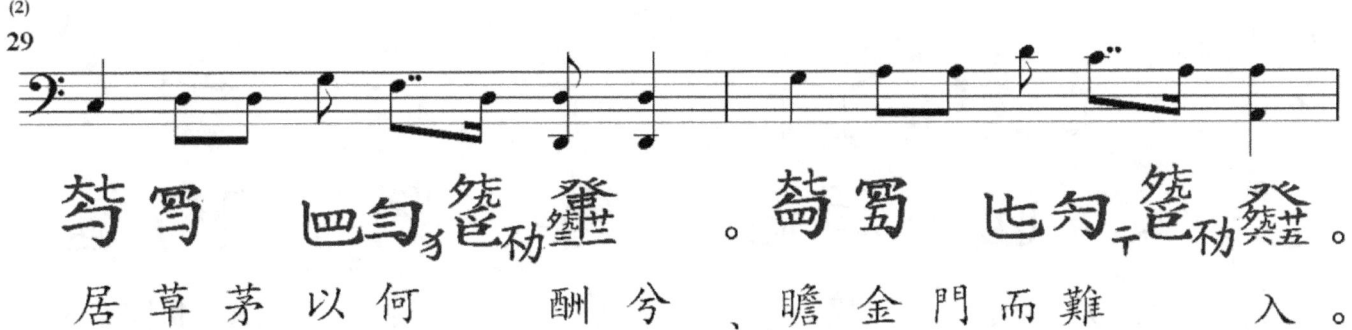

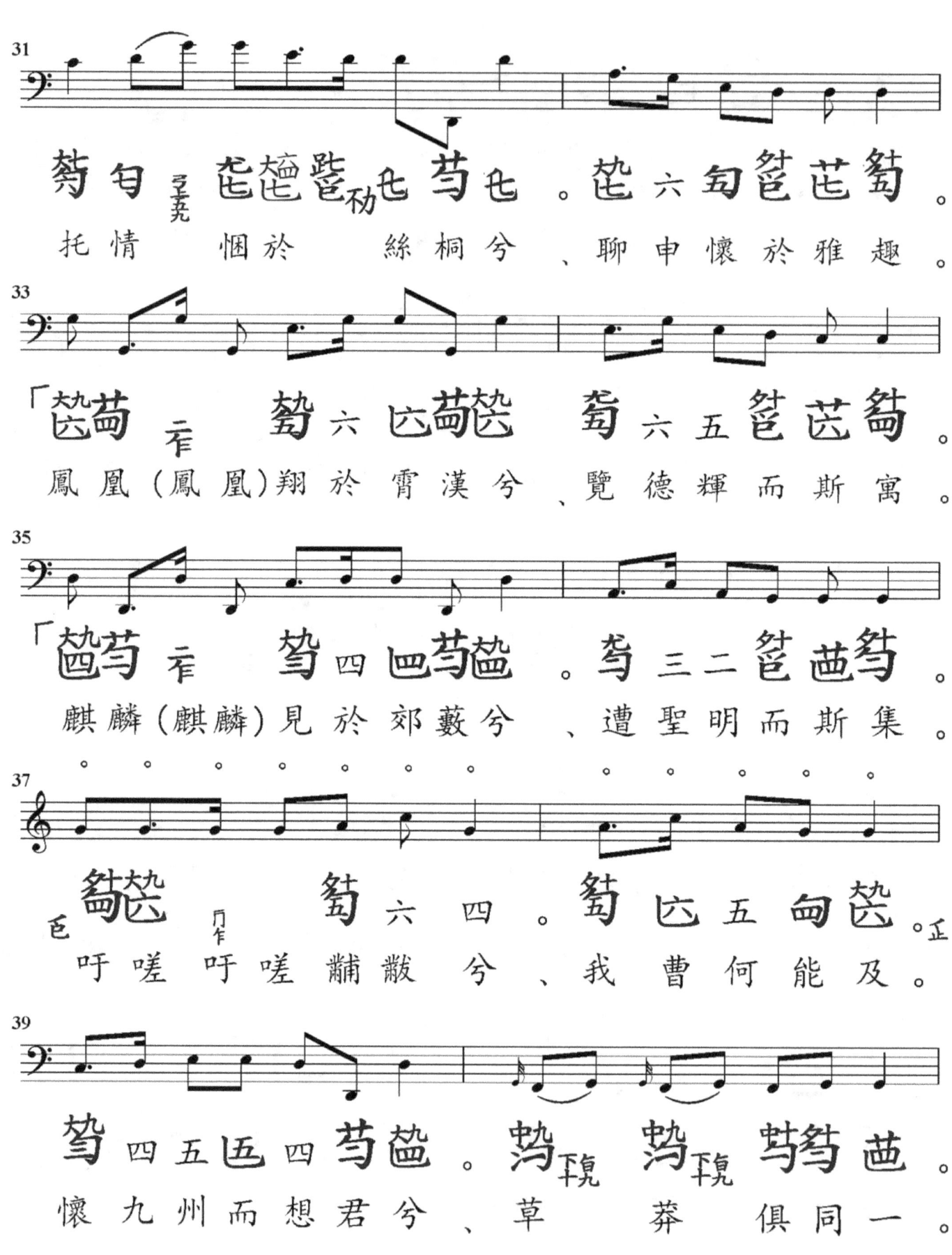

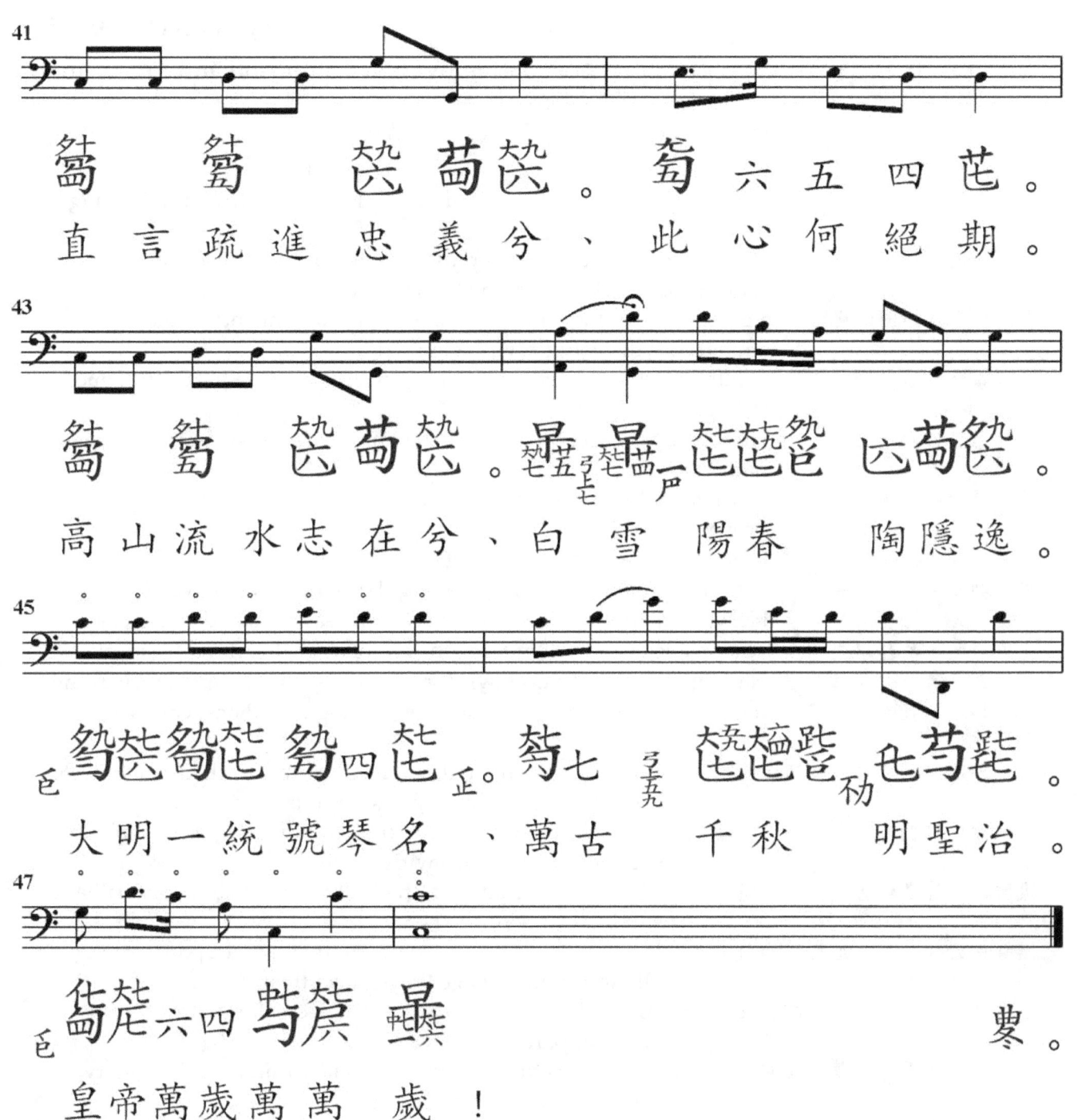

直言疏進忠義兮、此心何絕期。

高山流水志在兮、白雪陽春　陶隱逸。

大明一統號琴名　、萬古　千秋　明聖治。

皇帝萬歲萬萬　歲！

| | |
|---|---|
| 大明一統，聖壽萬年。 | Hail, United Ming, may the emperor live myriad years! |
| 有詔頒降，許人直言。 | He decrees from above: people are allowed to speak frankly. |
| 君量寬海，聖德光天。 | The ruler's capacity is magnanimous, His sacred virtue brightening the firmament. |
| 賞善罰惡，納諫任賢。 | He rewards the good while punishing the bad, He accepts reprimands while rewarding the worthy. |
| 崇儒鑒史，固國輕權。 | Venerating Confucian thought and examining history, He strengthens the country with gentle power. |
| 清心寡慾，益壽彌堅。 | A pure heart with few desires, may he add years to his life full and strong. |
| 踐祚念苦，欲民從輕。 | He recalls his bitter and humble beginnings, and wishes to be lenient with common folk, |
| 用度節儉，儲積豐盈。 | When spending He is careful and frugal, accumulations bringing prosperity. |
| 隄防邊塞，操練精兵。 | Defending the frontier, drilling skilled soldiers, |
| 明正綱紀，太平風聲。 | Clear and just principles, spreading the clarion call of peace. |
| 天長地久，海晏河清。 | Heaven and earth will last forever, with seas calm and rivers clear. |
| 兆民賴之，萬邦以貞。 | The people have trust in Him, the nations rely to Him as example. |
| 有德皇猷，無憂羽翼。 | Having virtuous imperial wisdom, He does not distress his assistants. |
| 百事具忠，直言諫勑。 | In a hundred affairs we are devoted, giving our honest counsel. |

| | |
|---|---|
| 居草茅以何酬兮，瞻金門而難入。 | What can one repay to Him from our thatched homes? We can gaze at the golden gates but it is hard to enter. |
| 托情悃於絲桐兮，聊申懷於雅趣。 | So we bind our sincerity to silk and wood (of the qin); and expand our emotions with elegant taste. |
| 鳳凰翔於霄漢兮，覽德輝而斯寓。 | The phoenixes soars in the Milky Way, and to His brilliant shining virtue reside here. |
| 麒麟見於郊藪兮，遭聖明而斯集。 | Unicorns are seen in remote marshes, and upon meeting His sacred personage they collect there. |
| 吁嗟吁嗟黼黻兮，我曹何能及。 | Alas! Alas! O ancient sacrificial dress: how can my rough rags compare? |
| 懷九州而想君兮，草莽俱同一。 | We cherish the country and fondly think of His majesty, even people living in the wild think the same. |
| 直言疏進忠義兮，此心何絕期。 | Having spoken honestly words to give advice with loyalty and righteousness, how could this heart forget you? |
| 高山流水志在兮，白雪陽春陶隱逸。 | High Mountains and Flowing Streams: the aim is here; White Snow and Sunny Spring: pleased to hide in retirement. |
| 大明一統號琴名，萬古千秋明聖治。 | We call out with our qins to The Great Ming's United Realm, through all eternity shall it hold its bright, sacred reign. |

| | |
|---|---|
| 皇帝萬歲萬萬歲！ | To the emperor: long life! Long long life! |

英語琴統初階

# Sanmin Zhuyi

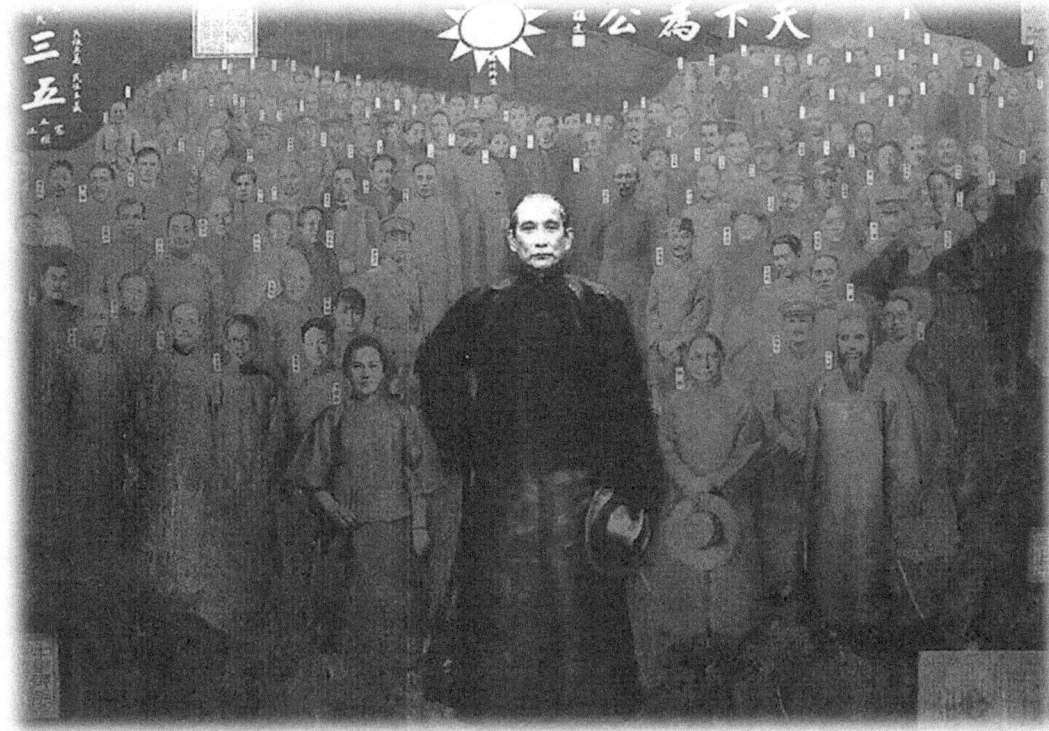

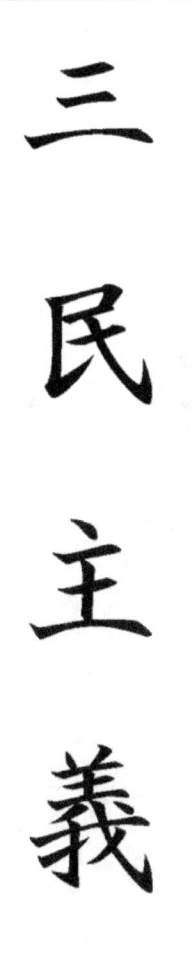

As the fourth (and as of 2024, the current) official national anthem of the Republic of China, *Three Principles of the People* was adopted in March 1930 and officially recognized as the official anthem in June 1937, and was originally the official song of the Kuomintang (KMT). The anthem's place was cemented with the onset of the Second Sino-Japanese War (1937-1945), and its use still continues today.

The piece is composed in a court music style, accompanied by the 4-character lines and Shijing-style stanzas. This form of music makes it naturally compatible with the guqin's natural tuning. Dynamics are treated with harmonics as a staccato piano, while double-string movements give extra volume. Open and pressed strings are used interspersed in the same style as actual court music guqin scores from previous eras, and shows a rare example of 20th century composition where authentic Chinese musical forms are respected.

# 三民主義 Three Principles of the People

Composed by Cheng Maoyun 程懋筠

Qin transcription by Juni L. Yeung 楊儁立

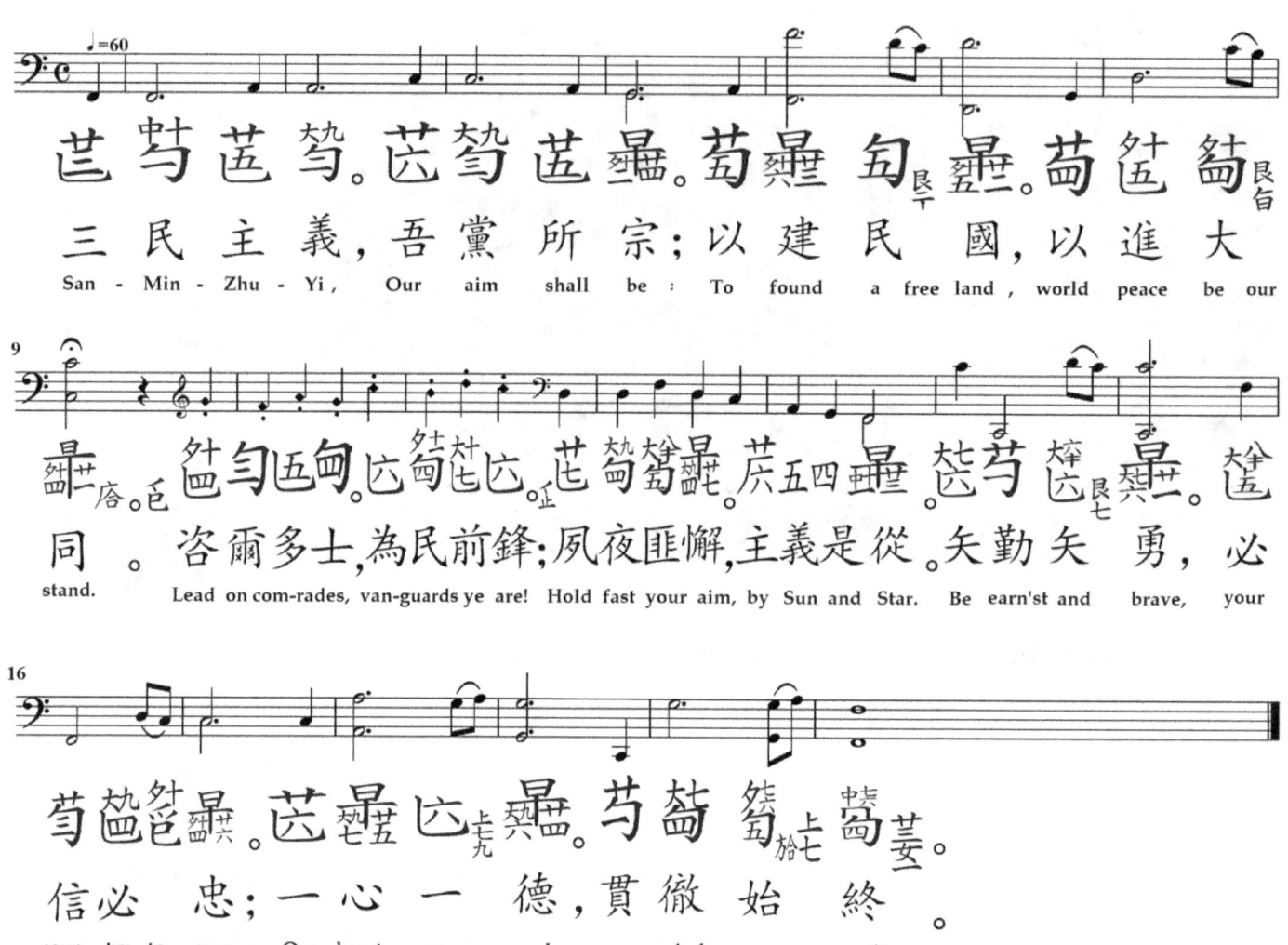

三民主義，吾黨所宗；以建民國，以進大
San - Min - Zhu - Yi, Our aim shall be : To found a free land, world peace be our

同 。咨爾多士，為民前鋒；夙夜匪懈，主義是從。矢勤矢 勇，必
stand. Lead on com-rades, van-guards ye are! Hold fast your aim, by Sun and Star. Be earn'st and brave, your

信必 忠；一心一 德，貫徹始 終 。
coun - try to save ; One heart one soul , one mind on -e goal!

# O Canada

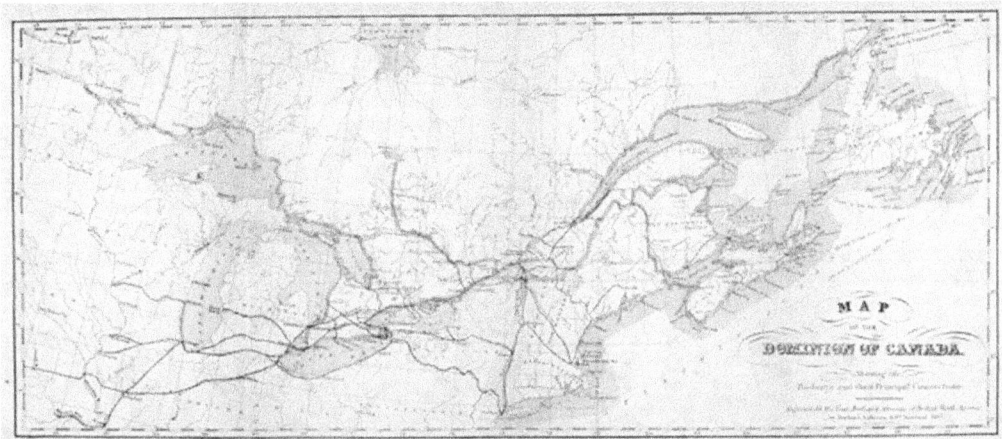

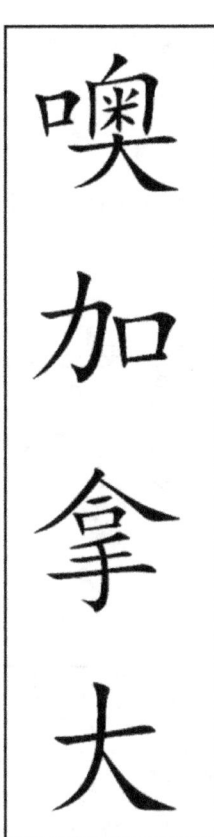

First commissioned by Québec Lieutenant-Governor Théodore Robitaille in 1880 for St. Jean-Baptiste Day, *O Canada* with French lyrics was among several candidates as national song in the early 20th century. With the English lyrics written in 1906 and revised in 1914 by Robert Stanley Weir, it became the *defacto* anthem in the 1930's when King George VI stood in attention to the song, and was selected as the national anthem in 1967, the centennial of Canada's confederation. The National Anthem Act did not pass Royal Assent until 1980, when the rights to Weir's lyrics were sold by Gordon v. Thompson Music, where it is now public domain. The English lyrics were made gender-neutral in 2018, and the 4th edition now reflects that change.

As an adaptation of a piece of Western music onto the qin, the occurance of non-pentatonic tones, especially accidental sharps, will require extra attention to achieve accuracy in performance. Set in E flat major, the B flat modal Qiliang tuning is used instead to allow performing accidentals in harmonics.

| *Official English Lyrics*<br>*By Robert Stanley Weir* | *Official French Lyrics*<br>*By Sir Adolphe-Basile Routhier* |
| :---: | :---: |
| O Canada! | Ô Canada! |
| Our home and native land! | Terre de nos aïeux, |
| True patriot love in all of us command. | Ton front est ceint de fleurons glorieux! |
| With glowing hearts we see thee rise, | Car ton bras sait porter l'épée, |
| The True North strong and free! | Il sait porter la croix! |
| From far and wide, | Ton histoire est une épopée |
| O Canada, we stand on guard for thee. | Des plus brillants exploits. |
| God keep our land glorious and free! | Et ta valeur, de foi trempée, |
| O Canada, we stand on guard for thee. | Protégera nos foyers et nos droits. |
| O Canada, we stand on guard for thee. | Protégera nos foyers et nos droits. |

# 噢加拿大 O Canada

By Calixa Lavallée (1880)
Adapted to guqin by Juni Yeung

Chushang (Qiliang) Tuning 楚商 (淒涼) 調

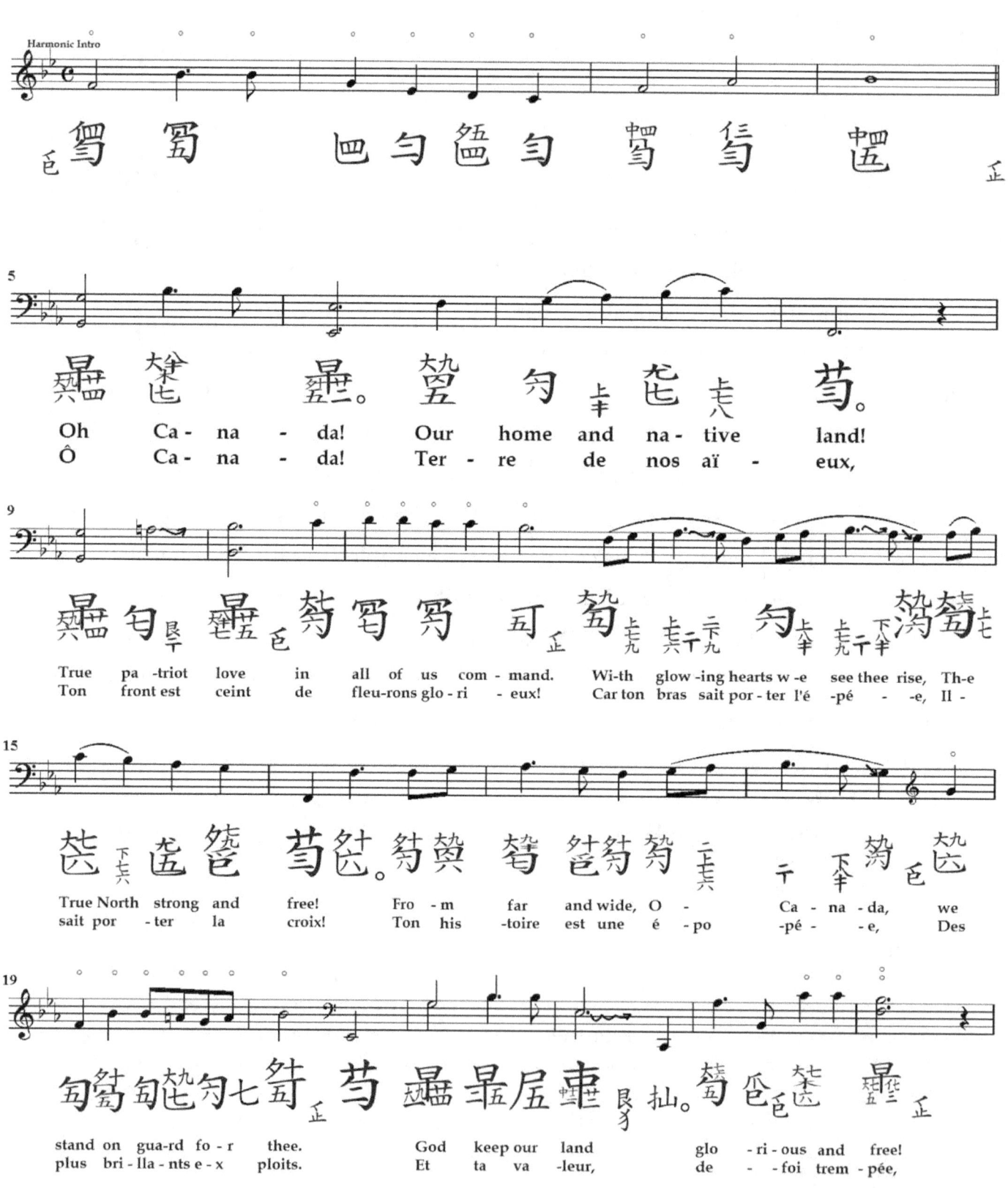

英語琴統初階

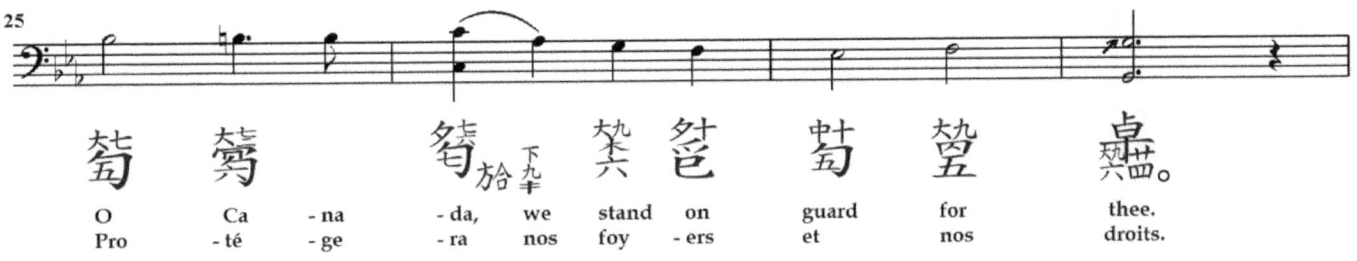

O Ca - na - da, we stand on guard for thee.
Pro - té - ge - ra nos foy - ers et nos droits.

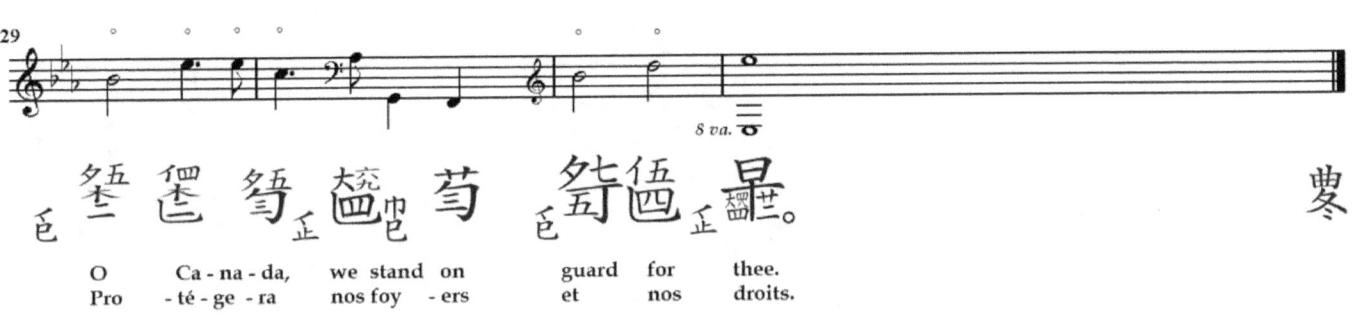

O Ca - na - da, we stand on guard for thee.
Pro - té - ge - ra nos foy - ers et nos droits.

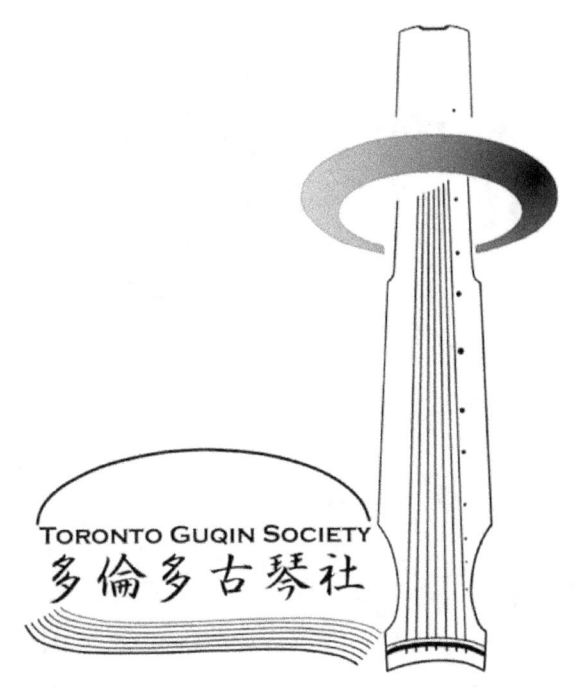

TORONTO GUQIN SOCIETY
多倫多古琴社

Standards of the Guqin